The Mismeasure of Education

The Mismeasure of Education

Jim Horn
Denise Wilburn

INFORMATION AGE PUBLISHING, INC.
Charlotte, NC • www.infoagepub.com

Library of Congress Cataloging-in-Publication Data

A CIP record for this book is available from the Library of Congress
http://www.loc.gov

ISBN: 978-1-62396-391-0 (Paperback)
978-1-62396-392-7 (Hardcover)
978-1-62396-393-4 (ebook)

Printed in the United States of America

Contents

Acknowledgements

The contours of this book came together during the Spring of 2011, and by the Fall we had a rough outline. Having worked together on previous projects, we could move forward without the personal politics and ego issues that sometimes slow joint writing ventures. We both wish to thank one another first for making this effort an ongoing series of insightful and reflective encounters that characterizes the best of shared learning and teaching.

We want to acknowledge the work of Bent Flyvbjerg, whose core questions for social science researchers in *Making Social Science Matter: Why Social Inquiry Fails and How it Can Succeed Again* provided the template for the four main sections of the book. We wish to thank, too, Paul Changas, Anna Meredith Westman, and Dale Ballou for their conversations and technical advice. For the patient and insightful assistance of Vincent McGrath at the Tennessee State Library and Archives, a big thank you. We want to deeply thank Peter McLaren, David Berliner, Gary Orfield, and Susan Ohanian for reading and generously commenting on the manuscript.

For the enthusiasm and encouragement by George Johnson at Information Age Publishing, we extend our gratitude. And we want to especially thank Gene Glass for his encouragement and guidance in getting this idea to finished book form. Finally, we want to thank, in a big way, Janeene Larkin and Bill Wilburn for the patience, support, love, advice, and psychic space they have afforded these two very grateful authors.

—**Jim Horn** and **Denise Wilburn**

Prologue

The Mismeasure of Education

The title of this book, *The Mismeasure of Education,* is deliberately chosen as a very deep bow to the great paleontologist, Stephen Jay Gould (1996), whose *The Mismeasure of Man* offers a critical history of the all-too-human fixation by scientists to try to derive a measurement for human intelligence, or IQ, that can be expressed as a "single quantity." Gould's "Mismeasure" focused on exposing for social scientists the dangers of an obsessive kind of "physics envy," at the same time that he applied a very effective battering ram to the various arguments for biological determinism—the belief that intelligence and social class are biologically based, genetically determined, and inheritable. Our more modest volume here is focused on how the vestiges of this dangerous ideology and this obsessive practice of quantification among education policy people has molded the dominant dogma of testing that has held sway from the very beginnings of educational measurement and testing even to today.

There are distinctions we should make up front, however, between then and now, between the contemporary fixation to distill learning to the purported purity of a value-added test score today, and the earlier and cruder attempts by various forms of pseudoscience during the past hundred years "to rank people in a single series of worthiness, efforts that invariably found that oppressed and disadvantaged groups—race, classes, or sexes—are in-

The Mismeasure of Education, pages xi–xiv

nately inferior and deserve their status" (Gould, 1996, p. 21). The picture is more nuanced and paradoxical today, though no less misguided. We can see this, in fact, as a kind of inner contradiction among many of today's growth model/value-added testing advocates, those of the psychometric set who espouse the seemingly egalitarian belief that despite the fact that students begin at different places, all children, nonetheless, can learn the same body of facts and can demonstrate that learning in the same way upon command, even if at different rates. Yet, these same value-added modeling (VAM) advocates continue to use measurement instruments that just as reliably label the poor and disadvantaged as learning laggards today, as did the horribly biased IQ tests used during the 1920s.

For even the most vaunted of inheritors of those earlier attempts to efficiently sort and track students, the modern SAT clearly demonstrates, as did its predecessors, the direct and continuing correlation between economic privilege and resulting SAT scores. (See the historical discussion of testing in Part 1 for a graphic analysis of these correlations, which is similarly mirrored, too, by any other standardized achievement test used in or out of schools today).

So what does it mean, then, to proclaim that we should hold everyone to the same high standard, and that there are "no excuses" for not reaching them, if the standard is almost always attained only by those with the economic, cultural, and social capital to boost them up to meet that standard? As we will show, particularly in Part 2, "Who wins and who loses?", the results for poor and immigrant children are sadly predictable, with millions of elementary children held back because they could not attain what their level of economic disadvantage or cultural difference put out of reach for them. So no, we as a society are no longer regularly administering IQ tests to Mexican children in a language they can't read in order to place them into industrial schools, as was common practice, for instance, in Los Angeles schools in the 1920s (Stern, 2005, pp. 95–99). But we are engaged, as we were during the first decades of the last century, in an "orgy of tabulation" with very high stakes for failure that include repeating grades or not receiving diplomas among children, or losing pay and even careers among teachers.

Twenty years have passed since Tennessee became the first state to mandate relatively new value-added modeling (VAM) of using standardized test scores to measure student achievement gains in public schools. The new assessment system was developed and marketed by University of Tennessee agricultural statistician, William Sanders. When Dr. Sanders managed to get his proprietary statistical model written into state law in 1992, it became the Tennessee Value Added Assessment System (TVAAS).

That amazing feat provided the focal point for a policy history of the TVAAS by Wilburn in 1996, and it is that policy history that provides the case study (Wilburn, 1996) that is here reexamined, expanded, and contextualized to the present day to reflect the increasingly prominent roles of VAM in state and federal policies for assessing student learning and evaluating schools and teachers.

The plan for this book is inspired by a challenge presented in the brilliant and provocative work of Danish social scientist Bent Flyvbjerg (2001), *Making Social Science Matter: Why Social Science Fails and How It Can Succeed Again.* Flyvbjerg's theoretical and applied social science manual provides impetus and the tools to engage in a kind of investigative social science that deftly poses the necessary questions to help the public beneficiaries of social science to understand underlying values expressed in social policy advocacy and implementation, while tracing out sources and expressions of power in social steering that most often remain hidden behind technocratic and normative rhetoric. Flyvbjerg throws down the gauntlet to all social policy researchers to aim for an understanding of social organizations and systems as products of human actions that occur within multiple contexts of expressed power and values, which make the traditional natural science goals of "explanation and prediction" impossible to attain. For social scientists attempting to understand policies and actions that are at the center of concern for "the local, national, and global communities in which we live" (p. 166), Flyvbjerg advocates and models a case study approach to allow understanding of social organizations such as education systems. To do so requires a close focus on the values and power relations that often are ignored in social policy research that conforms to research methods better suited for situations less messy than making education policy and implementing it.

The organization of the book, then, follows Flyvbjerg's four central questions to examine our current case study, which uses the Tennessee Value-Added Assessment System (TVAAS) as a central case for understanding the current directions in testing policy within U.S. schools. Part 1 asks and attempts to answer, "where are we going with educational assessment in the United States?" To come to a sensible answer, we first provide an overview of where we have been with testing as it developed over the past century in U.S. schools, a period that marks the emergence of education as a late entry in the race among social disciplines to attain the designation as a science. In understanding where education policy is today and where it may be going, we make that case that the succession of education reforms during the past century represent the institutionalization of an historically repetitive motion that serves to reproduce dominant power relations and values within society, while advancing more technically sophisticated versions of the same tools and strategies for achieving increasingly ambitious ends that, meanwhile, move further out of reach as we grapple toward them.

Part 2 examines the question, "who gains, and who loses, and by which mechanisms of power?" In this section, we specifically examine, using Tennessee as a case, how and why assessment has come to dominate both school curriculum and instruction during the last half century. Too, we trace the losers and the winners in the struggle to control the steering of public school policy, as well as those winners and losers who are directly affected by the struggle. In doing so, we attempt to clarify the roles played by the media, business interests, corporate foundations, think tanks, unions, political parties, federal and state officials, the university, and schools and teachers.

Part 3 asks the question, "is it desirable?" We closely examine various evaluations and critiques of the TVAAS and the Sanders version of VAM over the past 20 years. We begin, however, by attempting to tease out the various assumptions by different constituencies that are used to judge what is desirable and what is not. Beyond weighing the desirability of VAM based upon scientific veracity and logical argument, we also examine the consequences and unintended outcomes emanating from the Tennessee case that must be understood in judging its desirability as a national model.

Finally, Part 4 asks and attempts to answer the question "what should be done?" In so doing, we hope to contribute to further opening of the dialogue and debate that places educational measurement within a larger discussion of (a) what constitutes learning; and (b) what purposes of schooling are consistent with how learning occurs. If readers note a tone of urgency in what we put forward in this final section, it is likely based on our core belief that learning and schooling must first and foremost acknowledge the required sustainability of the planet, and that the more familiar goals emanating from the overarching one we often hear of "preparing children to compete in the global economy" must be tempered by the realization that sustainable economies only exist where human civilization is present. In the end, we shamelessly advocate for what Bateson (1972, 1979) called an "Ecology of Mind" that would allow learning and schools to be put to work for the greater selfish interest of human survival. In pursuing this path, we hope to promote and inspire others, perhaps, toward the further development of social research as "a practical, intellectual activity aimed at clarifying the problems, risks, and possibilities we face as humans and societies, and at contributing to social and political praxis" (Flyvbjerg, 2001, p. 4).

1

Where Have We Been and Where Are We Going With Educational Assessment Policy in U.S. Schools?

What was once educationally significant, but difficult to measure, has been replaced by what is insignificant and easy to measure. So now we test how well we have taught what we do not value.

—Art Costa, professor emeritus at Cal State–Fullerton

If poverty makes people lower-class, if being lower-class causes children not to learn and achieve, if not achieving causes people to remain poor, then... it is doubtful whether the school alone can break the cycle. If schools are deprived of the remedial and special programs they now have, it is likely that the achievement gap between classes will grow larger. It also seems that the cycle will not be broken until the problem of poverty is confronted directly, not as a cultural manifestation or a racial aberration, but on economic grounds.

—Dianne Ravitch (1972)

The Mismeasure of Education, pages 1–54

New Twists to Old Plots

On October 5, 2009, the Board of Testing and Assessment (BOTA) of the National Research Council (NRC) delivered a 17-page letter (National Academy of Sciences, 2009) to U.S. Education Secretary Arne Duncan that offered some solicited feedback on the Obama Administration's proposed Race to the Top (RTTT) plan. The plan had been posted July 29 on the Federal Register website for a ninety day public comment period. A number of BOTA's remarks represented affirmations and points of agreement with the Education Department (ED), but the NRC had some serious concerns as well, particularly about an assessment method known as "value added modeling" (VAM). VAM, which measures growth in student test scores over time, represents a small genus of quantitative methods vying for ascendancy in the scramble to measure student achievement growth and teacher effectiveness by using standardized test scores of students.

Secretary Duncan and his team of advisors, many of whom had left jobs from corporate foundations or were on loan to ED from the Gates and Broad Foundations, hoped the new plan of financial incentives based largely on Bush Administration priorities of more testing, accountability, and charter schools would provide a more popular successor to the widely reviled No Child Left Behind Act (NCLB). In 2009, NCLB was already three years past due for reauthorization, and many educators and policymakers viewed NCLB's obsessive focus on high stakes test scores, increasingly unattainable testing targets, and punishing sanctions as a hideous morphing of the original Elementary and Secondary Education Act (ESEA) passed in 1965. With a large majority of American children expected to fail to reach proficiency in reading and math in 2014, RTTT would, perhaps, provide a measure of relief that could be enacted at the Executive Cabinet level without Congressional action. Of equal importance, a new initiative based on test score growth, rather than impossible proficiency targets, could provide an escape valve for some of the steam building among opposition forces to NCLB and high-stakes testing.

Of most concern to the panel of testing experts at BOTA, who had been dedicated to testing and assessment issues since the mid-1990s, were RTTT plans to require states (if their grant applications were to be viewed favorably) to devise systems that would use student test scores for teacher and principal performance evaluations. The NRC group (National Academy of Sciences, 2009) got right to the point of their disagreement with this approach:

> BOTA has significant concerns that the Department's proposal places too much emphasis on measures of growth in student achievement (1) that have not yet been adequately studied for the purposes of evaluating teachers

> and principals and (2) that face substantial practical barriers to being successfully deployed in an operational personnel system that is fair, reliable, and valid. (p. 8)

BOTA concluded the section on the use of "growth data" by recommending that if VAM were to be used at all for evaluation purposes, then closely monitored pilot projects would be needed prior to any large scale launch. In any case, said the NRC, "VAM estimates of teacher effectiveness that are based on data for a single class of students should not be used to make operational decisions because such estimates are far too unstable to be considered fair or reliable" (p. 10).

Just over four months after the NRC warning letter to Secretary Duncan, Tennessee and Delaware became the first two winners of RTTT grants in March 2010, with successful applications that promised to do exactly what the NRC had warned against in October 2009 (i.e., to use "measures of growth in student achievement" to make high stakes decisions for teacher and principal performance evaluation). While Delaware moved more deliberately to implement its plan, Tennessee was not waiting, having adopted the motto of "First to the Top" three months before officially winning the larger grant worth $501,000,000. As if to demonstrate that the NRC warnings had fallen on deaf ears, in January 2010 the Tennessee General Assembly met in special session to give its VAM-based teacher and principal evaluation scheme the sanction of state law, along and other RTTT priorities that included unlimited charter school growth capacity, commitment to school turnaround strategies for low scoring schools, expanded and consolidated data gathering system for teachers and students, and commitment to adopt the Common Core State Standards and tests to go with them.

These new tests would be based on more "rigorous standards" than students were accustomed to in most states, and they would be administered as in a variety of dry runs throughout the school year, leading up to the big end-of-year exam. Tests would be developed for more subjects than just reading and math, and the test development work would be paid for with another $330 million of RTTT funds aimed specifically at producing new tests to replace state tests used under NCLB. Hoping to avoid any perception of federal oversight in what was quickly becoming national curriculum standards and national tests to go along them, the new Obama Administration gave credit to the state governors and their appointed bureaucrats. Ever since the Reagan Revolution of the 1980s had created a lasting and deepening suspicion of federal intervention in education issues, subsequent administrations had funneled federal and big business education policy priorities to the National Governors' Association (NGA) and the

Council of Chief School Officers (CCSO). We will have more to say about this shift later in the chapter.

Tennessee's successful RTTT application was aided, too, by close linkages, both directly and indirectly, with the Bill and Melinda Gates Foundation (BMGF), which had taken on multiple educational policy roles on the national stage, all of them related to choosing RTTT winners whose goals were consistent with those of the BMGF and ED. Secretary Duncan, in fact, had recruited some of the BMGF's key people (Libby, 2010) to serve in important roles at ED, and in October 2009 the *New York Times* quoted Florida State Senator and Education Committee Chair, Nancy Detert, as saying that "the Gates program and the Arne Duncan program are pretty much the same program" (Dillon, 2009, para. 12). Noting, too, the unprecedented influence by the BMGF in shaping public education policy, an Associated Press story (Quaid & Blankinship, 2009) that same month began with "the real secretary of education, the joke goes, is Bill Gates" (para. 1).

In Tennessee, the Gates influence was no joke. Tennessee's education reform history since 1980, along with its use of value-added testing (Tennessee Value Added Assessment System [TVAAS]) since 1992, had not escaped the attention of the BMGF. Having satisfied all of the BMGF reform criteria for favorable consideration for grants, including the demand for "no firewall barring the use of student achievement data in teacher evaluations" (McNeil, 2009, para. 4), Tennessee, indeed, was one of 15 states hand-picked in August 2009 to receive a $250,000 Gates Foundation grant to help prepare the lengthy RTTT applications, which BMGF personnel had helped to construct. Then, in addition to receiving assistance from the BMGF, the organization that had helped establish RTTT goals, the criteria for selection, and the application assistance grants, Tennessee recently received another plum advantage from the BMGF during the frenetic weeks leading up the announcement of winners in the RTTT contest. In November 2009, Gates had established a beachhead in Memphis City Schools, with $90 million in grant money "to improve teaching in the district" (Roberts, 2009). The new program was focused on attempting to isolate teacher influence on raising test scores, to the exclusion of other influences that affect student achievement.

On the day the Memphis City School Board accepted the Gates Foundation grant, Superintendent Kriner Cash's rapturous response (Roberts, 2009) did not forget to mention the key Gates talking point:[1]

> "This is huge, this is huge, this puts Memphis City Schools in very elite territory, on the front page of the nation," said an exultant Supt. Kriner Cash,

> adding that teachers were the "most important single factor in the education of a child." (para. 4)

The influence of the BMGF did not end, however, with Tennessee's winning the $501 million RTTT grant in March 2010. The speedy design and implementation of a teacher evaluation plan based on the Gates criteria was greatly assisted, too, by a non-profit consulting company, Education First, whose founder, Jennifer Vranek, was a former Gates Foundation employee whose profile was high among contenders for RTTT consulting work with grant winners. With Education First's assistance, Tennessee developed and began actual implementation of the new evaluation scheme in August 2011, with value added student scores counting 50% of an educator's evaluation, with the other 50% based on multiple classroom observations that designers hoped would match the state test score results.[2] What quickly emerged by late 2011 was a labyrinthine system of multiple observations, conferences, and testing that brought immediate and withering criticism from teachers as well as principals, who were charged with completing four observations per year for all faculty members, without exception. To complicate matters further, all teachers were to be evaluated using student test scores, whether or not they taught a subject that was tested:

> Because there are no student test scores with which to evaluate over half of Tennessee's teachers . . . the state has created a bewildering set of assessment rules. Math specialists can be evaluated by their school's English scores, music teachers by the school's writing scores." (Winerip, 2011a, para. 8)

One middle school principal, Will Shelton, told the *New York Times* (Winerip, 2011a), "I have never seen such nonsense," and a school board member in the same district wondered aloud "I don't know why they felt they had to rush. . . . Clearly this wasn't well thought out." If Tennessee was going to be the "first to the top," as their new motto claimed, then it was clear that the quick ascent would need to ignore all warning signs, even of potential avalanche, with the treacherous risks to teachers who never had a chance to vote on whether or not to engage in this new kind of harrowing forced march up such a slippery slope.

By July 2012, state officials had completed their first analysis of how classroom observations based on an official evaluation rubric/checklist matched up with the state value-added, or TVAAS, test score ratings. Comparisons showed wide disparities, with 75% of teachers receiving a 4 or 5 on classroom evaluations, while 50% scored 4 or 5 based as determined by the TVAAS system. On the low end of the scale, differences were even greater, with "fewer than 2.5% scor[ing] as 1 or 2 when observed, while 16% scored a 1 or 2 when judged by learning gains" (Gonzalez, 2012, para. 4). In a report issued by the state in July 2012, the Tennessee Department of Education questioned the veracity and abilities of the classroom observations, while never hinting that the test scores or that the state test or the TVAAS might be questioned for accuracy. Principals (where the largest discrepancies occurred), however, would undergo additional training during the coming years in clinical observation techniques to bring them more in line with conclusions reached by using student test scores.

In a twist of irony that remains largely unappreciated, had Tennessee instituted its evaluation scheme before 2010 when new cut score for the state test were established, it would have found principal observations not higher, but lower, than the state test results. In a state where 80 to 90% of children were shown to be proficient on state tests in 2009, one year later following the setting of new cut scores, 40 to 50% of the same children were judged proficient (Roberts, 2010). The inventive, though entirely arbitrary, nature of these changes in testing reality did not alter the State's resolve, however, to lean even more heavily upon them, as the first year state report (2012) recommended that teachers with high value-added ratings should be able, in fact, to disregard entirely any evaluative conclusions reached by human observers:

> Teachers with individual value-added scores who receive a 4 or 5 on TVAAS should be allowed to use that score to count for 100% of their total evaluation score. Because the TVAAS score comes at the end of the year, these teachers would still receive feedback from observations during the year. (p. 6)

With some of the lowest SAT and NAEP scores in the nation to match the history of being near the bottom in per pupil spending when compared to other states, it may seem unlikely that a state like Tennessee would be at the head of the pack in the Race to the Top, when so many better-funded states failed to win grant awards. However, RTTT's corporate-inspired education policy agenda demanded a willingness to do politically what was needed to gain the most favorable status for consideration, and Tennessee's frugality, along with its 30 year affair with business solutions to education problems, put it at the forefront of consideration for the next rendition of corporate education interventions, once again with the imprimatur of the U.S. Department of Education. The state's historical connections with the growing influence of corporate education solutions are deep and numerous, and Tennessee's increasing visibility over the past twenty years in this area is due significantly to the tireless public relations and marketing nets cast by developer of Tennessee's value-added testing system (TVAAS), William Sanders. The role of Sanders and his statistical modeling figure significantly in our story, particularly in Parts 2 and 3.

The Tennessee case, then, provides the specific contemporaneous example that we use in this book to examine the role of standardized testing to measure learning in American schools. Much has changed in K–12 education during the past 20 years to make schools very different places than they were in 1992, when Tennessee first adopted the Tennessee Value Added Assessment System (TVAAS), and part of our task here is to make visible the changes that can be credited to, or blamed on, educational assessment via high stakes testing, value-added modeling (VAM), and the TVAAS in particular. More important than the past two decades for value-added modeling, however, will be in the next ten years or so, for there are clear signs emerging that, despite strong reservations and compelling caveats within the scientific community and education policy arena, VAM could play an even more prominent role in this generation's production of the school testing drama, revived as it is every generation with evermore sophisticated technical savvy, contemporized language, and appropriate costuming aimed to save an outdated script from the educational dustbin.

A number of things have not changed in the repeated revival of the testing drama for which we offer our present interpretation and critique. Most prominent is the recurring theme of science of some quantifiable variety applied for personal and public betterment, a theme that historically has suffused each subsequent production of our recurring drama—or as some observers (Bracey, 2004; 2009) would prefer to call an unending farce. The impacts of abstracting socioeconomic, cultural, and political experience into a quantifiable format that can be efficiently conveyed in the name of scientific-based education have had lasting effects on the way schooling is conducted and the purpose we attach to education in general. In large part, standardized testing has paved the road to a quantifiable variety of what may be generously referred to as science, and the application of that educational science has always been used to express and to justify the values for which educationists' own peculiar variety of science was created to serve. The fact that testing, standardized for the masses, became the primary tool to sort the privileged from those under the privileged is no mistake or fluke of nature, and to this day, the replication of the vocational and social ordering derived from previous centuries may be remedied by any means other than dispensing with the measure that assures the continuation of the same vocational and social sorting. As E. M. Forster (1927/1956) so eloquently quipped in regards to the British system of standardized tests and their "power to ban and bless,"

> As long as learning is connected with earning, as long as certain jobs can only be reached through exams, so long must we take the examination system seriously. If another ladder to employment was contrived, much so-called education would disappear, and no one would be a penny the stupider (Chapter I, para. 11).

From Certain Suspicions to Suspicious Certainty

As a nation that saw itself built on the principles of freedom, we had to tell ourselves that there was something about the slave that justified slavery.

—James Horton[3]

By the turn of the twentieth century, the crusade by Horace Mann and other nineteenth century school reformers to provide all classes of American White children access to decent and free public schools had been largely won in the northern states, due largely to successful strategies by Mann to sell the concept of public schools to social and economic elites as good for social stability and industrial productivity (Taylor, 2010). Mann's own motivation for free public schools grew from a deep anxiety regarding the possibility of class warfare breaking out between the increasingly unequal American citizens (Urban & Wagoner, 2008). By the twentieth century, too, Mann's espousal that schools would function as the "the great equalizer of the conditions of men, the balance wheel of the social machinery" (Sigler, 1997, p. 78) were giving way to an older Jeffersonian meritocratic notion that schools would function "to rake a few geniuses from the rubbish" (Mondale & Patton, 2001, p. 23). School and social reformers were looking to science, as did Jefferson, to help them to create their vision of a more perfect union, or at least a society that would be run most efficiently by those most fit to do so.

Unfortunately, Jefferson's views on meritocracy and his rhetorical commitment to create a more perfect union depended greatly on the economic advantages that accrued from the grim reality of slaveholding. The colonial political economy demanded enslavement for some to assure liberty for others, and by Jefferson's time, slavery based on race had come to require a thorough marginalization and unalterable othering of African-Americans. With distancing of came de-empathizing, so that the common White belief in African-American inferiority was legally codified without regard to any broken moral code, as slaves were reduced by 1705 to the status of property for life (Beverley, 1722) that, if need be, could be used as collateral for a loan on a new carriage or silver set. We find these sentiments expressed in *Notes on the State of Virginia* (1787/1853), wherein Jefferson's "suspicion only" of African-American inferiority set down the challenge for future scientists to make "Black and Red men . . . subjects of natural history":

> I advance it therefore as a suspicion only, that the Blacks, whether originally a distinct race, or made distinct by time and circumstances, are inferior to the Whites in the endowments both of body and mind. It is not against experience to suppose, that different species of the same genus, or varieties of the same species, may possess different qualifications. Will not a lover of natural history then, one who views the gradations in all the races of animals with the eye of philosophy, excuse an effort to keep those in the department of man as distinct as nature has formed them? This unfortunate difference of colour, and perhaps of faculty, is a powerful obstacle to the emancipation of these people. Many of their advocates, while they wish to vindicate the liberty of human nature, are anxious also to preserve its dignity and beauty. Some of these, embarrassed by the question 'What further is to be done with them?' join themselves in opposition with those who are actuated by sordid avarice only. Among the Romans emancipation required but one effort. The slave, when made free, might mix with, without staining the blood of his master. But with us a second is necessary, unknown to history. When freed, he is to be removed beyond the reach of mixture. (p. 153)

For one harboring suspicion only, Jefferson's commitment to complete separation in order to avoid "staining the blood" of Whites (in the event that slavery was to end) sounds particularly adamant and insistent. For sure, Jefferson's challenge to the science of the future was taken up by his successors, some in an obsessive fashion, and the cataloging of those efforts provides the subject matter for Gould's *The Mismeasure of Man (TMoM).*

It is not our task here to retrace Gould's archeological dig into the scientific missteps and ideological investigations posing as science, but there is an important lesson to be learned from Gould's own flawed treatment of the prejudicial ponderings and calculations of Dr. Samuel Morton (Menand, 2001–2002), whose rankings of human intelligence based on the size of human skulls during the 1840s were intended to respond in his own way to Jefferson's challenge, thus demonstrating the superiority of Americans of Northern European ancestry over African-Americans: "In descending order of volume, these were: Caucasian, Mongolian, Malay, Native American, and Negro" (p. 110).

Gould begins *TMoM* by tracing his own detective work to demonstrate that Morton had allowed his racial prejudice to overtake his scientific curiosity, and Gould's results, indeed, showed that Morton's statistics were fudged. Louis Menand (2001–2002), too, has documented Morton's "seat-of-the-pants adjustments. In the case of Morton's measurements of Caucasian skulls, some of the skulls "belonged . . . to men who had been hanged for murder; Morton argued that the Caucasian mean therefore be adjusted upward, on the assumption that murderers have smaller cranial capacity than law-abiding persons" (pp. 110–111).

Most recently, however, scholars have examined Gould's work (Saletan, 2012) and found that Morton's calculations were largely correct and that Gould, in fact, was the one guilty of the offense for which he had accused Morton. It was Gould's own statistical errors that were used to show that Morton's numbers were wrong, when, in fact, they were quite right. So, while Gould was unable, perhaps, to check his own biases, intentional or otherwise, so also was Morton, but in a different way; specifically by falling prey to attributing accurate correlations to faulty causations, which then were used to project his racist belief in Black inferiority, rather than demonstrating by factual means.

For while Morton and the illustrious Louis Agassiz were crisscrossing the lecture circuits during the late antebellum period with their "scientific" data to demonstrate Black inferiority based on skull size, German biologist, Carl Bergmann, was observing in 1847 that "within the same species of warm-blooded animals, populations having less massive individuals are more often found in warm climates near the equator, while those with greater bulk, or mass, are found further from the equator in colder regions" (O'Neil, 1998–2012, para. 5). What Morton did not know and what his attentive slave-holding lecture audiences in the South did not want to know is that skull size and body size are correlated to geography rather than to intelligence, so that humans as well as other vertebrates from colder climates generally have more body volume, including cranial capacity, than those that live in warmer climes. Bergmann's observations have since been substantiated and codified into what is known as Bergmann's Law, which now explains why Northern European cranial capacity is on average greater than that of Africans. Skull size, then, had always been about preserving or shedding caloric heat, notwithstanding an impressive array of numbers by Morton to "scientifically" justify a racist "suspicion" begun by the man who penned the Declaration of Independence.

In similar ways to Morton's scientific racism, the classism and racism of the early twentieth century became even more self-justified and psychically embedded through the creation and use of intelligence (IQ) tests and achievement tests that verified, while concealing, the bias from those within the "scientific" community who found in testing a way, once again, to acceptably express their prejudices under the auspices of science. When we look at the rankings on early IQ tests developed for the U.S. Army by a team of psychologists led by eugenicist and racialist, Lewis Terman and Robert Yerkes, we see national origin rankings that neatly overlay the racial types from Morton's hierarchy of intelligence based on skull size: U.S. (officers England, Holland, Germany, United States (White), Canada, Norway, Ireland, Greece, Russia, Italy, Poland, United States (Colored) (Mondale & Patton, 2001, p. 101). But rather than providing a scientific basis for a belief that is even older than Jefferson that White children of the elite are more intelligent than poor or Black ones, and especially poor *and* Black ones, the IQ tests and the subsequent SAT test that first appeared in 1926 simply confirm the suspicions of another generation of the privileged who, like Jefferson in his day, had substantial reasons involving both conscience and capital for ignoring the fact that African-Americans, immigrants, or the poor suffer unfairly and disproportionately from the continued use of scientific measures to justify deep socio-cultural preconceptions.

Zealots for the Elimination of Waste

> The educational significance of the results to be obtained from careful measurements of the intelligence of children can hardly be overestimated. Questions relating to the choice of studies, vocational guidance, schoolroom procedure, the grading of pupils, promotional schemes, the study of the retardation of children in the schools, juvenile delinquency, and the proper handling of subnormals on the one hand and gifted children on the other—all alike acquire new meaning and significance when viewed in the light of the measurement of intelligence as outlined in this volume.... More than all other forms of data combined, such tests give the necessary information from which a pupil's possibilities of future mental growth can be foretold, and upon which his further education can be most profitably directed.
>
> —Elwood P. Cubberley, from foreword for Terman's *The Measurement of Intelligence*, 1916 (p. viii)

Following the importation of British statistical procedures by American psychologist Edward Thorndike in 1903, "standards of deviation and correlations of coefficients were in the air" (Rugg, 1975, p. 295) by 1910, so much so that the study of education, which was preoccupied with becoming the newest of the social sciences, henceforth, would be driven by the urge to quantify and tabulate all aspects of schooling, as noted here in Harold Rugg's summary of developments in the early twentieth century:

> The steps by which the new educational measurers began to apply methods of research to the study of the curriculum were: first, the construction and use of tests in arithmetic, spelling, language, algebra, etc.: second, the inventory of the current curriculum by the tabular analysis of "courses" of study and textbooks: third, the determination of socially worthwhile skills and knowledge by the tabulation of actual human activities; fourth,... the

careful determination of trends in social development, the chief institutions and problems of contemporary life, standards of appreciation, etc. (p. 296)

Accompanied, too, by hopes that scientific quantification could make social problems efficiently manageable, something new called intelligence testing was seen as a godsend toward achieving the task, despite the fact that inventors of intelligence tests had something else in mind. When Alfred Binet, for instance, developed the first intelligence tests at the behest of the French education ministry (Black, 2003, pp. 76–78) during the first decade of the twentieth century, it was to help identify those children needing special assistance in schools where attendance had recently been made compulsory. By 1912, however, a prominent leader of the American eugenics movement, Henry Goddard, had adapted Binet's intelligence test for use in screening and sorting Eastern European immigrants, many of whom were Jewish. Goddard and other eugenicists found in the intelligence test a purportedly objective way to quantify the structural racism of the day and to have it accepted as scientific, all the while protecting the American citizenry from the continued influx of impure and unfit immigrants, who were viewed as threats to the health of the American gene pool. In 1916, a colleague of Goddard's, Robert Yerkes, developed the Alpha A and Alpha B intelligence tests, which were used to screen and efficiently sort enlistees for the U.S. Army leading up to World War I. Those with high scores were more likely to end up with desk jobs, and those with low scores were more likely to end up in combat roles. That same year, Stanford psychologist, Lewis Terman (1916), published, *The Measurement of Intelligence,* wherein he established his vision for test use in schools based on the fine-grained sorting of "defectives," which he believed could be calibrated by using tests:

> ... intelligence tests are rapidly extending our conception of "feeble-mindedness" to include milder degrees of defect than have generally been associated with this term. The earlier methods of diagnosis caused a majority of the higher grade defectives to be overlooked. Previous to the development of psychological methods the low-grade moron was about as high a type of defective as most physicians or even psychologists were able to identify as feeble-minded.... It is safe to predict that in the near future intelligence tests will bring tens of thousands of these high-grade defectives under the surveillance and protection of society. This will ultimately result in curtailing the reproduction of feeble-mindedness and in the elimination of an enormous amount of crime, pauperism, and industrial inefficiency. It is hardly necessary to emphasize that the high-grade cases, of the type now so frequently overlooked, are precisely the ones whose guardianship it is most important for the State to assume. (p. 7)

By 1922, Columbia College was using E. L. Thorndike's *Tests for Mental Alertness* (Synnott, 2010, p. 18) to limit the number of Jews among its student body. Incensed by what he considered a racist portrayal of the new Ivy League testing policy by reporters from *The Nation*, Columbia's Dean Herbert E. Hawkes, a mathematician by training, shared his rationale (Columbia Documents, n. d.) for the "mental test" in a letter to Professor E. B. Wilson:

> What we have been trying to do is to eliminate the low grade boy.... We have not eliminated boys because they were Jews and do not propose to do so. We have honestly attempted to eliminate the lowest grade of applicant and it turns out that a good many of the low grade men are New York City Jews. It is a fact that boys of foreign parentage who have no background in many cases attempt to educate themselves beyond their intelligence.... I do not believe however that a College would do well to admit too many men of low mentality who have ambition but not brains. At any rate this is the principle on which we are going.

The primitive and biased tests effectively reduced Jewish enrollment by half, from 40% to around 20% (Synnott, 2010, p. 18), and the "mental test" remained a screening tool until the late 1930s, when the grip of the eugenics craze stateside began to give way as the German fascist mirror finally allowed Americans to glimpse where their own social engineering could be headed.

By the 1920s Terman's Stanford-Binet intelligence test was being administered to over a million children a year (Mondale & Patton, 2001) in order to sort school children into curriculum tracks that would funnel them into adult job roles. Ostensibly to differentiate the learning needs of students and to increase American economic competitiveness with the rest of the world, many immigrant children, particularly Mexican children in California (Stern, 2005, pp. 95–99), were given the test in a language they did not understand and placed in the kinds of industrial training programs first introduced following the Civil War and the Indian Wars for former slaves and American Indian children at boarding schools like Hampton Institute (Anderson, 1988). Others were slotted into vocational programs, business curriculums, and college prep, all under the banner of progressive social policy and social efficiency.

The early twentieth century era of school testing was driven, then, by psychologists looking to expand the influence of intelligence testing and by a new generation of school administrators seeking to apply scientific management techniques developed by Frederick Winslow Taylor (1911/1967) for industry and business to all areas of school operations. These new disciples of social efficiency became "zealot[s] for the elimination of waste"

(Kliebard, 2004, p. 20), from curriculum making to the sorting of students. Kliebard cites former muckraker and self-proclaimed efficiency expert, Joseph Mayer Rice, as advocating in 1913[4] for what sounds much like today's corporate education reform goal of "a scientific system of pedagogical management [that] would demand fundamentally the measurement of results in the light of fixed standards" (p. 20). Rice (1913) called for "a system of management specifically directed toward the elimination of waste in teaching, so that the children attending the schools may be duly rewarded for the expenditure of their time and effort" (p. viii). The assembly line became the metaphor for school production, and IQ testing provided the scientific analysis for which line the raw material ended up in to be molded into one of several models. If the new social engineers had their way and could see their dream realized, such differentiated instruction would assure efficiency and the elimination of waste. As we shall see, the "elimination of waste" takes on a darker meaning as we examine ideology-driven social sorting on an industrial scale.

What resulted from that first generation of testing and sorting was a system that continues today to provide "scientific" rationalization for the creation and maintenance of measures whereby children of the privileged display test results, on average, consistently higher than those children under the privileged on tests that were devised to show as much. By using measures stamped with the seal of science, then, high test scorers are guaranteed seemingly legitimized access to the a legacy of privilege that accompanies higher performance, thus reproducing social and economic dominance by descendants of the middle class elites who first established their dominion in the Colonies during the seventeenth and eighteenth centuries. Some who read this will surely doubt such a claim, but we hope that by the time readers finish the book, this contention will be an indisputable, though unacceptable, fact. For those less skeptical now, we hope this book will provide a deeper understanding as to how the mismeasure of children became standard pedagogical practice.

Zealots for the Elimination of the Unfit

Developing from within a long tradition of social Darwinism, whereby those who are fittest are destined to rise to the top, intelligence tests and achievement tests simply confirmed what was commonly believed: Those who occupy the top rungs, or the bottom rungs, of the societal ladder are there because the natural order has ordained it. And, thus, modern science provided the privileged with a scientific rationale and a moral balm of justification during the late nineteenth and early twentieth century, an era of extreme and growing income inequality, exploitative factory life among urban slums, economic upheaval, economic depression that lasted from 1893 to 1898, and new waves of Jewish, Slav, and Italian immigrants from eastern and southern Europe. Essentially, the business, religious, and social elites of the Gilded Age found a justification in a new science of eugenics that solidified and quantified the exuberant biological and social determinism expressed by nineteenth century economist, Herbert Spencer, who argued throughout the last half of the nineteenth century that Laws of Nature, no less, have ordained the "survival of the fittest" in all spheres of life, from biology to economics. Unlike Darwin, however, whose views acknowledged many more species extinctions than successfully adaptive ones, Spencer molded his philosophy to fit the unfailing optimism of laissez-faire capitalism. Importantly, Spencer's philosophy of perpetual progress offered comfort to people like Andrew Carnegie by providing a "philosophical justification for Carnegie's unabashed pursuit of personal riches in the world of business, freeing him from the moral reservations about financial acquisition that he had inherited from his egalitarian Scottish relatives" (PBS/WGBH, 1999, para. 2). Carnegie, an avid reader, was once asked which author he would take to a desert island if he could have only one. Carnegie didn't hesitate: Herbert Spencer would be his choice (para. 1).

The social efficiency education reformers who rose to prominence just after Herbert Spencer's death in 1903 inherited from social Darwinism the unwavering belief in increasing "differentiation" at every level of existence, from the physical to the social sphere, from the evolution of the physical and biological worlds, even down to the proliferation and classification of social and work roles. Spencer saw a pattern of differentiation everywhere he looked, which was for him a sign of progress. Human-assisted differentiation was, for Spencer, what Man could do to help Nature along toward that destination: "From the earliest traceable cosmical changes down to the latest results of civilization, we shall find that the transformation of the homogeneous into the heterogeneous, is that in which Progress essentially consists" (Halsall, 1997, para. 3).

In 1857, Spencer (Halsall, 1997) detailed a number of examples of "differentiation at work," from the political to the religious, but the sorting and segregating of worker classes is the form of differentiation that the social and economic efficiency reformers of the early twentieth century seized upon:

> Simultaneously there has been going on a second differentiation of a still more familiar kind; that, namely, by which the mass of the community has become segregated into distinct classes and orders of workers. While the governing part has been undergoing... [its own] complex development...,

> the governed part has been undergoing an equally complex development, which has resulted in that minute division of labour characterizing advanced nations. (para. 6)

By the twentieth century, then, industrialists and philanthropists inspired by Spencer's hierarchical social philosophy, turned Spencerian science toward a scientific approach to dividing labor, a turn that was accompanied by the maturing needs of America's industrial economic engine and the mass production of goods. Taylor's (1911/1967) *Principles of Scientific Management* was unerringly based on the principles of analyzing and dividing job tasks into their most differentiated and efficient components so that that simplified job assignments could be accomplished by interchangeable workers with minimal training whenever possible. Increased efficiency and industrial production demanded, in fact, the elimination of skilled artisans who made products from start to finish and who could demand higher pay for their services as a result. The emerging national economy of industrial scale would not allow for such pastoral excesses or the kind of differentiation based on skilled trades. Each trade, in fact, required analysis and further dividing of labor, if differentiation and progress were to be fully engaged.

By 1920, the social efficiency social control ideology based on differentiation through scientific management provided a central rationale for the "progressive" use of intelligence tests and achievement tests to measure, sort, and segregate school children in ways that upheld social structures based on class and race prejudices. Social efficiency based on racial and socioeconomic differentiation became defined and advanced by scientific educationists, researchers, and psychologists, many of whom were eugenics enthusiasts and who constituted a small group of the most influential social and education reformers of the early twentieth century. They included luminaries like John Franklin Bobbitt, Elwood P. Cubberley, G. Stanley Hall, Edward Thorndike, Lewis Terman, Robert Yerkes, and Robert Goddard. Their work provided a rationale for the new scientific schooling set forth in books like Bobbitt's (1918) *The Curriculum*, Terman's *The Measurement of Intelligence* (1916), and Thorndike's *The Principles of Teaching* (1906). Thorndike, who set for himself the immodest task of "conquering the new world of pedagogy" (Lagemann quoting Thorndike, 2000, p. 58), viewed the job of teachers, three quarters of whom were women in 1906 (p. 8), as carrying out the tasks as determined by the "higher authorities" of male administrators and psychologists such as himself, who were to be engaged in "decid[ing] what the schools shall try to achieve and to arrange plans for school work which will attain the desired ends" (p. 60).

Those "desired ends" would be the presented to children by a subordinated teacher corps and measured by standardized achievement tests, developed by a growing army of psychologists following Thorndike's lead. Subsequent to the massive evaluation survey of New York City public schools in 1911 and 1912, researchers viewed the use of "scientific tests" to evaluate achievement as a necessary component of evaluation research. These standardized achievement tests were developed for most every subject, from reading to handwriting to Latin grammar:

> The proliferation of achievement test was phenomenal: between 1917 and 1928, some 1,300 achievement tests were developed in the United States; by 1940, there were 2,600. The massive growth of these tests was fueled by the simultaneous development of "intelligence" tests. (Lagemann, 2000, p. 88)

What a Difference 25 Years Makes

To get an idea of the effects of the new scientific efficiency movement during the early twentieth century, particularly on curriculum and assessment, it is instructive to look at how curriculum priorities changed between 1893 and 1918. The earlier date marks the approval by the blue ribbon Committee of Ten's rather modest set of elective tracks of high school study, distinguished mainly by the amount of classical and modern languages required to fill out a list of subjects based within the liberal arts tradition. Harvard president Charles W. Eliot, who chaired the Committee of Ten, was insistent that any of the four tracks could ready high school students for a happy life, whether a high school diploma was the final educational destination or if college were to follow:

> . . . the right selection of subjects, along with the right way of teaching them, could develop citizens of all classes endowed in accordance with the humanist ideal—with the power of reason, sensitivity to beauty, and high moral character." (Kliebard, 2004, p. 10)

Twenty-five years later in 1918, another elite commission charged with the same mission and under the same NEA sponsorship came up with a radically different set of curriculum priorities that replaced the focus on traditional liberal arts curriculum subjects with a steadfast focus on preparing students for differentiated life roles that would be predicated by their learning capacity as measured by intelligence and achievement tests. In two and half decades, the Committee of Ten's humanistic ideal for high school graduates to enter the world with "the power of reason, sensitivity to beauty, and high moral character" (Kliebard, 2004, p. 10) was replaced by seven "cardinal principles" that reflected the growing influence of social engineers who viewed school as the primary tool to achieve efficient social steering and control. This new class of progressive technocrats was armed with statistical methods inspired to measure and quantify, predict, and control every aspect of economic and social life. They shared in the visionary prognostications of their leader, Thorndike, who believed that a new educational psychology, properly aimed, "would tell the effect of every possible stimulus and the cause of every possible response in every possible human being" (Lagemann quoting Thorndike, 2001, p. 60). In turn, every aspect of school was to be molded to serve a new social order as defined by a grandiose faith in science and schooling and a devotion to the highly contagious quackery of eugenics.

Entitled, *Cardinal Principles of Secondary Education* (U.S. Office of Education, 1918), the first lines of the report by the Commission on the Reorganization of Secondary Education (CRSE) makes the mission clear: "Secondary education should be determined by the needs of the society to be served, the character of the individuals to be educated, and the knowledge of educational theory and practice available" (p. 1). The "needs of the society" were determined by researchers conducting, among large and small school systems alike, extensive evaluation surveys and learning inventories of every sort in what Harold Rugg (1975) referred to as "an orgy of tabulation" (p. 298). The result was a list of priorities for the secondary curriculum that mentioned no specific school subject, classical or otherwise:

- Health
- Command of fundamental processes
- Worthy home membership
- Vocation
- Civic education
- Worthy use of leisure
- Ethical character

Just a few sentences into the Introduction of the Report by the Commission on the Reorganization of Secondary Education (Cardinal Principles), the authors, most of whom were professors in the new university departments of educational administration, noted the rationale for this tectonic curricular shift toward social utility: "The character of the secondary-school population has been modified by the entrance of large numbers of pupils of widely varying capacities, aptitudes, social heredity, and destinies in life" (p. 2). Readers today may wonder what role high school was to play if "destinies in life" had been pre-determined prior to "entrance" to high school, but assumptions in 1918 about the role of school were quite different from the one espoused by Horace Mann, who expressed the notion of the common school as the "great equalizer of the conditions of men—the balance wheel of the social machinery" (Sigler, 1996, p. 78). Such meritocratic idealism was not driving the Cardinal Principles, and the "scientific" sorting of children by testing was unabashedly celebrated as a progressive step toward an efficient society built with machine precision. In clearly discernible ways, the Cardinal Principles reflected decades of increasing social anxiety among elites regarding the threat to American bloodlines and social values from increasing immigration and unbridled heterogeneity that grew, in large part, from the unquenchable needs of the vast industrial melting pot born of scientific management. The irony of attempting to fix a social situation with the same tools that went into creating it was not lost on John Dewey (1907), who believed that everyone who desired it, either manager or worker, should have an education that left them equally prepared to appreciate life fully:

> Some are managers and others are subordinates. But the great thing for one as for the other is that each shall have had the education which enables him to see within his daily work all there is in it of large and human significance. How many of the employed are today mere appendages to the machines which they operate!... At present, the impulses which lie at the basis of the industrial system are either practically neglected or positively distorted during the school period. (pp. 38–39)

Although Dewey, George Counts, William James, and Boyd Bode spoke and wrote against the presumptions underlying the types of social sorting that were advocated by social efficiency and scientific management reformers, testing experts, and eugenicists, Dewey and the social democrats were fighting a rear guard action by 1918. Dewey's pragmatic blend of philosophy, experience, and the social sciences to improve democratic living did not fit the tenor of the day. As Thorndike represented a growing army of behavioral psychologists set about to "conquer the new world of pedagogy" (Lagemann, 2000, p. 58), Thorndike had declared the same year that "whatever exists, exists in some amount" (p. 57) whose quantity, as well as quality must be determined. Lagemann rightfully concludes that Thorndike's focus on controlled experiment and quantification (p. 58) signaled "a rise to prominence [that] made it unlikely that educational scholarship [or educational practice] would develop along the lines Dewey had advocated" (p. 57).

Even though the recommendations of the 1918 Commission advocated for comprehensive high schools that advanced civic unification through required general education courses, electives open to all students, as well as vocational specialization and career tracking, a sociocultural hierarchy quickly emerged in the new comprehensive high school (Wraga, 1998) that mirrored the underlying beliefs and thinly disguised intentions of the education efficiency experts who dominated the Cardinal Principles :

> Within the first decade following the release of the report it was already apparent that the specializing function would take precedence over the unifying function. This was evident in a marked emphasis on providing for a variety of specialized course while doing little to unite students of different backgrounds, abilities, and aspirations. Furthermore, when professional psychologists looked to the schools for a new clientele for their group (or standardized) testing practices developed during World War I, the result was a system of tracking that divided students in ways inimical to the unifying intent of the comprehensive model. (p. 125)

With the sorting tools available to separate the fittest from the less so, the beleaguered humanistic values that were central in the 1893 Committee of Ten Report became the principal learning domains of those middle class children with the test scores their worth in pursuit of the liberal arts curriculum that served, then and now, as pre-professional preparation. From that point forward, access to schooling that advanced the "power of reason, sensitivity to beauty, and high moral character" demanded a level of screening that economic advantage largely palliated. For the rest, there remained the other specializing functions of school to help adjust students to their appropriate "destinies in life." For Thorndike and those who followed his lead, those "destinies in life" were believed to be determined by inherited traits, so much so that "what anyone becomes by education depends on what he is by nature" (Lagemann quoting Thorndike, p. 58).

The Dark Side of Progress

> It is better for all the world, if instead of waiting to execute degenerate offspring for crime, or to let them starve for their imbecility, society can prevent those who are manifestly unfit from continuing their kind. The principle that sustains compulsory vaccination is broad enough to cover cutting the Fallopian tubes.
>
> —U.S. Supreme Court Justice Oliver Wendell Holmes, Jr.,
> *Buck v. Bell*, 274 U.S. 200 (1927)

On January 11, 2012, the *New York Times* (Severson, 2012) reported that a North Carolina state task force recommended a financial settlement for the victims of the state's involuntary sterilization law (Severson, 2011). Most of the 72 who remain alive are poor and disproportionately African American. Between 1929 and 1974, the state of North Carolina, alone, sterilized an estimated 7,600 of its citizens who were deemed feeble-minded, diseased, or otherwise defective by some trait thought to be inheritable. In offering to pay $50,000 to each of the identified victims or victims' families, North Carolina became the first state to suggest financial compensation to victims of involuntary sterilization from state Eugenics Boards that were once legal in 32 states and that claimed over 60,000 victims nationwide between 1909 and 1974. Even with the settlement that many considered an act of insult added to injury, North Carolina's victims were sure to face months and maybe years of further bureaucratic delays. In June, 2012, the most recent bill that would have provided the modest settlements (Severson, 2012) for North Carolina victims died in State Senate.[5] In California, where over 20,000 people were involuntarily sterilized, even such modest restitution is not on the horizon.

So that we remember the lessons from America's twentieth century adventures in eugenics, the discredited pseudoscience developed to justify containing, segregating, and/or sterilizing individuals for the benefit of societal improvement, there exists an extensive literature (Black, 2003; Rosen, 2004; Selden, 1999; Keveles, 1998; Stern, 2005; Lombardo, 2011) dedicated to deepening understanding of America's role in providing the ideological and logistical foundations for a form of social engineering that reached maturity on the most hideous scale during the Holocaust. No doubt families competing during the early years of the twentieth century at county fairs across America in the "Fitter Family" and "Better Baby" contests could never guess that their blue ribbons or letter grades for eugenics health could ever be prefigure the slaughter of millions deemed genetically defective; the policies propagated by the Nazis leading up to the World War II, however, were direct extensions of homegrown developments by American and British eugenicists intent upon encouraging the breeding of successful individuals of northern European ancestry (positive eugenics) and curtailing the breeding of unfit populations identified as carriers of defective "germ plasm" (negative eugenics).

The father of the eugenics movement, Sir Francis Galton, coined the word, eugenics (meaning "well born") in the 1880s as the umbrella term for what he planned as a new science that would demonstrate, firstly, that the British ruling class came to its appropriate social status as the result of biological inheritance. The argument was an extension of social Darwinism, which argued for a simplistic rendition of "survival of the fittest" to be applied in the social sphere, asserting that those of greatest worth should occupy the societal stations fitted to them by, well, their obvious fitness. Such fitness, or lack thereof, was thought to be passed to subsequent generations, for eugenicists followed, as did Spencer before them, the Lamarckian understanding of evolution, whereby acquired characteristics were thought to be inheritable through defective germ plasm. Eugenicists, then, not only advocated for strict immigration laws and universal intelligence testing to block entry by those deemed defective, but they successfully lobbied for mandatory sterilization as the most effective way to stem all sorts of human problems of the poor and downtrodden that were believed to hasten "racial decay."[6] As Assistant Director of the Carnegie-funded Eugenics Record Office at Cold Springs Harbor, Harry Laughlin (1922) published a model eugenical sterilization law in 1922 that provided guidance to the states, even though more than a dozen states already had laws on the books by 1920. By 1939, 31 states had enacted eugenical sterilization laws. Here is an excerpt from Laughlin's model law:

> AN ACT to prevent the procreation of persons socially inadequate from defective inheritance, by authorizing' and providing for the eugenical sterilization of certain potential parents carrying degenerate hereditary qualities.... The socially inadequate classes, regardless of etiology or prognosis, are the following: (1) Feeble-minded; (2) Insane, (including the psychopathic); (3) Criminalistic (including the delinquent and wayward); (4) Epileptic; (5) Inebriate (including drug habitues); (6) Diseased (including the tuberculous, the syphilitic, the leprous, and others with chronic, infectious and legally segregable diseases); (7) Blind (including those with seriously impaired vision); (8) Deaf (including those with seriously impaired hearing); (9) Deformed (including the crippled); and (10) Dependent (including orphans, ne'er-do-wells, the homeless, tramps and paupers). (p. 369)

Though cloaked as science, eugenics represented an ideological commitment to perfecting human pedigrees and eliminating threats to that utopian end. It was built around a set of scientific-sounding extrapolations from biology and agriculture, and as Garland Allen (1986) quotes Galton, eugenics focused on "the study of the agencies under social control that may improve or impair the racial qualities of future generations, either physically or mentally" (p. 225). Cutting and pasting from both social Darwinism and Lamarckian theory regarding the inheritability of acquired traits, eugenics was then placed into a statistical fortress that would shelter the new "science," with a public relations machine and research capacity paid for with large philanthropic donations. Such efforts could not have been sustained without early and ongoing financial assistance from the Carnegie Institution and the Rockefeller Foundation, (Black, 2003) which helped to establish for eugenicist "a gargantuan research establishment" (p. 219). Much of the widespread appeal of eugenics reinforced a new secular faith in science as advanced by cranks as well as the most respectable among society's elite, and it reinforced the bombastic belief in American exceptionalism and the capacity for unceasing progress and increased efficiency. Sadly, the broad appeal of eugenics was buoyed, too, by great reservoirs of class bigotry, fear, unbridled racism, and anti-democratic sentiments that were on the rise in the early years of the twentieth century, both here and abroad.

Since the eugenics chapter of American social history is rarely taught in schools where even the story of our slave-holding history remains controversial, most Americans do not know that eugenics was taught as a regular part of science curriculums in junior high and high schools, as well as at Princeton, Harvard, Yale, University of Chicago, Stanford, and dozens of other American colleges and universities (Black, 2003, p. 75). In fact, Stanford's first President, David S. Jordan, published a book in 1902 entitled *Blood of a Nation* that was seminal in advancing the notion that attributes such as pauperism and talent, industriousness and lassitude, are inheritable qualities.

With eugenics being propagated even by many religious leaders during the first decades of the last century (Rosen, 2004), it is not surprising that the race and class assumptions that drove the eugenics ideology and message found their way into cutting-edge education reform in the new twentieth century, embracing as it did the efficient ordering of society and the elimination of waste. Influential education professor and eugenicist, J. Franklin Bobbitt, whose "scientific curriculum making" provided the model for American school curriculum for almost 50 years, viewed social reformers' plans of his day to assist the poor, or the unfit, as "civilization's retrogressive policies." Black (2003) quotes Bobbitt as declaring that "schools and charities supply crutches to the weak in mind and morals... [and] corrupt the streams of heredity" (p. 29). For Bobbitt and other social efficiency education reformers, initiatives to educate and provide assistance to the poor got in the way of Nature's weeding process, which if allowed to operate freely in combination with eugenical sterilization, would eliminate the defective "worm-eaten stock" (p. 29). By 1912, Bobbitt was a leader of the new scientific curriculum standards and testing movement in education that marked the ascendance of social efficiency experts, or the "zealot[s] for the elimination of waste in the curriculum through the application of the kind of scientific management techniques that, presumably, had been so successful in industry" (Kliebard, 2004, p. 20).

Elwood P. Cubberley was another important advocate of eugenics and the science of social efficiency applied to education. As Stanford professor, colleague and friend of Lewis Terman, and Dean of the School of Education (1917–1933), Cubberley trained a generation of school administrators and wrote textbooks on school administration and the history of education that provided the standard interpretations for over 30 years. Cubberley's (1922) *A brief History of Education* provided the educational history for teacher and administrator preparation programs for two decades, and in a concluding chapter argued that advocates that the modern state's "humanitarian educational duties" (p. 451) demand that "defectives ... be sent to a state institution or be enrolled in a public-school class specialized for their training" (p. 450). Cubberley's main attention, however, was aimed toward the "the education of superior children":

> One child of superior intellectual capacity, educated as to utilize his talents, may confer greater benefit to mankind, and be far more educationally important, than a thousand of the feeble-minded children upon whom we have recently come to put so much educational effort and expense. (p. 451)

If any question remained in the minds of future educators as to how "superior" children would be identified, Cubberley immediately followed with a clarion call for intelligence testing to provide the solution to this and many other educational problems:

> Questions relating to the training of leaders for democracy's service attain new significance in terms of recent ability to measure and grade intelligence, as also do questions relating to grading, classification in school, choice of studies, rate of advancement, and the vocational guidance of children in schools. (p. 451)

Echoing Cubberley's unambiguous position was leading psychologist of the child study movement, G. Stanley Hall (1904), who attacked the liberal arts curriculum of schools in 1905 as unworkable because of the inherited defects of most students, who constituted

> ... the great army of incapables, shading down to those who should be in schools for dullards or subnormal children, for whose mental development heredity decrees a slow pace and early arrest, and for whom by general consent both studies and methods must be different. (p. 514)

Hall called for the weeding out of defectives and the breeding of a better race to populate a utopian superstate (Karier, 1983) that would be steered by psychologists like himself, for whom he created the term "heartformers":

> If farmers who can breed cattle, sheep and horses, can also learn how to breed good men and women, the problem is solved. Germ plasm [genetic material] is the most immortal thing in the physical world. Backward it connects us by direct unbroken lines of continuity with our remotest ancestor ... and the most optimistic law in the world is that the best survive and the worst perish. (p. 55)

Just as the eugenics message was clear in public lectures, college coursework, and teacher preparation texts such as Cubberley's, the new pseudoscience burrowed deeply, too, into high school biology textbooks, as recounted in Selden's (1999) *Inheriting Shame: The Story of Eugenics and Racism in America.* Selden examined six mainstream biology texts from 1914 to 1948. By using texts cited by Selden and others recently made available online, we may, in fact, trace the public expressions and beliefs of eugenics advocates during the first half of the twentieth century. That this ideology found its way into school books for the most widely offered science course in high school helps us to understand, perhaps, how sorting, testing, grouping, and segregation became an accepted and expected component within the "basic grammar of schooling" (Tyack & Cuban, 1995, p. 85).

Even though George W. Hunter is more remembered as the author of the biology text used by John Scopes when he was brought up on charges of teaching evolution in a Dayton, Tennessee high school, Hunter should be remembered, too, for his significant role in spreading the ideology of eugenics through his textbooks. In the 1914 high school textbook, *A Civic Biology: Presented in Problems,* George W. Hunter defined eugenics as "the science of being well born" (p. 261). And yet a few pages beyond this rather mild definition, Hunter offered flawed interpretations on inherited traits within two famous family case studies, the Jukes and the Kallikaks, to fuel the conclusion that

> Hundreds of families such . . . as [the Jukes and Kallikaks] exist today, spreading disease, immorality, and crime to all parts of this country. The cost to society of such families is very severe. . . . They not only do harm to others by corrupting, stealing, or spreading disease, but they are actually protected and cared for by the state out of public money. Largely for them the poorhouse and the asylum exist. They take from society, but they give nothing in return. They are true parasites.
>
> **The Remedy**—If such people were lower animals, we would probably kill them off to prevent them from spreading. Humanity will not allow this, but we do have a remedy of separating the sexes in asylums or other places and in various ways preventing intermarriage and the possibilities of perpetuating such a low and degenerate race. Remedies of this sort have been tried successfully in Europe and are now meeting with success in this country. (p. 263)

With the publication in 1922 of the junior high science text, *Civic Science in the Community,* the crisis that Hunter and co-author, Walter Whitman, foresaw took on an added urgency, and his broadcasting of the problem became more amplified. Using the same detailing of the Jukes and the Kallikaks cases from previous texts, Hunter claimed the problem was much more extensive than the "hundreds of families," as he had indicated in his 1914 text. By 1922, Hunter and Whitman have lumped into their estimate all of America's "200,000 feeble-minded persons" as part of their earlier category of parasites:

> If this [Jukes or Kallikaks] were but one case it would be bad enough, but there are over 200,000 feeble-minded persons in the United States to-day. These persons spread disease, crime, and immorality in all parts of the country, principally because they know no better. Just as certain plants and animals become parasitic on others so these people have become parasites on society. Largely for them the asylum and poorhouse exist. (p. 419)

Hunter and Whitman go on to cite, specifically this time, a European solution to the problem from the Italian village of Aosta, where "idiotic folk known as cretins" were segregated during the previous century into male and female asylums, thus preventing reproduction: "Since that time the race of cretins has gradually died out and one rarely sees any of them now. This is the only means by which feeble-mindedness can be eventually blotted out from the earth" (p. 419). Hunter and Whitman end their discussion of eugenics in *Civic Science in the Community* with a definition that reflects the grafting of eugenics presumptions based on Mendelian inheritance onto the terminology of research by early geneticist, Thomas Hunt Morgan, who had, in fact, scientifically discredited the assumptions of eugenics regarding the mechanisms of genetic inheritance. Somehow, Hunter does not seem to have noticed that the science had taken a different fork in the road from eugenics, or if he had, such new knowledge did not alter the authors' renewed confidence that eugenics was an ascendant science:

> The above paragraphs show us that blood will tell or rather, to put it scientifically, "that the chromosomes will tell the story." It is evident that if the race is to be improved, we must improve the stock. This is to be done in the same way that we would work on animals or plants, that is, we must check the reproduction of the poorest strains and mate individuals of the strongest stock. *Eugenics* [italics in the original] is the science of improving the human race by better heredity." (p. 422)

By 1930, advances in genetic science and the growing acceptance of environmental influences in shaping human characteristics, had shifted thinking within the scientific community away from the strict biological determinism argued by eugenicists. That did not stop school textbook writers, however, from continuing to push the eugenics agenda, and by 1935, Hunter and Whitman (1935) were at it again, this time with renewed vigor and enthusiasm for the measures being taken to segregate and sterilize those deemed unfit to reproduce, so that the defective and feeble-minded could, in Hunter and Whitman parlance, be "blotted out from the earth":

> This can only be done by segregation of such people into institutions and some means taken to prevent their reproduction. Several states and at least one country, Germany, have laws which allow such persons to be sterilized or rendered incapable of reproduction. (p. 484)

Such language remains ominous almost 80 years later, and the thought of it being taught in a high school biology class remains shocking, especially since open and official hostility in Germany toward Jews and other "unfit" groups was a matter of governmental policy and public record when Hunter and Whitman were praising the Germans for their foresightedness. In fact, a major movement was afoot in the United States in 1935 to boycott the 1936 Olympics in Berlin. These events, however, could not dissuade these textbook writers and shapers of children's values from their self-appointed tasks. Two pages further on, Hunter and Whitman adds this warning:

> If our country is to keep its place as a leader in world progress, we must prevent its overpopulation by defective or weak mental stock. We must, on the other hand, do all we can to have persons of the better stock mate and have children. (p. 486)

The authors end their chapter with a list of terms from which students are to choose in order to fill in the blanks on the end of chapter test. Here is the final item, with proper answers supplied: "Laws should prevent the breeding of the unfit, who would soon disappear from the earth" (p. 487). We may wonder if any young American boys taking this test in 1935 were there when the gates of Buchenwald and Auschwitz were opened in 1945 for the horrified young troopers to see to what "disappear from the earth" looks like when efficiently applied on an industrial scale.

For those who know something about this history of eugenics, there remains the common notion that the opening up of the German concentration camps and the subsequent horrors unveiled in testimony at Nuremburg served to stem homegrown enthusiasm for eugenic efforts to sort and segregate the fit from the unfit. Selden (1999) shows this assumption to be a myth, as does researcher, Ronald Ladouceur (2011), with examples from post-war high school (and college) biology texts that make it clear that what survived the Holocaust was what Selden (1999) calls a "reform eugenics" that dropped the avowals to strict biological determinism, even as it maintained a loyalty to social efficiency goals of social and vocational sorting. The reform eugenics textbook writers and testing disciples continued to use schools as the primary institutional tool to sort and segregate children, as well as the next generation of adults. In fact, any "discussion of human possibilities" was to be based on a "commitment to a hierarchical and corporate social order that placed students in social and vocational slots based on fatally flawed measures of 'hereditary worth'" (p. 82).

Selden (1999) ends his analysis of textbooks with *Animal Biology* (1948), a high school text by Dr. Robert Guyer, noted biologist at the University of Wisconsin, Madison. In important ways, Guyer demonstrates how little eugenics advocates had actually changed since the beginning of the twentieth century. Almost 40 years after the first wave of eugenic-inspired education reform, Guyer (as cited in Selden, 1999, p. 81) claimed that "certain hereditary types are more valuable to society and the race than others... [and] in many family strains the seeds of derangement and disability have become so firmly established that they menace the remainder of the population." Though the eugenics of mid-century ostensibly acknowledged the nurture side of the nature-nurture debate, Guyer advised against public or private assistance to the unfit, as he argued that "unwise charity... fosters the production of unfit strains" (Selden, 1999, p. 82). It is as if Dr. Guyer was disinterring arguments made by the new "scientists" of education, Bobbitt and Cubberley, 30 years before.

We will turn now to examine more closely where we have been and where we are going in regards to the overlapping and mutually reinforcing linkages among the rise of accountability and standards movement, high stakes standardized testing, and the latest manifestations of corporate education reform. We shall do so in a way that contextualizes these elements within the recurrent cultural and political policy markers that lead some to refer to our educational history metaphorically as a pendulum, or even a vicious circle. Our metaphor, hopefully, may be viewed as a spiral, for as Tyack and Cuban (1995) point out, the arrow of time upon which social evolution is carried, makes it impossible to return to exactly the same place, even if the ideas and motivations are drawn from previous eras and even if they have not changed.

The Road Beyond Eugenics: Technocratic Meritocracy

In the post-war glow of consumerist individualism in the United States, education policy makers were keen to tack away from earlier enthusiasms for social engineering via eugenics. As a liberal supporter of the comprehensive school as the "great engine of democracy," Harvard president, James Conant sought to revive the Jeffersonian democratic ideals based on meritocracy, which favored a system whereby, as Jefferson (1787/1853) put it, a small number of the "best geniuses will be raked from the rubbish annually" to receive a William and Mary education at public expense. As the first Harvard president from a "humble background" (Lemann, 1995), Conant set about creating a scholarship program during the 1930s to attract the most capable students from a national pool, regardless of economic background. Trained as a chemist and reared with an understanding of what life was like without inherited privilege, Conant "immediately moved to increase the representation of younger versions of himself" (para. 11). Seeking to derive an objective way to select Harvard students with the most academic potential, he recruited a young Harvard assistant dean and devoted testing enthusiast, Henry Chauncey, to help him decide how scholarship winners would be decided. Conant and Chauncey turned, predictably, to another test to help them rake a new generation of geniuses "from the rubbish." The test was the Scholastic Aptitude Test (SAT) (Lemann, 1999).

Though not in wide use until after World War II, the SAT was created a generation before by Carl Brigham, an assistant of Robert Yerkes, a leading eugenicist who was the chief developer and promoter of the Alpha and Beta intelligence tests administered during World War I. Brigham modeled the early versions of the SAT on the Army Alpha, which had been used to sort officer material from those recruits whose scores made them suited for the trenches in France. These early versions of the SAT remained largely intact even up through the outbreak of World War II, when the SAT finally replaced the more "labor-intensive essay exams" (Lemann, 1995, para. 36) and other "old-fashioned college admissions tests" (para. 38).

Chauncey had sold Conant on the notion that the SAT measured "pure intelligence," and Conant believed that such a test in wide circulation would offer all American high school students, Harvard bound or otherwise, an equal shot at college, regardless of the quality of their local high schools—which remained as inconsistent then as now. Even after he became a leading advocate for overhauling public high schools, the irony never seemed to register with Conant that a college admissions tool that purported to make high school quality irrelevant may, in fact, make public school improvement a less compelling need to those disposed toward socioeconomic efficiency.

Even with Chauncey and a second generation of testing advocates on board with Conant's plan, a formidable task remained for the supporters of the SAT as the chief tool for implementing the new meritocracy. The proportion of high school graduates attending college was still small by today's standards, and the model for achieving financial success did not involve getting a college degree. Most people in 1940 viewed college attendance as an activity of the children of those who had already arrived at their financial destinations, rather than as a chosen vehicle by those trying to get there:

> The idea that formal education was unnecessary or even inimical to economic success was a staple of American popular culture from Franklin's time until the mid-twentieth century. In works as adoring as Horatio Alger's novels and as condemnatory as Theodore Dreiser's *The Financier*, the self-made man always drops out of school and becomes a kind of apprentice to an older businessman as the first step on the road to riches. (Lemann, 1995, para. 44)

To be able to identify the new generation of potential "natural aristocrats" by testing measures would require, then, a strong case for the desirability of going to college. That case would be made by James Conant, himself, who did so in two pieces of patriotic outpouring and passionate verbal stirrings published by the *Atlantic Monthly* during the early 1940s.

The first article appeared in 1940, and in it Conant (1940) set out to reconnect the future of America with its Jeffersonian past, and in so doing, to realize for liberals like Conant the long-held Jeffersonian goal of challenging inherited privilege by creating a meritocracy that would be enabled by the modern technology of standardized tests. Conant does not mention testing until his cinched-up conclusion, which follows an explanation and interpretation of the three Jeffersonian verities that his essay proposes as a social and political middle ground for America moving forward, none of which, by the way, was generally accepted or widely operationalized during Jefferson's lifetime: "Freedom of the mind, social mobility through education, universal schooling—these . . . are the three fundamentals of the Jeffersonian tradition" (IV, para. 1).

For Conant (1940), to not accept the three elements of the Jeffersonian tradition meant choosing from the other three political options as he saw them: to be free, though class bound (as Great Britain); to be without caste, though not free (as the Soviet Union); or to neither free nor without caste (as Nazi Germany) (II, para. 13). The choice for America was clear, the implications clearer, and the path to get there indelibly marked:

> If we as educators accept the American ideal, then this acceptance must be the major premise for all our thinking. Without neglecting the older roads designed for those of academic brilliance, we must construct many new approaches to adult life, and we must do so very soon. Extreme differentiation of school programs seems essential—differentiation of instruction, but not necessarily a division into separate schools. From this, it follows that rapid improvement in our testing methods must be forthcoming; a much more conscientious and discriminating form of educational guidance must be developed soon if we are not to fail. In short, a horde of heterogeneous

> students has descended on our secondary schools; on our ability to handle all types intelligently depends in large measure the future of this country.

The month before Conant's (1943) second article appeared in the May issue of *Atlantic Monthly*, Henry Chauncey, on temporary leave from Harvard, helped lead an effort by the College Board on April 2, 1943 to administer, on the same day, an adapted version of Brigham's original SAT to 325,000 young men. The contract was paid for by the War Department, and the test was known as the Army-Navy College Qualifying Test. Though given under much more test security than the old Alpha and Beta tests of WWI, the results of the test would have the same "life and death" consequences, as high scorers were assured deferment for college or a Washington desk job and low scorers were labeled for induction (Lemann, 1995). In offering evidence that the SAT could be administered on a grand scale and efficiently scored with a new invention that electrically registered graphite marks on a multiple choice answer sheet, a new generation of scientific testers was born.

As Horace Mann had a hundred years before when he argued for education as "the great equalizer" and schools as "the great balance wheel of the social machinery," Conant's call for more equality of educational opportunity, rather than equality of result, aimed to stem the political polarization between Left and Right that he feared would worsen once the War was over. Following on the established secular faith in education (Tyack & Cuban, 1995) that had taken deep root early in the twentieth century, Conant (1943) argued for the creation of a North American variety of post-partisan radical who would be dedicated to universalizing educational opportunity as the path to equality:

> No one needs to be told that the American radical will be a fanatic believer in equality. Yet it will be a peculiar North American brand of doctrine.... He believes in equality of opportunity, not equality of rewards; but, on the other hand, he will be lusty in wielding the axe against the root of inherited privilege. To prevent the growth of a caste system, which he abhors he will be resolute in his demand to confiscate (by constitutional methods) all property once a generation.... He will favor public education, truly universal educational opportunity at every level. He will be little concerned with the future of private education, except as he values independent competing groups in every phase of American activity. (section 3, para. 5)

When it came time for Conant (1943), himself, to become a new American radical committed to "truly universal educational opportunity at every level" (section 3, para. 6) he took a decidedly more conservative stance. When Congress passed the new Servicemen's Readjustment Act of 1944 (GI Bill) to allow access to higher education for returning soldiers, Conant quickly urged revisions to the law to restrict the number of college admissions. He did not go so far as his fellow university president at the University of Chicago, Robert Maynard Hutchins, who warned of an influx of unemployed veterans that he referred to as "educational hoboes" ("Conant Suggests," 1945), but in his Annual Report to the Harvard Corporation Trustees in January 1945, Conant argued that the federal benefits should be based on "demonstrated ability," rather than length of service:

> Unless high standards of performance can be maintained in spite of sentimental pressures and financial temptation, we may find the least capable among the war generation, instead of the most capable, flooding the facilities for advanced education in the United States. (para. 5)

Two years later, and 10 years after Conant urged the creation of a single national testing organization, the Educational Testing Service (ETS) was chartered. With the help of Conant, Chauncey became its first President (PBS Frontline, 1995–2013, para. 9). In 1948, Conant became the first Chairman of the Board (para. 4).

Conant's legacy is not limited to his influence on the future of testing and measuring, for he went on to become a distinguished diplomat and respected voice in reforming the American high school. His influence, however, on the character of American higher education owes much to his years devoted to pushing forward and upward the fixation of standardization. Louis Menand (2002) sums us Conant's contribution thusly:

> The scientific standards he imposed on the selection of students and faculty at Harvard (and, through that example, on much of the rest of the country's institutions of higher education) reflect a certain impercipience about the variety of forms that contributions to knowledge and to the cultural life can take. He largely drove imagination out of the university, and he helped to quantify talents—such as "verbal aptitude"—which it is meaningless to assess in purely quantitative terms. You don't have to an enemy of logocentrism to have doubts about the system Conant helped to create. You only have to look around you at the people who have "made it." (pp. 105–06)

Even though the SAT continues to cast a very long shadow, the purported objectivity assigned to the SAT by the testing experts at ETS has not been able to erase the systemic problems that would eventually become impossible to ignore. Besides the cultural biases to which early SAT writers remained quite blind, there was then and remains today the unfairness of economic privilege in relation to academic achievement that had haunted earlier efforts to scientifically measure intelligence and academic worth.

As the chart below shows from an analysis published for all to see in the *New York Times* (Rampell, 2009), there remains no better predictor of SAT scores than family income and wealth, despite the ostensible intentions of James Conant, Henry Chauncey, and their psychometric descendants. The same close correlations between family income and standardized test scores are mirrored today at every level of education, from early elementary to graduate school. The likelihood of "raking a few geniuses from the rubbish each year" must be weighed against the cost of a continuing to maintain a college admissions system that perpetuates the advantage of the economically advantaged (see Figure 1).

Even less apparent, though more insidious, are long-standing disadvantages that accrue to those groups of test takers who have suffered from systematic discrimination or societal stereotyping. Claude Steele's (1997; 1999) and Joshua Aronson's (Steele & Aronson, 1995) ground-breaking

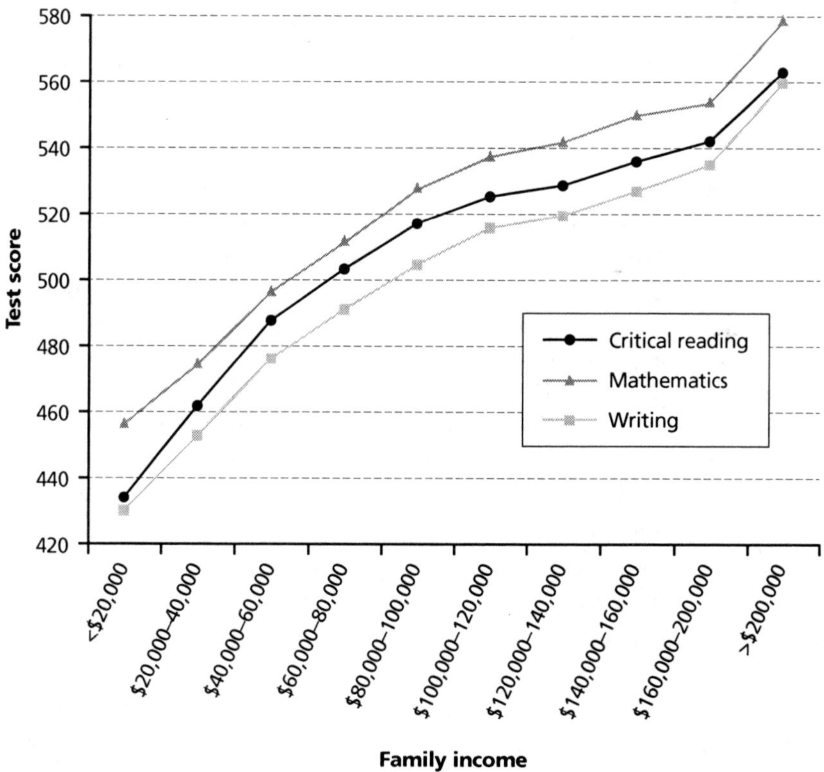

Figure 1 SAT scores and correlation to family income (*Data Source:* College Board, 2009, p. 4).

research on "stereotype threat" make these privileges and disadvantages clear, and in doing so, they raise questions that go to the core of testing practices at any level. Steele and Aronson show that negative stereotypes historically associated, for instance, with intelligence of African-Americans or the mathematical ability of women continue to function as a test score depressant in testing situations where mathematical reasoning or intelligence, respectively, are measured. In the words of Steele and Aronson, stereotype threat is

> ... a social-psychological predicament that can arise from widely known negative stereotypes about one's group.... the existence of such a stereotype means that anything one does or any of one's features that conform to it make the stereotype more plausible as a self-characterization in the eyes of others, and perhaps even in one's own eyes.
>
> ... whenever African American students perform an explicitly scholastic or intellectual task, they face the threat of confirming or being judged by a negative societal stereotype—a suspicion—about their group's intellectual ability and competence. This threat is not borne by people not stereotyped in this way. And the self-threat it causes—through a variety of mechanisms—may interfere with the intellectual functioning of these students, particularly during standardized tests (p. 797).

In experiments that have been replicated and widely disseminated, researchers (Aronson, Quinn, & Spencer, 1998; Schmader & Johns, 2003); Steele, 1997; Steele & Aronson, 1995) have shown that stereotype threat can affect performance by as much as a standard deviation on intelligence tests or high stakes aptitude tests such as the SAT, and this phenomenon may be triggered even by such subtle cues as identifying one's race or gender on a test form. In 2011, Steele told an audience at Stanford University, "I think the best account of it is when an African-American is taking a difficult IQ test, there's that stereotype out there that's ancient about intelligence, and you allocate some of your cognitive resources to defending against that stereotype" (Kenrick, 2011, para. 11).

In the end, the SAT and other standardized measures will fall short of attaining the objective and neutral status envisioned by their progressive proponents for as long as the effects of race and class privilege, bigotry, and discrimination remain alive in our society. They will, in fact, help sustain unfair advantages and sorting systems that many liberal SAT advocates would, otherwise, outlaw. History offers a prime example of this irony with the insistent demands for federal evaluation systems by Robert Kennedy, one of the chief architects of the original Elementary and Secondary Act (ESEA) of 1965.

The Modern Testing Era Begins

As noted earlier, education has not always been the chosen road to opportunity and upward mobility. The case had to be made, and the solution had to be sold, and James Conant was instrumental toward establishing education as the means to that end. Between the New Deal and the early 1960s, policy makers at the national level consciously chose to focus efforts to establish social and economic equity through increasing access to education (Kantor & Lowe, 1995), rather than the more expensive and politically unpopular route of wealth redistribution, job creation, guaranteed minimum income levels, and programs to disrupt segregated living patterns and inadequate health care provisions. Progressives in the United States had advocated during the 1930s for the kind of social and economic development efforts that became institutionalized in the social democracies of Western Europe and Scandinavia after World War II, and the "movement to expand government control of the market and to alter its distributional patterns seemed likely to succeed even in the United States" (p. 6). Following World War II, however, the GI Bill, the rhetorical messaging of leaders like Conant, and successes within the labor movement had, in effect, reduced the perceived need for direct government structural intervention in social equity efforts. The NAACP's focus, too, on school desegregation as the primary civil rights agenda added to the impetus already taking hold:

> By the late 1950s and early 1960s, the political space for active state intervention in the market had thus shrunken considerably. Although the Civil Rights movement sought to put full employment planning and income redistribution back on the public agenda, these policies generated little support from the middle class or from blue collar workers who received benefits mainly through the private sector. Consequently, when policy makers in the Kennedy and Johnson administrations began to formulate poverty policy, they ruled out active government intervention to create jobs and redistribute income because without widespread popular support they did not think they could win approval for such measures in Congress. (p. 7)

Even though the federal strategy of increasing educational opportunities with large infusions of cash was able to buy Southern support, finally, for the desegregation of schools, it set a precedent for future generations policy elites who continue to espouse the belief that "education is the civil rights issue of our generation" (Lewin, 2012, para. 5). This expression has taken on a deep sense irony in recent years, since federal education funding sets a high priority on the unlimited spread of charter schools, which have a clear segregative effect (Frankenberg, Siegel-Hawley, & Wang, 2010;

Miron, Urschel, Mathis, & Tornquist, 2010) on public schools, even in areas where schools were intensely segregated already.

The Elementary and Secondary Education Act (ESEA) came one year after the passage of the Civil Rights Act in 1964, and President Lyndon Johnson promoted ESEA as a hard-to-ignore financial incentive aimed to make palatable the non-discrimination requirements of the Civil Rights Act for Southern segregationists. Johnson hoped that the ESEA funds offered to states and cities that agreed to desegregate would finally break the back of Southern apartheid, which had remained largely undisturbed despite the 1954 unanimous Supreme Court decision in *Brown v Topeka Board of Education* decision. The plan was hugely successful, so much so that apartheid education largely disappeared in 17 Southern states by the late 1960s (Orfield, from Mondale & Patton, 2001). Distrustful, however, of the Southern political establishment in general and Lyndon Johnson in particular, Senator Robert Kennedy did not want to see the draining away of millions of Title I dollars before they could ever reach the malignantly and impoverished minority children for whom Title I was intended (Lagemann, 2000). Kennedy, in fact, argued for standardized procedures and uniform data gathering, and he called for a "good faith administration effort to hold educators responsive to their constituencies and to make educational achievement the touchstone of success in judging ESEA" (Mathison, 2009, p. 6). At a Senate hearing in 1965, Kennedy went so far as to propose "some testing system that would be established [by] which the people at the local community would know periodically as to what progress had been made" (Barone, 2007, p. 4). In advocating program evaluations for the original ESEA Title I programs, Kennedy unwittingly served to inspire the program accountability movement in education (p. 10).

Robert Kennedy's efforts to find out if poor children were actually learning to read were complicated by new federal budgeting requirements for implementing cost-benefit analyses aimed to increase efficiency in federal spending by identifying the most successful programs. Satisfying either aim would have been difficult for a single evaluation scheme, but satisfying both proved entirely too much. Further complicating efforts, as Ellen Lagemann (2000) has pointed out, were state fears and resentment related to potential federal control or state embarrassment for poor results. All of these concerns were on the table as a new national assessment was being developed, field tested, and administered in 1969. It was called the National Assessment of Educational Progress (NAEP), and today it is known as America's Report Card. More will be said about NAEP in Part 4, particularly as it relates to the use of arbitrary and unrealistic norming in order to then use the low test results for political purposes.

Another seminal event that unwittingly contributed to the growth of the educational accountability by testing is known today as the Coleman Report (Coleman, et al, 1966). The mandate for the Coleman report came from the Civil Rights Act of 1964, which required a research study be conducted within two years of passage to identify where educational resources in public educational institutions were lacking due to "race, color, religion, or national origin" (Lagemann, 2000, p. 193). Almost overnight, previous education program evaluation criteria based on resource inputs shifted to program outputs as the mandate for tracking education program effectiveness was written into federal legislation.

While everyone, including James Coleman, expected to find large differences in achievement based on large differences in resources between the 600,000 children that his study included in 4,000 Black and White schools, the findings confounded expectations. As Coleman scholar, Gerald Grant (2009) points out Coleman found discrepancies in spending between Black and White schools to be less than expected, due to infusions of cash by Southern states in hopes of maintaining the "separate but equal" apartheid systems. But, even where resource differences were large, Coleman found these disparities in Black schools influenced student achievement differences much less than "who you went to school with":

> Simply put, Coleman found that the achievement of both poor and rich children was depressed by attending a school where most children came from low-income families. More important to the goal of achieving equal educational opportunity, he found that the achievement of poor children was raised by attending a predominantly middle-class school, while the achievement of affluent children in the school was not harmed. This was true even if per-pupil expenditures were the same at both schools. No research over the past 40 years has overturned Coleman's finding.... (p. 159)

Coleman and his team (1966) found, too, that non-Asian minority children are more affected by social composition than are White children, and that "if a minority pupil from a home without much educational strength is put with schoolmates with strong educational backgrounds, his achievement is likely to increase" (p. 22). Though this finding is commonly cited in analyses and interpretations of the Coleman study, the dynamics that shape this social fact are most often attributed to the social capital that accrues for various reasons when poor children go to school with middle class children. Coleman, however, clearly introduces a race element beyond socioeconomic status that is related to the effects of oppression and demoralization that is rarely cited. Therefore, we include this rather lengthy quote below, which if attended to by policy makers, would doubtless create an added urgency to dust off long-neglected integration plans. Notice that Coleman remains loyal to and supportive of the charge given to him under Section 402 of Civil Rights Act of 1964 to provide data related to "the lack of equal educational opportunity for individuals by reason of race, color, religion, or national origin . . . ," even though his investigations have led him to findings that even Coleman could not have predicted:

> This analysis has concentrated on the educational opportunities offered by the schools in terms of the student body composition, facilities, curriculums, and teachers. This emphasis, while entirely appropriate as a response to the legislation for the survey, nevertheless neglects important factors in the variability between individual pupils within the same school: this variability is roughly four times as large as the variability between schools. For example, *a pupil attitude factor, which appears to have a stronger relationship to achievement than do all the "school" factors together, is the extent to which an individual feels that he has some control over his own destiny* [italics added]. . . . The responses of pupils, except for Orientals, have far less conviction than Whites that they can affect their own environments and futures. When they do, however, their achievement is higher than that of Whites who lack that conviction.
>
> Furthermore, while this characteristic shows little relationship to most school factors, it is related, for Negroes, to the proportion of Whites in the schools. Those Negroes in schools with a higher proportion of Whites have a greater sense of control. This finding suggests that the direction such an attitude takes may be associated with the pupil's school experience as well as the experience in the larger community. (p. 23)

Coleman found hope, then, strongly correlated with the presence of a sense of autonomy, which is more easily demonstrated, measured, and retained where racial and economic mixing prevails, rather than in racially and economically segregated environments—whether that segregation is sustained by antiquated beliefs, legal maneuvering, or by outdated school assessment practices. And it was this "pupil attitude factor" of hope that had a greater effect on achievement than all other school effects examined in the Coleman study, which remains the largest research undertaking of its kind in U.S. educational history.

The Coleman findings on socioeconomic status and school achievement echoed the findings of another large, longitudinal study a few years earlier, whose similar results on the topic were similarly ignored (for similar reasons, we may assume). The federal research project in 1960, Project Talent, involved detailed questionnaires in over 1,300 high schools and a series of tests for 440,000 students that included achievement, attitudinal, interest, and aptitude tests, surveys, and questionnaires. Instruments were administered in 1960 when students were ninth graders and again in 1963 when they were seniors. By 1973, it is clear that Washington's elite had digested the implications of these studies, as expressed here by fiscal and monetary expert, Alice Rivlin (1973):

> The most general result of these statistical studies [the Coleman Study and the Project Talent study] has been the finding that variables reflecting the socioeconomic characteristics of students and their families explain most of the variation in test scores, and variables reflecting school characteristics or resource inputs explain very little.
>
> These results should not be exaggerated—they do not prove that "schools don't matter"—but they certainly provide a basis for considerable skepticism about using test scores as measures of the output of the education industry as such. Test score changes may primarily reflect changes in the school population and the way it is mixed, rather than the productivity of school resources themselves. (p. 424)

Lagemann (2000) recounts the drama surrounding the release of the Coleman Report's initial findings in 1966, and the subsequent "firestorm" set off within the Johnson Administration, which knew that Coleman's findings could sabotage the Administration's strategy of using the federal purse to buy Southern support to end apartheid schooling in the South, as set forth by ESEA the year before. Johnson knew that Republicans, already resistant to more federal spending, would seize and exploit the counterintuitive fact that spending levels were clearly not the prime factor in performance discrepancies. Coleman's findings, too, offered a swipe at a core component of the American secular faith in education and educational opportunity as "the chief instrument for redressing the inequalities of American life" (Kantor, 1991, p. 50).

This lofty notion had, indeed, fed the Jeffersonian belief, later transferred to Horace Mann, that education may provide solutions to social problems that were thought to be the result of the poor's own shortcomings. Blaming the poor for their poverty is as traditional as our Calvinist forefathers of Puritan New England, who viewed the socioeconomically unfit as having earned their lack of status through their own moral failings (Rippa, 1996). These shortcomings, in turn, might signal the column of the celestial tally sheet to which all souls had been added who were not a part of the Elect, or God's elite. From this early theological base, there eventually grew the Protestant economic catechism of the Gilded Age, with ample doses thrown in of Social Darwinism, which "held that responsibility for poverty lay not with the business cycle or the existence of a capitalist reserve army of the unemployed, but with the moral failure of the poor themselves to conduct proper family economy" (Dawley, 1993, p. 27).

By the 1960s the poor's personal flaws and the lifestyles (Kantor, 1991) they spawned were bundled within a new and encompassing concept known as the "culture of poverty," which acknowledged structural barriers as well as the traditional blaming of the victim:[7]

> First, though it acknowledged the structural sources of deprivation, the culture of poverty thesis tended to focus attention more on the personal characteristics of the poor themselves.... Consequently, and this is the second point, because it implied that people were poor due to their own attitudes, behaviors, and life-styles, it suggested that changing the poor rather than redistributing income or creating jobs was the best way to eliminate the problem of poverty. (p. 55)

The third characteristic that Kantor (1991) attributes to the "culture-of-poverty thesis" was its belief that, since the economic and psychological conditions left the poor without the "will and capacity to attack the sources of their own deprivation" (p. 55), professional intervention was required, which assured a powerful role for the liberal public policy makers during the 1960s. Such interventions, however, did not disrupt the underlying assumptions of economic order, systems of privilege, or existing power relations, as initiatives to help the poor focused more on education and training programs. As noted earlier, these kinds of compensatory solutions could be provided without disrupting the social and economic structures that would have been challenged by job creation programs or other alterations to economic and socio-cultural patterns. The preferred compensatory strategies adopted by liberals could "compensate for capitalism's inevitable flaws and omissions without interfering with its internal workings" (Kantor quoting Brinkley, 1991, p. 56).

Coleman's findings, however, were not governed by any of these assumptions. His findings clearly suggest the need for structural alterations to the racial and socioeconomic organization of schools, while clearly pointing to the limited value of simply adding resources without structural modifications. The initial findings of the Coleman Report, therefore, were appropriately muted by Johnson's White House; the media, with no open controversy to sell copy and with its accepted narrative wisdom to protect, largely ignored the complete findings when they did appear late in 1966 (Coleman et al, 1966). Both liberal and conservative policy people, then, read the Coleman Report looking for ideological ammunition, and they found it. Conservatives centrally concerned with cutting costs and conserving the status quo cherry-picked Coleman's findings (Alexander, 1997) to argue that "throwing money"[8] at educational problems couldn't fix them, while liberals used Coleman's findings related to social capital and the importance of racial and economic mixing to argue for mandatory busing policies to achieve racial balance. Coleman remained disappointed (Coleman, 1972) at the reception of the study, and he remained throughout his life an advocate for removing all barriers to socioeconomic integration, even as an interim measure toward achieving equity and equality (Kahlenberg, 2001). Kahlenberg (2001) cites Coleman from a rare interview in 1972, in which his claim for the significance of social capital is made unequivocal:

> Coleman said that research continued to show that "a child's performance, especially a working-class child's performance, is greatly benefited by his going to a school with children who come from educationally stronger backgrounds." Coleman declared flatly: "A child's learning is a function more of the characteristics of his classmates than those of the teacher." (p. 62)

How different today's education reform agenda might be if Coleman's core finding had been acknowledged and taken to heart for its central truth: schools alone can never consistently close the gaps in achievement that reflect deep differences in levels of autonomy and privilege, wide disparities in opportunity, deep veins of racism, and an ongoing and deepening hope gap. How different our schools might be if we were to take seriously what good research already tells us, or if we as a society were to fund other social science research with the potential to matter in the health of our neighborhoods and our world. Or, how differently our schools and our perception of schools might be if we were to conceive of educational improvement as one important component of a comprehensive commitment to social and economic renewal, in a way that acknowledges the wisdom expressed by Jean Anyon's (1997) quip: "Attempting to fix inner city schools without fixing the city in which they are embedded is like trying to clean the air on one side of a screen door" (p. 168).

Instead, it would seem that another, though harsher, version of corporate education reform is now aimed toward U.S. schools. The latest testing/accountability scheme of Race to the Top continues to ignore Coleman's core research findings on how social and economic segregation impact achievement, even as today's corporate reformers continue to cite education[9] as the civil rights issue of the present era. If we are to believe, then, the mountain of scholarship[10] that validates Coleman's findings (Gamoran & Long, 2006) as they relate to the power of shared social capital and the limited capacity of schools alone to end output gaps as measured by test scores, we must surely find ways to counter the essential irrationality that says there are "no excuses" for children and teachers segregated by race and class, who must accomplish the impossible or, else, accept the punishing and inescapable consequences. Here we are reminded Richard Hofstadter's (1955) warning to those who dare challenge the status quo masked as reform:

> In determining whether... [social] ideas are accepted, truth and logic are less important criteria than suitability to the intellectual needs and preconceptions of social interests. This is one of the great difficulties that must be faced by rational strategists of social change. (p. 204)

Until such time that our society signals a return to common sense and humane values applied to education policymaking, we may wonder what calamities may be required to halt this generation's "revolving, reformist administrative shell game" (Martin, Overholt, & Urban, 1976, p. 71) to preserve the status quo while proclaiming change. During the first half of the previous century's "orgy of tabulation" (Rugg, 1975), it took an economic depression and a world war to interrupt the virulent social-efficiency engineering project that eventually threatened democracy and human rights everywhere. Will we, once again, choose the failed efforts and dangerous intoxicants of the past in a different guise, while ignoring the continuing retrenchment of structural inequality and social inequity that make our democratic ideals increasingly arcane and the hope that sustains us, adults and children alike, less likely with each passing school year?

"Sound and Cheap"

> *There is the fact that some skills are clearly more measurable than others, and that some most highly prized intellectual characteristics (creativity, ingenuity, motivation) are hard to measure at all.*
>
> —Alice Rivlin (1973)

By the end of the 1960s, a backlash was taking hold in both the South and the North to compensatory education programs and desegregation efforts. Analysis of the Coleman Report (Mosteller & Moynihan, 1972) zeroed in on the negative effects of families on test scores and the limited effects of additional resources to raise achievement in poor schools. On the national political stage, Richard Nixon used race as a wedge issue in 1968 and exploited resistance to the War on Poverty to peel off support among disaffected Southern Democrats angered by Democratic alignment with the Civil Rights Movement. By late 1969, Nixon had a name for the new permanent voting bloc he hoped to build for Republicans based on "the Southern Strategy," and in a speech (Nixon, 1969) on Vietnam in November of that year, he appealed to a new constituency he labeled the "Silent Majority" by declaring their rightful role in maintaining social order for the entire history of America,

> ...the policy of this Nation has been made under our Constitution by those leaders in the Congress and the White House elected by all of the people. If a vocal minority, however fervent its cause, prevails over reason and the will of the majority, this Nation has no future as a free society.

In 1970, the new champion of the Silent Majority was ready to challenge the compensatory education programs that had become the vehicle for delivering Lyndon Johnson's War on Poverty in schools. In a "Special Message to Congress on Education Reform" (Nixon, 1970) on March 3, Nixon began with "American education is in urgent need of reform," and directly came to the reasons why:

> We must stop letting wishes color our judgments about the educational effectiveness of many special compensatory programs, when—despite some dramatic and encouraging exceptions—there is growing evidence that most of them are not yet measurably improving the success of poor children in school.... Years of educational research, culminating in the Equal Educational Opportunity Survey of 1966 have, however, demonstrated that this direct, uncomplicated relationship does not exist.

The President's speech called for a new focus on school outputs rather than inputs, along with the creation of a new National Institute of Education to "lead in the development of educational output." In initiating "a new concept: accountability," Nixon called for new "dependable measures" even at the local level: "School administrators and school teachers alike are responsible for their performance, and it is in their interest as well as in the interest of their pupils that they be held accountable."

A year later, Nixon appointed Sidney Marland, Jr. to operationalize his new accountability concept within the Office of Education, and Marland proved eager to apply "management by objective" strategies toward creating a "science of evaluation" that sounded strikingly similar to Frederick Winslow Taylor's "scientific management principles" from 60 years earlier:

> Once large objectives have been hammered out, each must be broken into specific and carefully defined sub-objectives. Accountability is implicit from day to day and from month to month as all echelons in the Office of Education focus their energies on the objective and its sub-objectives and perform the various tasks which lead to their completion. (Marland, 1972, as cited in Martin, Overholt, & Urban, 1976, pp. 70–71)

Though Marland's further speculations on the future of accountability would be off in terms of timing, he could not have been more of a visionary in regards to the eventual outcome:

> Indeed, within our time—perhaps within the next ten years—there could well be a nationwide accounting process or institution which would act like a certified public accountant in business, objectively assessing the success and failure of our schools and reporting the findings to the public. . . . [on] how productively are our teachers being used. . . . (p. 71)

We may see, then, the die as cast in the first years of the Nixon Era for another generation of "objectively assessing" schools in ways that would continue to cast doubt on the effectiveness and efficiency of compensatory programs for the poor, while turning concerns for raising student achievement into an obsessive fixation on test scores for a shrinking number of subjects.

Accountabilism

Haney and Reczak (1994) found that the federal education clearinghouse and database, ERIC, began using "educational accountability" as a descriptor in 1970, when nine documents using the term were collected and made accessible by ERIC.

The graph in Figure 2 represents our recent search of all ERIC publications, including documents, journal articles, and books, from 1966 when ERIC was established through 2011. The second steepest increase in publication activity occurred from 1971 to 1972, when the number of found items increased from 142 to 440. That sharp increase cannot match, however, the rise in the number of found items between 2008 and 2009, when the number shot up from 1,591 to 1,934. In 2010, the number of items reached 2,200. It took 30 years, in fact, for the number of citations per year to reach a thousand, and it has taken only 13 years for the number of ERIC entries per year to go to over 2,200. Note, however, the sharpest one-year

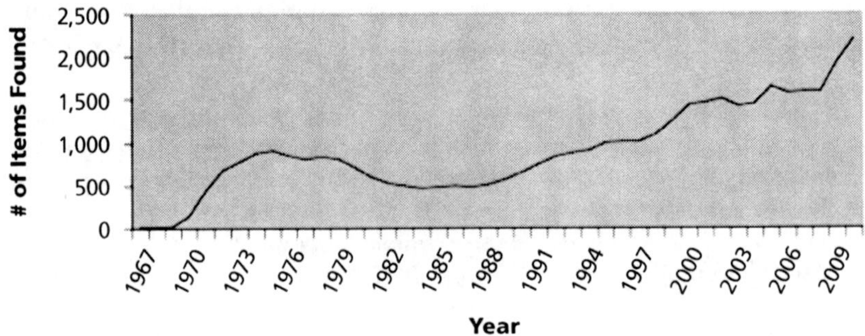

Figure 2 ERIC citations accountability and education.

decline ever in the number of citations for 2010–2011, when the number plummeted by over 400 entries.

"Accountability" means "the ability to deliver on promises" (Lessinger cited in Glass, 1972), and "an accountable relationship between seller and buyer involves three elements: 1) disclosure concerning the product or service being sold, 2) product or performances testing, 3) redress in the event of false disclosure or poor performance" (p. 636). Accountability has not always meant the same thing to all people in the many different situations for which the term has been applied, but the field of education in particular has developed more unique misuses of the term than could be expected, even of a sub-discipline that borrows liberally and regularly terms and concepts from more respected disciplines for which such facile transfer remains entirely inappropriate. Forty years ago, Glass noted that

> The term [accountability] drips with excess meaning. In recent months it has been applied variously to 1) the statement of instructional objectives, 2) performance contracting, 3) voucher systems, 4) economic input-output analysis, 5) accreditation, 6) community participation, and so forth. How can a word that means so much mean anything at all? (p. 636).

If the narrowing of focus over time can be counted as a virtue, then the last four decades have brought Goodness to the field of educational accountability, as the term's unmistakable usage in schools has come to be associated with the repeated performance testing of products for which the clerks (teachers) and even the customers (children and parents) are held liable, in this case for a product line for which the manufacturers (policy elites and the education industry) reap the rewards while accepting none of the responsibility for quality.

While 1970 signaled the beginning of the new era in which "accountability" would bleed into almost every thread of the schooling fabric, 1990 marks the beginning of a second generation of an accountability and standards movement. Before we go there to examine what happened to exhort accountability reformers at the end of the 1980s, we must first look briefly at what happened at the beginning of the decade. A 30-year fitful history of attempts to establish a more equitable public education system ended with a whimper during Ronald Reagan's first term as President. The shift came as no surprise, however, for Reagan had clearly signaled during early campaign swings throughout the South that he was a believer in "states' right," and if elected, he would work to "restore to the states and local communities those functions which properly belong there" (The Neshoba Democrat, Nov. 15, 2007). Education policy was at the top of Reagan's restoration list, and he was unambiguous that, if elected, federal attempts to steer education policy toward compensatory efforts would be seriously curtailed. In Meridian, Mississippi on August 3, 1980, Reagan warmed up the Neshoba County Fair crowd with one- liners aimed at Ted Kennedy, who at the time was mounting a challenge to President Jimmy Carter's incumbency: "They're having quite a fight in that convention that's coming up. Teddy Kennedy—I know why he's so interested in poverty: He never had any when he was a kid." With wife Nancy sitting near him on stage in a rocking chair, Reagan did not waste time getting to the message that the crowd came to hear:

> I believe that there are programs like . . . education and others, that should be turned back to the states and the local communities with the tax sources to fund them, and let the people [applause drowns out end of statement]. I believe in state's rights; I believe in people doing as much as they can for themselves at the community level and at the private level.

By 1983, Reagan had honed his message to clearly suggest that civil rights enforcement had been the culprit for what was described as a growing crisis in education, which the Administration's alarmist document, *A Nation at Risk* (ANAR; National Commission on Excellence in Education, 1983), declared as a national emergency. In a speech to build support for the reform agenda laid out in ANAR, the President implied that civil rights enforcement was responsible for the downturn in test scores:

> The schools were charged by the federal courts with leading in the correcting of long-standing injustices in our society. Racial segregation. Sex discrimination. Lack of support for the handicapped. Perhaps there was just too much to do in too little time. (Mondale & Patton, 2001, p. 186).

What Reagan's provocative remarks fail to acknowledge is that, between 1964 and 1980, the United States had gone from what Gary Orfield describes as an apartheid system of schooling in nineteen states to a largely integrated single system that included most racial groups, students with disabilities, and English language learners. And even *with* the influx of children whose educational opportunities had been sharply curtailed or denied previously, the National Assessment of Educational Progress (NAEP) showed trends in average scale scores in reading, math, and science either unchanged or slightly improving for 9 and 13 year olds from its inception in 1971 to 1983, when Reagan's Commission on Excellence declared in ANAR the nation's schools were in crisis, based on falling test scores. The drop in SAT and ACT scores, which had coincided with the end of apartheid schooling, was largely attributable to changing characteristics of test takers that, in fact, had bottomed out and started moving back up four years before Reagan came to Washington (Stedman & Kaestle, 1985). Even the NAEP averages for 17 year-olds, which had declined slightly in math and science, had bottomed out and started back up again prior to 1983, when ANAR offered this alarming assessment that went viral even before the internet:

> If an unfriendly power had attempted to impose on America the mediocre educational performance that exists today, we might very well have viewed it as an act of war. As it stands, we have allowed this to happen to ourselves.... We have, in effect, been committing an act of unilateral educational disarmament. (National Commission on Excellence in Education, 1983, p. 5)

As historian James Anderson (Mondale & Patton, 2001) points out, significant strides made by "groups that had lagged way behind and had not had access to good public education...was lost because of concern over the economy, which we blamed on the schools" (p. 186). In effect, policy elites pronounced an educational catastrophe that called for stronger accountability measures, school choice in the form of private school vouchers, and more the introduction of "market-driven" reforms (Berliner & Biddle, 1995) that disguised the effects of myopic economic policies and an insular arrogance by the U.S. auto industry, which failed to retool or adjust in the face of foreign competition. Too, the mythical school meltdown reported in ANAR created a policy space for new initiatives aimed to challenge the "the public school monopoly" (Everhart, 1982) and the social policy advances emanating from past federal actions such as the Civil Rights Act, ESEA, Title IX, the Bilingual Education Act, and IDEA. If there had been a meltdown in student test scores, it would have ended before the Reagan Revolution could ever come to Washington, intent as it was upon trading in the goals of equality and equity for the efficiency-seeking and less expensive ones of higher standards and more test based accountability.

Even though NAEP and SAT test scores were on the way back up to pre-desegregation levels before Republicans swept into office in 1980, Reagan's criticism of public schools escalated during his two terms. By 1988, when George H. W. Bush was elected as President, congressional Democrats had been successfully cowed by Reagan's aggressive attacks that were eagerly parroted by the mass media, which was eager to repeat Reagan's popular rhetorical flourishes, such as this one (Reagan, 1983) delivered to promote ANAR in 1983:

> You've [the Commission] found that our educational system is in the grip of a crisis caused by low standards, lack of purpose, ineffective use of resources, and a failure to challenge students to push performance to the boundaries of

> individual ability—and that is to strive for excellence.... So, we'll continue to work in the months ahead for passage of tuition tax credits, vouchers, educational savings accounts, voluntary school prayer, and abolishing the Department of Education. Our agenda is to restore quality to education by increasing competition and by strengthening parental choice and local control.

"Local Control" and Corporate Influence

As the Reagan "local control" agenda advanced and social policy steering moved away from Washington and toward the statehouses, governors and business leaders within the Business Roundtable assumed even more prominent roles in shaping education policy aimed toward national standards and tests (Vinoski, 1996). In fact, the education policy agenda was not so much decentralized, as Eva Baker (1994) has argued, as it was transferred from federal control to state and corporate control, with more concentrated and broad-based support for national standards and tests:

> The Reagan administration, with its recurring efforts to undo the Department of Education and close down its educational research function, pushed the education issue to the states and ironically permitted the development of a potentially broad-based national rather than a weakly supported federal policy on educational reform. (p. 451)

This shift in the locus of power was made tangible by the Charlottesville Education Summit in 1989, where President Reagan's successor, GHW Bush, convened a national policy conference with the National Governors' Association (NGA) and corporate CEOs of the Business Roundtable (BRT). Chairing the NGA was former Tennessee governor, Lamar Alexander, who had taken the Reagan call for reforms as a central element of his two terms as governor. Alexander had initiated a statewide student testing system, an annual high school proficiency exam, and a performance pay system known as the Career Ladder Program. When it came time for Bush to appoint a new Education Secretary, he selected Alexander. The co-chair of NGA at Charlottesville in 1989 was another Southern governor, Bill Clinton. Both would play key roles in supporting the ongoing revival of standardized assessments as the key tool for judging adequacy of schools, children, and teachers.

By the time GHW Bush took office in 1989, federal support for education had been rolled back below 1970s levels (Jennings, 1992), and desegregation of Black students in majority White schools had peaked and headed in the direction of "resegregation" (Orfield & Lee, 2006, p. 13), taking with it the gains that had been made in narrowing the Black-White achievement gaps as measured by NAEP (Barton & Coley, 2010). Jennings

(1992) argued in 1992 that Bush presented himself as the Education President with a more active education policy agenda than Reagan, for he had "detected that Reagan's passive view of federal involvement in education was no longer supportable, because of the growing public demand that the schools be improved" (p. 304). Though rhetorically committed, then, Bush's first two years produced few tangible results due to a lack of financial commitment to support significant new initiatives.

Following the Charlottesville Conference, Bush picked Alexander to replace the "lackluster" Lauro Cavazos as Secretary of Education (Jennings, 1992, p. 304). Alexander had experience in crafting splashy business-friendly reforms that embraced the kind of efficiencies that Bush supported, and he borrowed heavily from British education reforms enacted under Margaret Thatcher, with an emphasis on national curriculum standards, national testing based on those standards, "parental choice" in the form of school vouchers (p. 304), and a pilot project to create "535 radically different public schools, one in each Congressional district and two in each state," that would be selected under the direction of what Alexander called the New American Schools Development Corporation (Chira, 1992). Alexander packaged his new plan in a report entitled America 2000, and it generated a good deal of enthusiasm until the Democratically controlled Congress came to realize that there was not nearly enough in the plan in terms of resource allocation to allow Republicans to assume leadership on education issues in Washington. Widespread skepticism of the "New American Schools" (Jennings, 1992, p. 304) plan developed, too, when the *New York Times* reported in May 1992 that the federal guidance for these new schools' proposals looked very similar to the Edison Project schools developed and promoted by former Alexander business associate,[11] Chris Whittle (Chira, 1992, para. 11).

The part of the Alexander Plan that created the most pushback, however, was the emphasis on public support for private schools in the form of vouchers that would be paid to parents to send children to private schools. The public's skepticism of the Alexander voucher plan was likely aggravated by the fact that Whittle put his Edison School tuition at $5,500, which was the average per pupil amount paid for public education in the United States at that time (Chira, 1992). By the Spring of 1992, however, President Bush was fully onboard with the Alexander plan, as he was seeking to devote three-fourths of the $690 million for America 2000 for what Bush called the G. I. Bill for Children, "which was essentially a voucher program involving private schools" (Jennings, 1992, p. 305). The provision eventually failed in both the U.S. House and Senate in 1992, but school vouchers initiatives and battles would be reborn with the crafting of initial versions of No Child Left

Behind—which mandated private school vouchers for children in schools that failed to achieve the testing targets that came to be known as Adequate Yearly Progress (AYP). As they had done in 1992, however, Congress once again struck the voucher provision from the NCLBA prior to final passage (Bach, 2004). Had Congress failed to strike the voucher provision from NCLB, it is entirely reasonable to assume that the Business Roundtable's urgent twenty-first century embrace of charter schools could have been entirely avoided, as school privatization may have proceeded as it was envisioned by conservative economist, Milton Friedman, a half century before.

No Child Left Behind Act (NCLBA)

In 2002, the No Child Left Behind Act (NCLBA) became the first twenty-first century reauthorization of the Elementary and Secondary Act (ESEA) of 1965. As a result of NCLB's demands and sanctions, value-added modeling (VAM) became a more attractive next option than it would have been, otherwise. It was, in fact, NCLB's requirement of 100% proficiency by 2014 that, within a few years after passage, had education policy folks looking for a way to circumvent the certain failure that accompanied the impossible testing targets, while continuing to push for more testing as the road to improvement in student achievement. By 2006, even the U.S. Department of Education was touting something called "growth models" as the remedy for arbitrary achievement goals that most American children would have never reached by 2014 (Debray, 2006, pp. 115–116).

Acknowledging that children's achievement levels vary widely, growth models were to measure testing progress relative to where children began, rather than to expect all children to step into the testing stream at exactly the same spot and, then, to exit the stream when the 2014 clock ran out, with every student at grade level or, otherwise, proficient. As odd as it may seem in retrospect, the utter impossibility of 100% proficiency could not alter enthusiasm for the rhetorical commitment to leave no child behind, even if such a commitment would have devastating effects for urban schoolchildren, teachers and parents. So, within three years after passage, some politicians and their appointees had begun to acknowledge the fanciful nature of the goal, and by 2010 any politician who wanted to be considered in the education mainstream was decrying if not vilifying NCLB and the spreading virus of school failure that been seeded before the first test was administered.

Even before Congressional passage of No Child Left Behind in late 2001, the overarching NCLB goal of 100% reading and math proficiency was viewed by some as a dangerous fantasy, while it was championed by public education foes as a tool to impose sanctions that would result in undercutting public school support and subsequent school corporatization. Elizabeth Debray's (2006) excellent legislative history of NCLB documents the controversy, confusion, and conflict around the "acceptable growth trajectories" (p. 138), which would become something educators came to fear and loathe as NCLB's Adequate Yearly Progress (AYP) goals. Debray cites a number of prominent warnings of negative effects from researchers, governmental officials, and school administrators prior to the bill becoming law. She also notes that these warnings emerged after the Senate and House passed their separate versions of the bill earlier in 2001, due largely the fact that hearings were few and brief, with committee testimony often limited to those friendly to the Bush plan.

The Senate version that passed March 28, 2001 was called the *Better Education for Student and Teachers Act,* and it was 694 pages long. A few days later, the official in charge of overseeing compensatory education programs for the U.S. Department of Education, Dr. Joseph Johnson, told a audience of administrators two months before he resigned that "people are looking at the data and saying, 'This is going to be catastrophic because there are going to be so many low-performing schools and this isn't going to work'" (Debray, 2006, p. 138). In July 2001 Stephen Barr, Missouri's Assistant Commissioner of Education, called the 100% proficiency target "an impossible dream," and in the same *New York Times* story Pennsylvania's head of schools, Charles Zogby, concluded that "it's unrealistic to think that in some places where 90% of the children are below basic that we're going to turn this around in 10 years. And then everybody is going to throw up their hands and say none of this is possible" (Wilgoren, 2001). That same month LAUSD Superintendent, Roy Romer, predicted, accurately as it turned out, that states and school systems would lower proficiency targets in order to avoid sanctions.

In case Hill and Senate staffers missed these early warnings, a month later economists Thomas Kane and Douglas Staiger (2001) published a half-page op-ed in the *New York Times* on August 13 entitled "Rigid rules will damage schools." If Dartmouth and UCLA economists can get their hair on fire about an education issue, I guess this might be what it looks like:

> Unless Congress can agree to rewrite the formula for pinpointing a failing school, as some states and some members of Congress are now urging, this education bill—the most ambitious federal initiative in education in three decade and a centerpiece of President Bush's plans for his presidency—is likely to end in a fiasco.

> The central flaw is that both version of the bill place far too much emphasis on year-to-year changes in test scores. Under either, every school in America would have to generate an increase in test scores each and every year or face penalties like having to allow its students to transfer to another public school, being converted into a charter school or being taken over by a private contractor.... In their current bills, the House and Senate have set a very high bar—so high that it is likely that virtually all schools systems would be found to be inadequate, with many schools failing (para. 1–2).

Back to the Future, Again

In 2010, 38,000 of the 100,000 U.S. public schools (Dillon, 2011) were found "inadequate" based on NCLB testing targets. With many states delaying the pain until the last few years, those percentages were scheduled to quickly soar. Outside the closed House and Senate committee meetings during the late summer of 2001, there was no mention of the undergirding rationale for demonstrating public school failure in order to privatize and corporatize schools. Even though clear and highly visible evidence leads us to the conclusion that the most extensive experiment in American educational reform history set in motion from the beginning the widespread failures in urban schools across America, the media appeared impervious to the facts once NCLB was quickly passed amidst the smoking ruins of the national tragedy of September 11.

The academic community was clearly aware of what was going on, too, and assessment experts who had examined the new ESEA reauthorization plan knew that the built-in proficiency demands known as Adequate Yearly Progress (AYP) would wreak havoc as the nation's schools moved toward the 2014 mandate of 100% proficiency. One of those experts was assessment expert and AERA President, Robert Linn (2001), who focused part of his critique on the negative effects on the most vulnerable students of ignoring differences in socioeconomic status:

> The reason that SES adjustments are problematic is summarized concisely by Clotfelter and Ladd (1996) as follows: "If one uses socioeconomic status as a predictor, the effect is to set a lower threshold for success for poor students than rich ones" (p. 26). The problematic nature of SES adjustments is exacerbated by the fact that there is a strong relationship between SES and ethnicity. Consequently, lower standards for students from low SES background automatically mean lower standards for African American and Hispanic students because of the relationship between SES and ethnicity. (p. 13)

At the point here at which Linn is about to arrive at a profound truth about NCLB specifically and standardized testing in general, he spins away to focus on another weakness of the plan. Had Linn gone one step further, he would have laid bare the bankrupt history of testing in modern times, which has always had at its core the fact that "socioeconomic status is substantially related to student achievement" (p. 12). Instead, he gingerly steps around testing's inextricable link between the classism we disingenuously deny and the racism we studiously ignore. Of course, to admit the "strong relationship between SES and ethnicity" is to admit the racialist and classist underpinnings of standardized testing for as far back as minority children and children of the poor have been taking standardized "intelligence" and achievement tests.

If Linn and the rest of us were to admit that the tests we use to measure achievement are irredeemably biased against the poor and minority students, then what? If we were to adjust testing expectations to take into account this truth, then what? Could we have lower expectations for some at the same time that we seek to embrace the proposition that "all men are created equal," as Jefferson wrote? Should we not, therefore, have the same high expectations for all as evidence of that belief? To do less would be to challenge the American creed that Jefferson began, Mann promulgated, and Conant revived—would it not? And so we have the same high expectations even written into law that no child will be left behind, neither the well-heeled nor the homeless, not the child with the 160 IQ or the intellectually disabled child who can't write his name. We have declared, then, the same expectation for all, even as we blithely disregard the same predictable failure for those we stubbornly deny are disadvantaged by physical, psychological, or economic disability.

If Jefferson's slaves were born as inferior creatures, as he clearly suggested in *Notes on the State of Virginia*, then all men of the superior grade could, indeed, be created equal—just as the Declaration stated. And so have we, in a way no less troubling than Jefferson, sanctified our own rationalization for the inferiority that our conscious assessment policies and practices presume for the Black, the Brown, the poor, the disabled. This helps to explain why the value-added method for applying our rationalization is so amazingly popular, despite the fact that science remains entirely skeptical of its veracity. For, by focusing on test score growth, rather than on the arbitrary testing targets that make obvious (to anyone willing to look) class and race privilege, we are able to preserve our zeal for increased productivity and efficiency, even with scaled back testing targets for the poor based on their own inferior beginning points—not ours. With value-added models based on test score growth, we can still demand from poor children and their teachers a year's worth of test score growth while effectively camouflaging gaping disparities in achievement levels between groups defined by class, race, and handicap. At the same time, we can rest assured that the less privileged will not achieve at higher levels of the children whose SAT, ACT, GRE and LSAT scores do not require psychometric handouts to demonstrate their obvious merit or fitness for the best post-secondary opportunities.

2

The Tennessee Case

Who Wins and Who Loses, and by What Mechanisms of Power?

Initially, we use data as a way to think hard about difficult problems, but then we over rely on data as a way to avoid thinking hard about difficult problems. We surrender our better judgment and leave it to the algorithm.

—Joe Flood, author of *The Fires*

Equity Arguments Move to the States

As the Reagan federalist agenda of the 1980s took hold and education policy steering moved away from Washington, the centralized control by business and political leaders at the state level took on even more prominent roles in shaping education policy. At the same time, the fight for equality in educational opportunity opened new fronts at the state level, particularly in the courts. This development came on the heels of the first major loss[1] by federal civil rights plaintiffs in a decision rendered by the U.S. Supreme Court in 1973, following the appointment of three new justices who all shared President Richard Nixon's antipathy toward federal intervention in shaping social policy in general education funding policies in particular.

The Mismeasure of Education, pages 55–146

The 5–4 decision in *Rodriguez v. San Antonio Independent School District* reflected the arrival of a new conservative majority, and it signaled the beginning of a full-throated pushback against federal intervention in civil rights issues from the previous decade.

As recounted by Michael Rebell (2002) *Achieving High Educational Standards for All: Conference Summary* (2002), Rodriguez was initiated by a group of parents in the Edgewood, Texas school district to challenge the constitutionality of the Texas system for education financing. Texas, like many other states, bases its school funding on property tax revenues. With almost all of its citizens Mexican-American or African-American, and its assessed property values extremely low, Edgewood's per pupil allocation for schools was $356, compared with the neighboring mostly Anglo Alamo Heights's allocation of almost $600 (p. 222).

In a decision that surprised civil rights advocates, the conservative majority overturned the federal Appeals Court decision in favor of the plaintiffs. In a 5–4 decision, the Court concluded that "some inequality" was evident in the state financing scheme that, indeed, hindered local residents' ability to achieve good educational choices for their children. However, such inequities did not constitute "a sufficient basis for striking down the entire system" (Rebell, 2002, p. 222). *Rodriguez* clearly signaled that those seeking relief from state financing inequalities would be advised to seek relief in legal venues other than the federal courts.

If the *Rodriguez* case "effectively closed the federal courts' door to school finance claims" (Nickerson & Deenihan, 2002, p. 1343), the *Serrano v. Priest* decision in 1976 by the California Supreme Court re-opened the door for litigants seeking relief from inequitable education funding by states. In *Serrano*, the California high court upheld a lower court ruling that affirmed that California's school finance system created disparities that violated the equal protection clause of the state constitution. By the end of the 1980s, lawsuits had been filed in 16 states by local school systems seeking relief from inequitable funding structures, and by 2007 almost 100 "education reform cases had been brought before state supreme courts" (Tennessee Advisory Council on Intergovernmental Relations & The University of Tennessee Center for Business and Economic Research, 2008, p. 12). It was from within the context of these state lawsuits over education funding that this part of our story unfolds, and it takes us back once more to Tennessee.

Reforming Reforms

In 1992, the Education Improvement Act (EIA) moved toward passage with the Tennessee Value Added Assessment System (TVAAS) in tow. For our particular purposes of examining the birth and rise of the TVAAS and value-added standardized testing practices, we examine the power relations among various individuals and groups that shaped the policy talk, decision-making, and policy implementation within the Tennessee case. Although the EIA comprises four major reform components (accountability, management, funding, and curriculum), we focus on the accountability and funding components of the EIA. Because education funding in Tennessee has been inextricably tied to other public policy reforms, we examine state-sponsored social and economic reform going on in Tennessee during the 15 years leading up to the passage of the EIA and the beginning of the value-added testing era. As the TVAAS came to play a central role in influencing the national education reform agenda, so did initiatives in other areas, such as health and criminal justice. More importantly, we contend that reforms in these other areas and the financial attention they received impacted the contours, content, and outcomes of the education reforms that the State eventually codified.

Passed in 1992, the EIA represents the culmination of a decade of education reform experimenting in Tennessee, and it signaled a new era of policies ostensibly aimed toward more equitable resource allocation and justified by accountability practices intended to monitor those policies. Policymakers joined the debate leading up to the EIA with the expressed intent of improving student performance and decreasing the disparity in educational financing among state LEAs, and they came out of the process with a brand new statewide system for testing, data collection, and monitoring: the TVAAS. The TVAAS has significantly reshaped instructional practices and student, school, and teacher assessment statewide, and its value-added modeling (VAM) has become a central element in national education policy talk and implementation. Its statistical parameters, codified in Tennessee state law since 1992, make needed adjustments to assessments, whether based on best instructional practices or public pressure, next to impossible, and they make teaching to standardized tests a classroom reality.

The winners in the debate that began in Nashville in the months leading up to the passage of EIA were the socio-political elites and economic policy players who were bound by similar goals and standards of "efficiency" and "effectiveness" that had risen to dominance a hundred years earlier in the early twentieth century (see Part 1). They also shared a heavy dependence upon and faith in the "science" of standardized testing to be able to identify the "laggards" and high flyers (Ayres, 1909) in need of very different instructional interventions, as well as their teachers who would be diagnosed as proficient, average, or failing. Whether from the low end or the high end on the spectra of educational variables, all students were supposed to emerge from this new crucible representing an improved final product—students prepared for the Twenty-first Century workforce.

Undertaking the task with high hopes, policymakers, nonetheless, failed to confront their basic assumptions and biases about teaching, learning, and educational improvement. Much of the potential to advance new educational practices and school financing arrangements was eroded, then, by an absence of reflexivity mixed with a parading and posturing of long-held positions and beliefs, while resisting occasions for exposure to ideas that might challenge those positions. When caught between political risk of raising taxes to pay for new education spending and a court order to address the "inequitable distribution of state money to local school systems" (Edmiston & Murray, 1998), policymakers chose to modestly increase funding over time but not without an elaborate method to let their constituents know whether or not they were getting some return for increases in spending by holding teachers' and students' feet to the fire. The result, then, was a new self-declared mandate for the creation of "the most cutting-edge accountability plan in the country" (Legislative minutes, Tennessee Senate Education Committee, 4/17/91, Chairman Albright), which could possibly earn then-Governor Ned McWherter a reform reputation at least equal to the previous governor, Lamar Alexander, who had leveraged his own education reform work as Governor of Tennessee into a position as Secretary of Education for G. H. W. Bush.

"Education Governors" in Search of Solutions

Leading Tennessee Democrat, Ned Ray McWherter, saw education reform from two perspectives: legislative and executive. As Speaker of the Tennessee House of Representatives in 1984, he signed the Comprehensive Education Reform Act (CERA) under the administration of then-Governor Lamar Alexander. As Governor in 1992, McWherter signed the EIA into law. When McWherter took office in 1987, he brought a legislative perspective on the past education reform efforts of Lamar Alexander, who had drawn national attention during his campaign for governor in 1978 by walking "1,022 miles across Tennessee to talk and listen to citizens" (Darnell, 1995–1996, p. 463). Both Alexander and McWherter had sought to make their gubernatorial reputations as "education governors." Both saw education as a way to strengthen the Tennessee workforce, thereby improving the state's economic prosperity.

Having been labeled as out of touch from ordinary citizens during his 1974 unsuccessful race for Governor, the Vanderbilt-educated Alexander in 1978 wore a red and black plaid flannel shirt during his walkabouts across

Tennessee, choosing to adopt a homespun political persona. It worked. According to Darnell and others, Alexander, the son of educators, placed education as a top priority, and Alexander's Better Schools Program, along with his career ladder performance pay plan[2] for teachers, drew national attention and set a precedent for subsequent Tennessee governors who also sought to become "education governors."

Bolstered by the recommendations in *A Nation at Risk* and a political governance structure that ensured his policy decisions, Alexander convinced Tennesseans that the road to economic prosperity was by way of higher student achievement as measured by improved test scores. In 1984 the Tennessee General Assembly funded the Comprehensive Education Reform Act (CERA) with $350 million new dollars (Wissner, 1990). The new reform package was funded by a one-cent increase in Tennessee's sales tax and an increase in some business taxes (Edmiston & Murray, 1998, p. 159). By fiscal 1987, the Tennessee Department of Education was spending $1.4 billion and employing a staff of 1,305 (Snodgrass, 1990, p. i) to implement CERA, with a significant portion of the allocated funds going to pay for teacher evaluations and merit pay under the Career Ladder Program. With the infusion of new money came education policy changes that the State had not seen before.

As one of the most significant policy initiatives in education in Tennessee in the last half of the twentieth century, CERA introduced three "profound changes in educational practice" (Keese & Huffman, 1998, pp. 158, 161). The first big shift came in measurement of school effectiveness from inputs such as per pupil expenditure to outputs, as measured by the improvement of student test scores. Whereas previous improvement mandates for Tennessee school systems, schools, and teachers were designed using assessment for diagnostic purposes to target general areas of student academic deficiencies, CERA's new Basic Skills First criterion-referenced tests, aligned with the curriculum frameworks and composed of specific goals and objectives by grade and subject levels, were used to identify specific areas of student academic deficiencies in grades 3, 6, and 8 by subject level and objective level and the associated deficiencies in teaching performance. This shift in specificity moved testing from low-stakes to high-stakes for students with passing the eighth grade test determining promotion to ninth grade (French, Dec 1984/Jan 1985, p. 10). CERA also called for nationally normed tests to be administered at three grades with a five-year performance goal of better than the national average. While student testing did not determine teacher advancement in CERA, the law did establish a process using observational and professional skills measurement instruments for teacher evaluation of specific teaching competencies, tied those competencies to teacher advancement, and teacher advancement to merit pay (French, Dec 1984/Jan 1985, pp. 11–12). The law did, however, mandate a study by the newly created State Certification Commission who had oversight responsibilities for teacher certification and evaluation to

> study the use of student progress or achievement, as measured by standardized testing or other appropriate measures, as an indicator of successful teaching and effective schools, and to review periodically the standards and criteria used for teacher and principal evaluation in view of the findings resulting from such study. (Public Acts 1984, Chapter No. 7, p. 31)

This requirement appeared in the early legislative discussions leading up to the development of the EIA.

Paying teachers "by performance rather than exclusively by training and experience" (p. 161) represented the second profound change created by CERA and a new first for Tennessee, even though educational history is replete with failed efforts to establish teacher performance incentives to raise student achievement. One of the longest lasting merit pay systems involved extra pay for better test scores in England (Wilms & Chapleau, 1999), and it lasted from 1862 to the mid-1890s:

> As historical accounts show, English teachers and administrators became obsessed with the system's financial rewards and punishments. It was dubbed the "cult of the [cash] register." Schools' curricula were narrowed to include just the easily measured basics. Drawing, science, singing, and even school gardening simply disappeared. Teaching became increasingly mechanical, as teachers found that drill and rote repetition produced the "best" results. One schools inspector wrote an account of children reading flawlessly for him while holding their books upside down. (para. 4)

CERA's resulting evaluation of teachers examined their performance in using a direct instructional model (based on Madeline Hunter's *Master Teaching*, 1982). Under the new Tennessee merit pay plan based on number of years of experience, evaluation performance, and portfolio submissions, teachers could apply for Career Ladder Levels I, II, or III. Successful applicants received merit pay based on the level of their awards, and they could earn additional money for additional work special needs students or with other related projects before school, after school, or in the summer.

The third big shift created by CERA involved a centralization of power in education policy development and implementation. It moved the locus of control from educators at the school system and university levels to legislators at the state level. The Public Education Governance Reform Act (PEGRA) of 1984 empowered the legislature by having the State Board of

Education report directly to the legislature instead of the commissioner of education and "disallowed professional educators from serving" on the Board (Keese & Huffman, 1998, p. 160). PEGRA, too, empowered the Governor to appoint members of the State Board of Education, subject to confirmation by the Senate and House, who were responsible for developing education policy that directed the operation of the State Department of Education. In the years following PEGRA, jockeying for control of education policy continued among elected state officials and their own appointees on the State Board and within the Department of Education. With the passage of CERA, though political costs were high when increasing state taxes, policymakers targeted areas of educational need—low student achievement, teacher and school accountability, and school funding—thus improving their political favor with constituents and advancing the state to a leadership position in national education reform efforts.

In 1987, the McWherter Administration acted quickly to establish its own education policy with studies of the CERA policies initiated under Alexander. The General Assembly called for resolutions to study the Career Ladder program, specifically, the effectiveness of teacher evaluation and its resulting merit pay and extended contract eligibility based on teachers achieving Level I, II, or III on the Career Ladder. Dr. Jerry Bellon, an expert in evaluation from University of Tennessee, directed the studies. On December 1987, members of the Joint Education Committee came together to discuss the preliminary findings of the research and to debate the effectiveness of the Career Ladder teacher evaluation system. During the meeting, disagreement broke out among legislators regarding the purpose of Career Ladder extended contracts, as Bellon had found that Career Ladder extended contract money was going to districts with greater numbers of Level II and III teachers and not to districts that had the greatest student need. Some remembered the legislated purpose of extended contracts being to "pay more for better teachers" in the state and some remembered its purpose to raise student test scores.

While the session offered ample opportunity for legislators to vent their concerns about the Career Ladder, the one action item that required a vote had nothing to do with fixing past reforms but, rather, anticipating what was to come. Prior to the Career Ladder debate by members of the Joint Education Committee, Sen. Leonard Dunavant had handed to members of the committee a resolution to study the use of "student progress," on standardized tests as an "indicator of successful teaching and effective schools." When called on by Chairman Gene Davidson to present his resolution, Dunavant's reading expressed his belief that "the use of student progress or achievement as a factor in the evaluation of teachers has not yet received the attention which it requires..." Dunavant added that student academic advancement "is the purpose of education and is the reasonable expectation of parents, taxpayers, and the business community for the massive commitment of money and effort which is made in the name of education reform." Therefore, Dunavant argued, student progress should be used as a component of teacher evaluation. Dunavant's language throughout the discussion of the resolution foreshadowed language in the final version of the EIA. He spoke of "student progress," "evaluation of teachers," "a method that is fair and reasonable and predictable in assessing what happens to the child as they move from year to year," (Legislative minutes, Joint Education Oversight Committee, 12/17/87, Senator Leonard Dunavant). The final language of the 1992 EIA read as follows:

> On or before July 1, 1995, and annually thereafter data from the TCAP tests, or their future replacements, will be used to provide as estimate of the statistical distribution of teacher effects on the educational progress of students within school districts for grades three (3) through eight (8) (TCA 49-1-2(g)(4)(C)).

To estimate teacher effects, the EIA also provided for the specific statistical system to be used, having "the capability of providing mixed model methodologies which provide for best linear unbiased prediction for the teacher, school and school district...." (TCA 49-1-2).

Concerned with the many factors that impact student learning and of which teachers have no control, Representative Leslie Winningham's pointedly responded that "if you are going to give an adequate evaluation of a teacher based on student performance you are almost going to have to determine the movement of that student 24 hours a day..." (Legislative minutes, Joint Education Committee, 12/17/87, Representative Leslie Winningham). Dunavant countered that in his own district some Career Level II and III teachers' students had poor academic achievement and some teachers whose students had outstanding performance were unable to reach even Career Level I. While sympathetic to Rep. Winningham's concerns about using standardized tests to measure student and teacher progress, Senator Bob Rochelle, understood the resolution as a focus on the "product" (student achievement), which he viewed as a "valid factor in considering the progress of the teacher, just as a lawyer is judged partially among other things by how many times he wins a lawsuit and dentists are judged among a lot of other things by whether the fillings they put in stay in" (Legislative Minutes, Joint Education Committee, 12/17/87, Senator Bob Rochell).

Dunavant's resolution[3] passed on a voice vote, and Chairman Davidson moved on to a question from Rep. Copeland concerning the criteria that other states used for the equitable distribution of educational funding to school districts. Mark Musick, Vice President of the Southern Regional Education Board (SREB), responded to the question by highlighting that of the 15 SREB states, Virginia and five others were threatened with lawsuits for inequitable distribution of education funding. A proposal from the Virginia Governor's office would "essentially take money from the wealthier counties and send that to the poorer counties" which, according to Musick, was the intended outcome of all the lawsuits. The cycle, he explained to the committee members, was one in which the court declared the funding formula unconstitutional, which then precipitated a change in the formula to narrow the funding gap between richer and poorer districts. When revisited by the judge five years later, then, there would still be an inequitable distribution of funds based on each county's taxing capacity, resulting in another round of lawsuits.

If the Dunavant amendment served to prefigure the shape of education reform in Tennessee, then Senator J. B. Shockley's concluding remarks to the long session introduced professional concerns that would also become more prominent during the coming decades. Referring to Bellon's review of the Basic Skills First Program of CERA, Sen. Shockley belatedly observed

> we are probably mired so deeply in tests, testing for skills and repeating and testing and what have you, that we are probably not doing or leaving little time for addressing more of the very essential parts of learning such as creative thinking or problem solving... We are testing and testing and testing and testing and really leaving out some of the real important parts of learning... it's a point that we need to address.

With Shockley's concerns duly noted and no action taken, the December 1987 Joint Education Committee session was adjourned.

As the legislative committees offered justifications for tighter accountability measures, Tennessee's Department of Education developed new proposals that would modify the state-mandated Basic Skills First testing program begun in 1984 (Smith, 1988, *News Release*). The new proposals called for:

1. Combining the existing Basic Skills First criterion-referenced test with new norm-referenced test items for each grade level from second through eighth grade.
2. Increasing collaboration between the curriculum staff and the testing staff in the development of the test items.

3. Implementing a writing assessment by 1990.

What resulted in 1990 was the Tennessee Comprehensive Assessment Program (TCAP), and it was hailed by Assistant Commissioner for School Success, Tom Cannon, as the "optimal testing program" that was designed to "make the testing program more efficient and more useful to educators" and that would "relieve teachers from feeling they must teach to the test" (Smith, 1988, *News Release*). The TCAP was an outgrowth of Senator Dunavant's resolution discussed above, and it came to provide a "systematic" assessment for the purpose of providing "diagnostic data" to identify and correct "student, teacher, or curriculum deficiencies" (Smith, 1990, pp. 9–10). By 1990, a "value-added" component was called for in the State Department of Education's *Twenty-first Century Challenge Plan* (Smith, 1990) to "determine more precisely the degree to which schools are increasing knowledge and comprehension among students they serve" (pp. 14–15).

Dr. William L. Sanders, an adjunct professor at the University of Tennessee College of Business Administration and station statistician at the UT Agricultural Institute, devised such a "value-added" statistical model for assessing student achievement with standardized tests in the early 1980s, in hopes of being able to parse out and quantify school and teacher effects on student achievement as measured by standardized tests. Helped with political access and logistics by East Tennessee Senator Ray Albright (Grounard, 2006) and Representative Frank Niceley (Humphreys, 2010), Dr. Sanders had shopped his value-added model to Commissioner Smith, the State Board of Education, Governor McWherter, and to members of the General Assembly from January 1990 to April 1991. With a uncanny knack for honing in on what policymakers were looking for, a talent that would serve him in the years to come, Dr. Sanders presented an assessment plan for accountability purposes that assured the General Assembly, as well as the general public, that they could reasonably expect significant levels of gains on test scores regardless of socioeconomic or ability differences. Rather than concentrating on the wide gap in raw test scores between students from underfunded communities and those in richer communities with adequate educational resources, Sanders urged the General Assembly to focus their efforts on rate of student progress on tests, which he argued could be measured independent of structural inadequacies responsible for vast disparities in achievement levels. Equally important to state officials, politicians, and to the business community, was Dr. Sanders' claim that his assessment model could reliably identify and quantify the effects of teachers on student test score gains, thus providing a method for applying accountability that could be directed toward educators for whatever results ensued. In short, Sanders' claims offered policy makers a surefire rationale for turning attention further from financial inputs for education and toward student test score outputs. In short, the Sanders Model offered the missing link to a coherent legislative package for education reform based on accountability and measurable results that minimized political and economic risk for policymakers and the business community, while offering the media and the public an easily readable measuring stick that could be used against schools, teachers, and students, as situations might merit. As a result, the attention that may have accrued in earlier years to the continued shrinkage in education funding in Tennessee was effectively shifted toward outcomes that allowed disparities in learning opportunities to continue largely unchallenged by a public bedazzled by charts, graphs, and numbers that plotted winners and losers in an undeclared race with increasingly high stakes and no finish line in sight.

Meanwhile, in Kentucky...

Four years after the Council for Better Education and 66 of Kentucky's school districts filed their lawsuit on November 20, 1985, the Kentucky Supreme Court ruled Kentucky's "entire system of common schools... unconstitutional" (National Education Access Network, 2008). In the decision, the Court noted the following disparities that mirrored realities in the state schools of its southern neighbor, Tennessee:

> The achievement test scores in the poorer districts are lower than those in the richer districts and expert opinion clearly established that there is a correlation between those scores and the wealth of the district. Student-teacher ratios are higher in the poorer districts. Moreover, although Kentucky's per capita income is low, it makes an even lower per capita effort to support the common schools. Students in property poor districts receive inadequate and inferior educational opportunities as compared to those offered to those students in the more affluent districts. (*Rose v. Council*, 790 S.W.2d 186, 60 Ed. Law Rep. 1289 (1989), p. 10)

As a result of the 1989 ruling, the Kentucky Supreme Court assigned the "sole responsibility" for equal educational opportunities for all children squarely on the shoulders of the Kentucky General Assembly. With a decision requiring the State to re-design and re-build a system of adequate and equal education for all children of Kentucky (McCarthy, 1994, p. 92), the Tennessee General Assembly felt the hot breath of court-ordered reform from next door. As a result, both the State Senate and the House intensified criticism of the State Board of Education and the Department of Education for failing to fulfill their legislated responsibilities, even as the State

Board and State Department of Education continued to devise improvement plans. Despite finger pointing by Tennessee legislators, the public grew more critical of the General Assembly, and some accused legislators of being more interested in politics than educational progress. That view had been expressed in an editorial a week after a group of small school systems in Tennessee filed their own lawsuit (*Tennessee Small School Sys. v. McWherter*, 851 SW 2d 139 (1993) against the State and its system for financing public schools on July 7, 1988: "Three years ago the state's prison system was in court. Now it is the schools. If Tennessee had more leadership in the General Assembly, it wouldn't have to spend so much time pleading its case before a judge" ("An unfair school system," 7/13/88).

In November of 1988, the State Board of Education approved the BEP to improve education funding in Tennessee, with Brent Poulton, Executive Director of the Tennessee State Board of Education Poulton, predicting that "a basic education" would be provided equally everywhere in the state: "As it now stands, quality of education is based partly on each city or county's ability to supplement funding that educators say is inadequate" *("Full new funding,"* 11/18/88). The *Tennessean* reported that many state officials did not share Poulton's optimism:

> . . . many state officials privately hope the case [the Tennessee Small School Systems lawsuit] will be lost so the courts, rather than politicians, can be blamed for tax increases that will be necessary to equalize education funding across Tennessee. ("No guarantee for poor areas," 11/27/88)

Prior to the Comptroller's Office performance audit of 1990, an outside consultant's report, and the small school systems' lawsuit, no one, from the Governor to elementary school students, escaped blame for the poor shape of education in Tennessee. While fingers were pointed in many different directions, all stakeholders could agree that accountability had to be the "key" or the "heart" of any new education legislation aimed to address the situation. The Tennessee Education Association, too, favored increased accountability measures, but TEA President, Ann Robertson, challenged policymakers' basic assumption that teachers are ultimately responsible for improved student performance when she said, "Accountability is an interesting word. Generally, when it is used in connection with teachers, it is synonymous with blame" ("TEA to tell teachers' view," 11/3/89).

In Need of New Management

As required by state law, the Comptroller of the Treasury completed a performance audit of both the Department and Board of Education in 1990.

The report was "intended to aid the Joint Government Operations Committee in its review to determine whether the Department and the Board should be continued, abolished, or restructured" (Snodgrass, 1990). Investigating the lack of progress in reaching the goals for improved academic performance in Tennessee's schools under CERA, the Comptroller's Performance Audit report (Snodgrass, 1990) offered a sobering appraisal of the schools: "Some of the measures indicate the state as a whole has improved. For almost every measure, some systems have not improved at all and some have worsened" (p. iii). The audit highlighted problems with both the State Board of Education's policies and the State Department of Education's implementation of those policies. It also cited a lack of specificity in policies related to monitoring Tennessee schools, an inadequate school rating system for compliance with State Board rules and regulations, and an insufficient information system. Due to the vague policies of the State Board and the inadequate monitoring of the Department of Education, the audit reported that 41% of the specific educational performance goals of the Better Schools Program would not be met by the April 1989 statutory deadline (p. iii). This particular finding would have a large impact on the development of the EIA in terms of the accountability indicators used to show progress in meeting education goals.

As overall state spending for education shrank in the early 1980s, the cost of implementing the merit pay Career Ladder Program caused other areas of state education spending to suffer as well. Despite new K–12 spending for statewide testing systems and the Career Ladder Program of CERA, the overall state spending for education between 1980 and 1985 fell by almost 30%, from $2.127 billion to $1.489 billion (Edmiston & Murray, 1998, p. 198). Funding did not return to the 1980 level until 1995. From 1977 to 1995, education spending in Tennessee had the smallest rate of growth (0.6%) of all state functions, which averaged 4%. In terms of the percentage of the state budget spent on education, by 1995 that number fell precipitously from 40% to 22.3%, which put Tennessee behind all other Southeastern states except Florida—whose disproportionately large retired population helps explain their weak standing. So, even though Governor Alexander was quick to point out that the first year of CERA brought the largest one-year increase in education spending that the State had ever witnessed, that fact masked a political reality of shifting interest and focus, accompanied by shrinking education spending. And, though the State Board was working quickly to revamp its current funding formula to avoid a lawsuit, the Comptroller's Performance Audit found the board's proposal inadequate and that it would not "resolve the disparity in dollars expended per pupil among Tennessee's local school systems because it leaves in place the existing tax structure with its disparities in tax rates and its opportunities for additional taxation" (p. 69).

The Comptroller's Performance Audit also examined the new teacher evaluation system that was central to the Career Ladder program. The evaluations were not always successful in distinguishing the best teachers for merit pay, and wealthier districts could pay teachers higher salaries, thus attracting many of the best teachers to their schools. The teachers in wealthier counties, then, were applying for Career Ladder II and III status and receiving extended contract money. The money, therefore, was not following student need, necessarily, but was following Career Ladder II and III teachers to wealthier districts. A University of Tennessee professor and consultant hired to study the Career Ladder evaluation, Dr. Jerry Bellon, called the career ladder evaluation "demeaning" because it "attempts to reduce teaching—a complex process—to seven or eight simple principles." Bellon concluded his negative appraisal by pointing out that "we have never found a state mandate that has improved education. It may have improved test scores but not learning" ("Bellon Report," 1988, pp. 4–5).

Improving test scores was not a sure thing, either. The sporadic testing schedule of the Basic Skills First Program, the lack of a data management system, and the reporting system for deficiencies within schools and school systems, made it difficult to target schools or school systems for improvement. With its lack of timely feedback on performance, lack of guidance for improved performance, and lack of local input in evaluation procedures, the Career Ladder evaluation system for teachers and administrators diminished the institutional capacity and narrowed teachers' perception of improvement to "teaching the test" (Snodgrass, 1990, p. 48). The Career Ladder evaluation system increased administrative and bureaucratic burden for everyone, from teachers to State Department of Education and State Board of Education personnel. By 1987, teachers were asking for changes in the evaluation and testing programs, and political risk was increasing as policymakers discussed the need for additional revenues to continue the education reform started under Alexander. Challenged by a lack of validity, accuracy and completeness in the academic measurement system it used to monitor student progress, the State Board proposed a new TCAP test that would track student progress, or added value, in grades 2 through 8 and in grade 10 (p. 91). The State Board planned to introduce "accountability at the local level by having local boards appoint superintendents" and by "strengthening the role of the principal," and it hoped to address funding inequities by establishing a new statewide funding formula (p. 117).

While focused on pushing measures that would demonstrate increases in measurable return on educational investment, Governor McWherter moved to devise an educational funding formula that could pass constitutional muster in regards to the continuing disparity between rich and poor counties in the state. McWherter ordered a study of the state's education funding policy, and to get the job done, he brought in Donald Thomas in 1990, an educational consultant who also directed the Division of Public Accountability in the State Department of Education in South Carolina. Coming from a state with even greater disparities between rich and poor school districts, Thomas quickly identified inadequate funding as the overriding problem in Tennessee, while assuring the Governor that the current State funding method did not violate the Tennessee Constitution: "There is no illegality. All it says in the constitution is that the state shall set up a system of free public schools. It has done that." (Wilson, 1990). Thomas was shocked to find that the provision for a "system" of free public schools had become part of the state constitution only a few years before: "It's under Miscellaneous. That blows my mind—education in an afterthought." Thomas found, in fact, the section of the Constitution mandating a state system of education appeared after the "Personal Property Exemptions" and just before the "Protection and Preservation of Game and Fish."

Thomas, a nationally recognized figure in education reform efforts, made broad recommendations to McWherter in a 20-page report (1990), "Tennessee Education for the Twenty-first Century," which he delivered in November 1990. He recommended that state policymakers shift the accountability and school governance focus from process to results and "to concentrate on standards to be achieved and not methods for achieving them, to hold people accountable for results and to take action when results are not attained, to encourage and support the separation of the public will [what schools should teach] from the professional prerogatives [how schools should be organized and how teachers should teach]" (p. 8). Thomas recommended "that the State Department of Education and the State Board of Education be strengthened in their accountability functions" and that "their current resources and structures [should] support their ability to take on these responsibilities" (p. 18).

Thomas' recommendations related to adequate and sustained funding for education called on the legislature to "provide adequate financial support for all children, regardless of where they live" in ways that would reflect a "partnership between the state and local districts," with the state carrying the major burden. Thomas recommended that the state funding structure "should be built on stable tax sources and have revenues that were to be placed in a dedicated trust fund for education" (p. 15). Thomas challenged the policymakers "to establish adequate financial support on a continuing basis—one that goes beyond the basic education program and incorporates all the components of an appropriate and adequate state educational system" (p. 15). Upon hearing Thomas' challenge to policy makers "to hold people accountable for results and to take action when results are not attained (p. 8)," the legislative education committees took a greater interest in Dr. Sanders' value-added model.

"We Come As Two Statisticians Saying You Can Measure It"

In an impressive salesmanship coup that represents a critical event in the Dr. Sanders and TVAAS story, the Tennessee General Assembly specified the Sanders value-added TVAAS model as a core component of the Education Improvement Act (EIA) of 1992. This action sanctioned the first statewide value-added assessment system, and it gave Sanders' continued contracting with the State by authority of state statute. And, even though a number of challengers to the continuation of the TVAAS have stepped forward over the years, as we recount in more detail in Part 3, Sanders' growing reputation among business leaders as an accountability hawk with quantifiable solutions has helped the Sanders team to solidify their position even in the face of growing skepticism among scholars, as well as the public and the media.

When Horace Mann faced the prospect of promoting the crazy-sounding notion of publicly funded common schools in Massachusetts almost 175 years ago, he had to convince multiple constituencies of the benefits of his idea by pointing out what was in it for each of his audiences, from the business and civic Brahmin of Boston, to the yeoman farmers, to the factory workers and immigrants of Lowell. Sanders, in selling the TVAAS in the days leading up the passage of the EIA in 1992, faced a similar task for his own radical idea, and he was no less politically savvy. Sanders made customized pitches to his varied audiences whose support he needed to get the value-added plan approved. He started with the business community, whose vocal majority in the Tennessee Legislature he had to recruit for any proposition to be approved. It was, in fact, two businessmen from East Tennessee—a State Representative and a State Senator—who got Sanders the fateful audience with the recently elected Governor Ned McWherter.

For instance, the Sanders claims that (a) socioeconomic status is irrelevant to test score gains, and that (b) a teacher's influence is the most important factor in determining student achievement, have both resonated with the majority of business elites whose educational policy steering goals for the past 100 years have been aimed at minimal expenditure for maximal return (see Part 1). As Sanders came to minimize the importance of class size, student diversity, or any other factor other than teacher effect, his star among business leaders rose even higher. When the Sanders Team (Wright, Horn & Sanders, 1997) declared that "teacher effects are dominant factors affecting academic gain and that classroom context variables of heterogeneity among students and class sizes have relatively little influence on academic gain" (p. 57), he offered a message to a national audience that corporate-styled education reformers from both political parties could heartily embrace. Democratic members of the Business Roundtable could find validation in Sanders' claims for their continued insistence that teachers should simply redouble their efforts to reach oft-neglected cohorts of disabled, poor, and minority children, while Republican businessmen could continue to focus on bottom line economic issues without the appearance of being penurious or uncaring in terms of the needs of the poor. And politicians without the conviction or courage to do something substantive about socioeconomic disparities or about segregation based on class, race, and ability could put forward a solution that was much easier to sell than more expensive structural interventions that could carry high political costs.

When Dr. Sanders journeyed from Knoxville to Nashville to sell his plan to the General Assembly in early 1990, he carried with him a very thin research portfolio to substantiate his claims or to buttress his case for the creation of a state system based on his statistical algorithms. In terms of research, his case rested on a single monograph (McLean & Sanders, 1983) for which he was second author, and it was printed in 1983 by the State of Tennessee without benefit of the kind of peer review that a reputable academic journal would require. The title, *Objective Component of Teacher Evaluation : A Feasibility Study*, offers a clear indicator of Sanders' original intent to use a statistical model to "objectively" evaluate teachers, a plan that would have to wait almost 30 years for the first statewide scheme (announced first in Tennessee's Race to the Top Application, no less) to evaluate teachers using value-added modeling (VAM). It was from this single study that Dr. Sanders arrived at his far-reaching claim that student, school, and teacher accountability could all be objectively established by his methods. In answering the question of "whether or not the influences of teachers on student learning can be unbiased and reliably estimated," Sanders did not answer directly but, rather, listed the "definition and construction of appropriate metrics" and the "nonrandom assignment of students" to teacher classrooms as problems in assuring a "fair and reliable system for teacher evaluation" (p. 1). Using Millman's (1981) criteria for "accurate assessment of teachers effectiveness using student achievement indicators" (p. 1) and Henderson's (1979) mixed model solution, Sanders suggested that an evaluation system could be devised in which student characteristics like race or socioeconomic status were considered to be "continuous fixed effects" and teacher effects "considered to be random" (p. 5). In short, this means he could devise a formula for measuring teacher effectiveness without also measuring student characteristics in that formula.

Sanders' data for this study included only the California Achievement Test from grades 2, 3, 4, and 5 of all Knox County Schools in 1981, 1982, and 1983. SAS software (PROC FSEDIT, 1982) was used to edit and match 34,000 individual student records. The final sample size for Sanders original study (p. 16) is given in Table 1.

In closely examining the McLean and Sanders (1983) study, we learn nothing of student characteristics except grade level, nothing of the vertical scaling properties of the CAT, nothing in regards to missing data or how it was treated, nothing of the test security, and nothing on how the students were assigned to teachers (i.e., randomly or otherwise). The total K–12 student population of Tennessee in 1983 was 860,708 (Center for Business and Economic Research, 2003) making Sanders' sample size less than 1% of the total state student population and entirely from Knox County Schools. In essence, we have no guarantees concerning the reliability and validity of the test scores and the resulting gain scores. Sanders and McLean offer no information, either, regarding alignment between the CAT and the curriculum in the schools, or where the test was administered. The only assurance we have concerning the validity of the scores is that "Knox County has a written curriculum and considerable attention had been given by the county educational specialists in the selection of a standardized test which reflected their curriculum" (p. 7).[4]

Based on the sample in Table 1, the McLean and Sanders (1983) study concluded

1. "There were significant teacher effects for all three subjects in all three grades;"

TABLE 1 Number of Teachers and Number of Student Gain Scores by Subject and Grade

	Math		Reading		Language	
Grade	# of teachers	# of students	# of teachers	# of students	# of teachers	# of students
3	78	2,104	79	2,107	79	2,197
4	86	2,670	86	2,700	86	2,704
5	76	1,986	82	1,987	80	1,989
Total	240	6,760	247	6,794	245	6,890

Source: McLean & Sanders, 1983, p. 16

2. "since data from only three grades were available, it is not possible to generalize these observations" concerning the variance among teachers related to grade;
3. "there is no doubt that data accumulated over a three-five year period for teachers teaching similar grade levels would provide very high levels of reliability of teacher effects;"
4. no covariates "were found to be of importance," including the nonrandom assignment of students;
5. teachers profiling high in one subject profiled high in the other subjects; and
6. "superior teachers were found throughout the county, not clustered in any particular geographical area" (pp. 8–11).

For independent corroboration, the statisticians chose four local administrators "to comment on the ranking" of teachers in terms of the size of their effect on test score growth (p. 12). The supervisors were in 100% agreement with the top ten teachers selected from each grade level and 90% in agreement with the ten that ranked at the bottom. In his conclusions, then, Sanders contended that evaluating teachers based on student achievement scores was "theoretically and computationally feasible," but the development of such a system would require "talent, time and monetary resources to develop, test, and implement" with the "primary hurdle to overcome" being the development of a state-wide criterion-referenced test with a "test-bank containing equivalent test items which will permit non-redundant tests over years" (pp. 12–13). One may wonder why such an extensive and expensive system may be necessary if local administrators could arrive at the same conclusions regarding teacher quality with equal veracity at much less pain and expense.

Following the McLean & Sanders (1983) study, Sanders published nothing related to value added modeling until 1994 (Sanders & Horn, 1994), even though he began offering expert testimony to the Tennessee legislature in January of 1990. According to a Sanders account offered some years later (Humphrey, 2010), his access to centers of influence in Nashville was assisted greatly in 1989 and 1990 by State Representative Frank Niceley (R), who represented the geographical area of Knox County where Sanders had collected data for the 1983 study on value-added possibilities. Though accounts vary (Grounard, 2006; Stewart, 2006; Humphreys, 2010), Niceley likely put in a call in late 1989 to Senate Education Committee Chairman, Ray Albright (R), who pushed increased accountability for education to the center of every legislative reform discussion. Albright would have then introduced Dr. Sanders to Governor McWherter and the recently elected State Senator Andy

Womack (D), who was interested in doing something for education and for his own visibility in Nashville during what would be his first legislative session. In interviews for a study on the history of the TVAAS (Grounard, 2006), Albright proudly acknowledged his role on pushing for value-added as a way to achieve accountability in schools, and he acknowledged a bipartisan effort, as he and the Senate freshman, Womack, spoke to one another's caucuses in favor of the Sanders plan. Albright also credited the Chamber of Commerce, the Tennessee Business Roundtable, and the Tennessee Chamber of Commerce and Industry "in getting value-added initiated" (pp. 98–99). Support from these powerful constituencies helped assure approval for the Sanders Model during the lead-up to passage of EIA in 1992.[5]

Having been ignored by the previous administration of Governor Lamar Alexander when approached with his accountability model, Sanders at first believed the initial phone call from the Governor McWherter's office was a hoax. "I thought it was a joke," Sanders told *Knoxville News-Sentinel* reporter, Tom Humphrey, in 2010. Sanders recalled that McWherter, in particular, was "in search of something fresh to put into the mix" (Humphrey, 2010, para. 9). Sanders noted to another interviewer that Tennessee policymakers "[who] were looking for a different approach to accountability... [had] bought into the notion that it's more fair to evaluate schools based on the progress rates of students than on standardized test results" (Stewart, 2006, p. 6).

The idea of measuring "progress rates," rather than raw test scores, remains intuitively attractive, for it speaks to a sense of fairness that most all of us embrace as long as such sentiments remain less expensive than doing otherwise. What the Tennessee legislators either failed to understand or preferred to ignore is that value-added calculations are based on standardized test results, too, so that any flaw or shortcoming in the standardized tests are necessarily reflected in the value added machinations of the test scores that follow. Considering the possibility that testing expert, James Popham, may be close in his estimation that 90% of the tests used in schools are "junk" (Horn, 2005), legislators and non-legislators, alike, should probably delay any self-nominated fairness awards for embracing value-added modeling. If a test is "junk," measuring student progress on it remains as misguided and unfair as expecting the economically underprivileged students to have the same scores at economically advantaged ones.

Almost overnight, then, Dr. Sanders went from a spurned political outsider with another unsuccessful accountability scheme to an invited guest of the Tennessee governor. First testifying before the state's House Education Committee January 23, 1990, Sanders hit his mark by telling lawmakers that he believed teachers could not be held responsible for all the ability differences among children that are determined by influences beyond the school, but that these ability differences can be statistically adjusted so that a teacher's influence on "progress rates" could be accurately measured. In short, Sanders claimed that a teacher could be held accountable for student achievement gains regardless of student background, disability, or any other mediating factor:

> . . . an individual teacher or an individual school is only responsible for the improvement that a child makes while that child is in that individual class . . . Teachers and schools . . . cannot be responsible for all the environmental influences that create differences among abilities of children. They are only responsible for the improvement that child makes . . . What we found is there's virtually no relationship between the ability levels of the kids and the gain [in academic achievement] except for the teacher effects. The teacher effects are the single most important factor that we have found determining how much the children gain or how much they learn in the course of the year . . . Statistically, it's rather easy to fairly adjust for the ability levels of the children to give you a fair assessment of the educational outcome without worrying about what the ability levels of the children are.

Dr. Sanders' message resonated deeply in Nashville, where legislators were most eager to hear that there may be other avenues to school improvement that did not involve expensive remedies ordered by judges to equalize funding between poor and rich districts. If economic deprivation could be statistically adjusted for and the influence of teachers on "progress rates" could be determined and closely monitored, and if some teachers were getting better "progress rates" than others, independent of where the school was located, then it stood to reason that holding teachers accountable for "progress rates" made sense. Clearly, then, the education answer for Tennessee policy elites lay in teacher improvement and more accountability measures, rather than in expensive interventions to equalize funding that may or may not work; the Sanders Model, framed as it was in 1990, offered the remedy for a serious problem that remained unspoken, even if it was on every legislator's radar screen.

The Sanders value-added plan became the talk of Nashville in 1990 and 1991, and Dr. Sanders' star has continued to rise ever since, as the political and economic implications of VAM have been advanced nationally by the same business and corporate entities that were behind his original rise from obscurity in Tennessee. By 1992, when Tennessee passed the Education Improvement Act (EIA), the Sanders value-added testing plan known as the TVAAS was a part of the state statute that established EIA.

No one can say how Tennessee might stack up today in achievement comparisons if the state had chosen other education reform strategies in 1990. What we do know, and what is presented in some detail later in this section, is that Tennessee's achievement gaps between rich and poor remain no better and in some cases worse than they were in 1992, when the Sanders plan became law, notwithstanding Dr. Sanders' purported ability to "fairly adjust for the ability levels." What we know, too, is that Sanders' TVAAS set the policy context for an ongoing diminution of education funding, as policy makers became focused on raising test "progress rates," rather than dealing with growing socioeconomic disparities that were mirrored in student achievement gaps.

Immediately following the Sanders presentation in January 1990, Rep. John Bragg challenged Sanders about the necessity of using the value-added process to improve education—indicating that there were just three things the state really needed to worry about in education: "1) we get the best teachers we can find and we pay them as professionals, 2) we keep instructional time sacred, 3) we adapt our work to the culture of the community." Sanders offered a masterful response that combined both humility and confidence, offered as an outside expert who could not be credited nor blamed for any education decision that may ensue from his recommendations:

> That sounds like very good guidelines. Dr. McLean [co-author of original value-added study] and I come before you today speaking not as experts in education administration. We come as two statisticians saying you can measure it [student progress rates and teacher influence on them]. But I think the results of what we're showing here is that the time that teacher spends in that classroom is powerful. (Legislative minutes, Tennessee House Education Committee, 1/23/90, William L. Sanders)

During the 1990–91 flurry of presentations to various constituencies that led up to EIA passage in 1992, Sanders also had something to offer the influential Tennessee Education Association, the state affiliate of the NEA, whose lack of support could have sunk his efforts in those early days. Sanders knew that the TEA had made an otherwise-smooth road difficult for Governor Lamar Alexander's Career Ladder program, and he was eager to get the TEA onboard the value-added train. What the Sanders Model offered to an organization representing teachers was the possibility, at least, of some relief from the mounting pressure being applied by more emphasis on standards, accountability, and the increasingly visible state tests that were based on proficiency targets that regularly did not match the realities in the schools. In short, the push for accountability was pushing one way—down, and TEA representatives were eager to discuss a testing system that acknowledged that all children will not register the same test scores, notwithstanding the ramped up achievement goals and high-visibility political posturing by those imposing those goals. The Sanders Model seemed to offer that kind of option, and Sanders was quick to emphasize to his teacher audiences his oft-repeated phrase that "an individual teacher or an individual school is only responsible for the improvement that a child makes while that child is in that individual class." Who could argue with that?

In Sanders' presentations during the days leading up to the EIA passage, the Sanders claim that teachers are the single most important factor determining student achievement has since become a widely published talking point, without the benefit of the qualifier, "that we have found." There is no record, in fact, of any effort by the Sanders team to correct the mistaken notion that teachers account for more variance in student test scores than any other factor. Rather, Sanders and his team (Wright, Horn, & Sanders, 1997) declared in 1997 that "the results of this study well document that the most important factor affecting student learning is the teacher" (p. 63).

Notwithstanding Dr. Sanders' claim, we know, rather, that teacher effectiveness constitutes the most important *school-based factor* to variations in test score achievement (Goldhaber, Liddle, Theobald, & Walch, 2010), with the exact percentage dependent upon the methodology used. Goldhaber (2002), for instance, found that teacher characteristics account for 8.5% of the "variation in student achievement" (para. 8), while analyses by Nye and her colleagues (Nye, Konstantopoulos, & Hedges, 2004) found among 17 studies that "7% to 21% of the variance in achievement gains is associated with variation in teacher effectiveness" (p. 240). What we know, too, is that that other factors have much more influence on student achievement variations than do teachers. Goldhaber and his colleagues (Goldhaber, 2002) have found that additional factors involving family background, peer composition, and other social capital influences make up 60% of the variance in student test scores.

McWherter Takes Reform Plan on the Road

Although Governor McWherter directed Education Commissioner Charles Smith to visit all 139 districts across the state in 1987 to gather ideas for school improvement, he, too, embarked on a tour across the state in 1990 (Smith, 2004). According to the Governor's Press Office in 1989, education policy would reflect the concerns and ideas of "anyone who has any relationship to our schools" ("TEA plan similar to governor's goals," 11/3/89), and during this time, policy elites were developing the next major education reform legislation known as the Education Improvement Act of 1992. The educators that Smith heard from during his listening tour spoke of the need for more dollars, fewer state regulations, and more time and greater flexibility in implementing state-mandated programs; they wanted a voice in curriculum matters and an evaluation process for teachers that would allow more local input and that would provide more guidance for teacher improvement. Smith heard a repeated plea from teachers up to superintendents for "freedom to be creative in the classroom and to be freed from the necessity of teaching to the test" (Smith, 1987, pp. 9–10). A majority of local educators believed the Basic Skills program (the testing program of CERA) to be "flawed by too much structure, too much paperwork, and too much testing… [and] that creativity in the classroom [had] been negatively impacted by the program" (Smith, 1987, p. 12).

On the other hand, business leadership and the general public expressed concern about accountability in public education and the inequitable state funding formula for schools. The business community demanded better preparation for the high school graduates, and their chosen vehicle to achieve that end was greater accountability and efficiency in school leadership and operations, rather than increasing educational resources. Policymakers were faced once again with the unlikely prospect of offering children equal educational opportunities without raising taxes during a period of sluggish economic conditions that would later worsen. The state was facing a $46 million revenue shortfall. According to Finance Commissioner, David Manning, sales tax growth was below budget estimates "primarily due to a slump in sales that [had] been seen across the nation" ("Tighter budget control," 11/15/88). This revenue shortfall presented a significant problem because changes in welfare laws under the federal Catastrophic Health Care Act and the Welfare Reform Act required some major state appropriations over which the state had virtually no control ("Tighter budget control," 11/15/88). A study completed in 1990 by Stan Chervin, director of research for the Tennessee Department of Revenue, explained that the state's tax structure had not been generating enough revenue to keep up with inflation because "consumers are spending an increasingly large share of their money on services, which are exempt from sales tax" ("Lawmakers may stay for school reform," 11/18/90). Then, as now, Tennessee's heavy reliance on sales tax for needed revenue put the state among those with the most regressive tax structures. In 2007, for instance, those with the lowest 20% of family incomes paid over 9% of total income for state and local taxes, while those with the top 20% of family incomes paid just over 4% to total income in taxes (Institute on Taxation & Economic Policy, 2009).

With input from stakeholders across the state and a new funding formula developed by the State Board of Education, Commissioner Smith directed the State Department of Education to draft the *Twenty-first Century Challenge*. The plan was released in 1990 and contained 12 goals that, when combined with State Board's 1990 Master Plan, comprised the primary elements of the Education Improvement Act. As Governor McWherter and SDE staff toured the state to sell his K–12 education plan (Smith, 2004), McWherter also proposed a state income tax as an alternate to an increase in sales tax to fund his education reform. An immediate outcry arose from the Tennesseans for Limited Taxation Association in testimony to the House Education Committee:

> In the country in general, we just had a $500 billion federal tax increase, postage rates went up, the savings and loan bailout is not yet concluded, we don't know what the Gulf War is going to cost, and we are in the middle of the recession still and when you add to that pot a proposed state income tax, which is a massive tax increase, that is why legislators are having trouble with constituents not trusting what they're going to do. (Legislative minutes, Tennessee House Education Committee, 4/8/91, Tennesseans for Limited Taxation Association)

Historically, increasing taxes for educational improvement in Tennessee had never fared well during poor economic times, and this was no exception. Public opinion sided with income tax opponents, and by 1991 it was clear that any needed education changes would be accomplished without a new income tax.

While focused on education issues and courting European companies to invest in Tennessee as Alexander had done in the Far East, McWherter's vision for future education reform played off the sweeping utopian pronouncements from the 1989 Charlottesville Summit,[6] which cemented the relations of the business executives and state governors in developing a new set of ambitious federal goals that would be cemented in Goals 2000. Anticipating the rhetoric of Goals 2000 that included the promise that by 2000 "every adult American will be literate and will possess the knowledge and skills necessary to compete in a global economy," McWherter aimed "to give every young person in Tennessee an equal opportunity to compete with the best students anywhere in the world" ("Twenty-first Century Schools," 1/27/90.)

McWherter sought to distinguish himself from other Tennessee governors with a promise that he would be accountable for the increased revenues for education and for the success or failure of his plan, and he proposed including for the first time a designated education account in the state budget:

> In the 18 years that I served the General Assembly, I observed tax increases from time to time under different administrations and the taxes . . . the revenue increases . . . would all be sold in the name of education. And in most cases that I can remember, thousands and thousands and thousands of dollars got into other state programs other than in the name of what they were raised for. When I ask for revenue for education in K–12 or higher education . . . and when I ask for accountability . . . I will be accountable to see that those dollars go into education. Accountability will reach all of us. (McWherter, 9/25/89)

Despite gubernatorial assurances, the type of accountability and educational fixes that provided the dominant theme for the EIA debate focused on students and teachers, and the Sanders explanation of teachers' responsibility for improved progress rates of children "regardless of the ability level of that child" loomed large in the thinking of the most influential state legislators. Fixing education quickly came to be associated with fixing educators and students alike, with Senator Dunavant suggesting that "maybe [value-added] will be a self-winnowing factor to cause those teachers to improve and do better and find ways to do better and if they can't to eliminate themselves" (Legislative minutes, Tennessee House Education Committee, 1/23/90. Senator Leonard Dunavant).

The EIA continued at the statewide level the shift of accountability measures that began with earlier federal efforts toward "effective procedures, including provision for appropriate objective measurements of educational achievement, [that] will be adopted for evaluating at least annually the effectiveness of the programs in meeting the special educational needs of educationally deprived children" (Elementary and Secondary Education Act, *U.S. Statutes at Large*, 1965, p. 31). In Tennessee, the new generation of accountability began with CERA in 1984, which supplied specific instructions for effective evaluation procedures based on outputs from standardized test scores. It specified a study for the:

> use of student progress or achievement as measured by standardized testing or appropriate measures, as an indicator of successful teaching and effective schools and to review periodically the standards and criteria used for teacher and principal evaluation in view of the findings resulting for such study. (Comprehensive Education Reform Act, *Tennessee Public Acts*, 1984, p. 31)

"... What We Call The Corporate Model"

Under the direction of Commissioner Charles Smith (1987–1993) and at the behest of the General Assembly, the Tennessee State Department of Education crafted goals that offered taxpayers and the business community a path that hopefully would avoid further litigation by underfunded school systems, while imposing ample accountability markers to justify minimal increases in education funding ("Assembly to consider funding," 9/25/89). In February 1990, Smith presented to and won approval for his *Twenty-first Century Challenge* from the General Assembly's Education Oversight Committee. The plan was tweaked and approved by the State Board of Education in March 1990. In highlighting the plan "to shift education governance from 'process control' to 'outcomes assessment, Smith told *Education Week* (Bradley, 1990) that

> Over the years, we have tried to tinker with our educational system.... Every six or eight years we've increased taxes and thrown more money at the problem. It is an approach that simply has not worked. (para. 6)

Charles Smith was a busy man during this time, for while serving as Tennessee's Commissioner of Education from 1987 to 1993, Dr. Smith was on the Board of Trustees of the American College and Testing Program, Inc. (ACT), where he served on the Executive Committee while chairing ACT's Budget and Finance Committee. The same month Dr. Smith completed work on the *Twenty-first Century Challenge,* he also met a member of the ACT Board of Directors to approve two new ACT projects, one to create a new assessment system for workplace readiness (WorkKeys) that measured applied math skills, reading for information skills, and information location skills, and the other a data collection, analysis, and reporting system for use by employees, employers, and educators (ACT, 2009, p. 88). According to ACT's official history, Smith arranged a meeting with Tennessee's business and education leaders to introduce WorkKeys in 1990, and by April 1991, Tennessee had contracted to become the first state in ACT's WorkKeys system (ACT, 2009, p. 91).

Other states followed Tennessee's lead, and by 1999, WorkKeys was responsible for $5.4 million of ACT's revenue. Between 2005 and 2010, ACT administered over 7 million WorkKey tests, and in 2011, alone, American students took 2.3 million WorkKey tests. The self-paced KeyTrain workbook costs $85, and for those who buy the workbook, the WorkKeys tests cost $40. Otherwise, the tests cost $65. Dr. Smith became Vice-President of ACT, Inc. in 2008.

Smith's *Twenty-first Century Challenge* portended the goal of preparing tomorrow's society to compete in a global marketplace. Commissioner Smith focused on industrial expansion as the chief utilitarian outcome of educational improvement in the State, an end product that brought with it the added benefit of reducing public expenditures for social welfare and criminal justice:

> It is their [children's] education which will determine in large measure whether our state improves its per capita income and enlarges its industrial base. It is their education which will determine whether our communities improve the quality of life of our citizens. It is their education which will determine whether we increase or decrease our public welfare rolls and our prison population... Today America's economic power is being challenged and tested by Japan, Korea, and many other countries. Today industries are demanding an educated work force as a prerequisite for any plant location.... No longer is attainment of an education simply a personal goal, valued only by a student and his or her family. It has become—out of necessity—a goal of society as a whole. This is true because the young people who pass through our schools today will be our communities' voters of the future. They will become our communities' work force of the future. And if they fail, they will become our communities' welfare recipients and jail inmates of the future.... (Smith, 1990, pp. 1–4)

Smith delivered the message policymakers wanted to hear. No one was to blame for the state's poor academic performance. The culprit was a structural problem in the educational management organization, and Smith got right to his solution:

> We want to restructure our schools in ways that will permit them to be run more like successful businesses... We are blessed across this state with an outstanding and dedicated core of teachers and administrators... The people are not the problem. The real culprit is the structure.... In far too many communities, schools are being run in a state of near anarchy—no one really in charge, no one truly accountable. But should we be surprised about such a circumstance? That's what happens when policymaking boards at the local level get involved in day-to-day management and personnel matters. That's what happens when governing boards have no control over the selection of the chief executive officer. That's what happens when superintendents have their hands tied in day-to-day management judgments. That's what happens when front-line administrators have no effective voice in governance... I have seen... the hard cold reality of the chaos that results when the school structure collapses under the weight of disorganization. (Legislative minutes, Tennessee House Education Committee, 2/12/91, Commissioner Charles Smith)

In an effort to bring focus to the many variables that affect student learning other than a school or a district's management plan, TEA's president, Relzie Payton, reminded legislators of what the "bottom line" of accountability was and was not:

> Everyone wants accountability. But let's face it; people want it for different reasons. Some see it as a way to avoid being held accountable themselves—a way to blame poor schools and poor performance on someone else, not me. Others see accountability as a way to punish someone—a teacher, a principal, a board, a superintendent. Still others want accountability in a business sense—show me that my tax dollars have been well spent. I want accountability in the hope that finally, people will realize that it takes all of us working together to successfully educate a room full of children, or even an individual child. The bottom line is—this will require a collaborative partnership... I want to conclude by asking you to keep three things in mind as you examine and shape the accountability sections of this legislation: 1) On behalf of the teachers of Tennessee, give us the tools, the time, and the authority to do the job and *then* hold us accountable, not the other way around; 2) Make students' interests the focal point of all accountability systems; and, 3) Remember, those students are human beings, just like you and me. And just like us, they are shaped by a variety of experiences. They are not cheaply or easily molded into the adults we all hope they will become. (Payton, 1991)

In the following weeks, after the Commissioner Smith's economic framing of the educational argument, the business community heavily influenced the legislative decisions in formulating the EIA accountability clauses. For example, Dan Frierson, a Chattanooga businessman who served as Chairman of the Education Committee for the Tennessee Association of Business (TAB), spoke to the Senate Education Committee (3/6/91) in support of increased costs to continue education reform *only if* the elements of a "corporate management system" were put into place. Sen. Ray Albright, Chairman of the Education Committee, reiterated those needed elements when he summarized the position of the TAB:

> ...I find your statement "that without a sufficient system of management in place, the cost of these [reform efforts] cannot be justified. I anticipate that that's a pretty strong statement... The corporate management system, what we call the corporate model, is the elected school board, appointed superintendent, principal's not being part of the bargaining unit, value-added testing for our students,... sufficient rewards and sanctions for those who perform and those who do not perform, [to eliminate] the Chancery Court appeal, [and] an audit by a professional outside the system and recommended by the Comptroller of the State of Tennessee... These are what need to be, in your opinion, a management [system] in place if this bill

> is to have support of your organization or of your education committee. I interpret that from your remarks sir. (Legislative minutes, Tennessee Senate Education Committee, 3/6/91, Chairman Ray Albright)

Frierson responded, "Mr. Chairman you've gone to the heart of it."

John Parish, a Tullahoma businessman speaking for the Tennessee Business Roundtable, pressed for more accountability as the most cost-efficient reform, when he made his case before the Senate Education Committee:

> I think [accountability] is by far the key ingredient [to education reform]. A good step in that direction is to create a system that holds the school board accountable for policy; the school superintendent for execution, that is, carrying out the policy; teachers who teach and students who learn. If you do nothing else but change the way we select school superintendents, you will have taken a good step in the right direction in improving education in Tennessee. Also, I might add, that this costs nothing, no new revenues are needed and no new revenues are required... And I can assure you [that if you fail to pass this part] the support for [education reform] by the business community would be in serious doubt, as well as, the support to pay for it. (Legislative minutes, Tennessee Senate Education Committee, 3/6/91, John Parish)

So it was that the EIA (1992) abolished the "elected office of county superintendent of public instruction" and replaced that office with "an administrative position filled by the applicable local board of education" [TCA 49-2-301 (c) & (d)]. Once the responsibility of the local school board, the new "director of schools" would "employ, transfer, suspend, non-renew and dismiss all personnel within the approved budget" [TCA 49-2-301 (f)] making the lines of authority and accountability clear. If teachers and principals couldn't get the job done, the director of schools would replace them and if the director of schools didn't get the job done, the local board of education would replace him/her. And if the local board couldn't get the job accomplished?

> If after two consecutive years a system remains on probation [for not making required academic progress], the Commissioner [of Education] is authorized to recommend to the State Board of Education that both the local board of education and the [director of schools] be removed from office. [TCA 49-1-2 (e)]

With the State Board of Education reporting directly to the legislature, as mandated by PEGRA (1984), the legislature had complete control of education policy in Tennessee. Since 1992, over 30 bills have been introduced to reverse the highly controversial portion of the EIA that ended the possibility for elected school superintendents (Smith, 2004).

The management information system in the EIA provided information to the State Department of Education "to be used in evaluating the fiscal operations of local school systems" based on meeting performance goals "determined by the value added assessment" (Title 49-1-2, Section 4). Section 4 continues to describe the expected rate of progress for schools and school districts; penalties for not making the expected progress; the definition of value added assessment that requires some statistical training to understand; characteristics of the achievement tests school districts would use in calculating value added scores; and most interesting of all, specific journal articles defining Sanders' value added methodology, including even the title of the first journal article on the Sanders Model: "A Unified Approach to Mixed Linear Models" by Mclean, Sanders, and Stroup (1991). Notably, early supporter of Sanders, Senator Andy Womack, later called the specificity of the state statute an "error" in 2004. In testimony before the Tennessee House Education Committee (3/3/2004), Womack claimed that the language of the EIA had given a monopoly to one value-added model and to one individual, Dr. Sanders. Despite a concerted effort to derail the Sanders Model in 2004, the same management system for accountability remains in place and is likely to remain so for some time, especially since the Sanders Model was reified by Tennessee's Race to the Top federal grant worth $501 million.

In reflecting on the passage of the EIA, Commissioner of Education, Charles E. Smith later shared (Grounard, 2006) with a doctoral student what he learned politically from the Tennessee reform effort: "the advice I would give would be that on something this complex and on something as substantive as it is, it needs to be part of a bigger package." Grounard concluded from his interview with Smith that putting together a complex bill with many parts that had some desired element for all stakeholders allowed the value-added system to survive: "the TEA was not comfortable with value-added but there were so many things in the Education Improvement Bill that they wanted they did not put up much of a fight" (pp. 102–103).

The Sanders Model within the EIA provided the linchpin for an accountability structure that tied together curriculum, textbooks, and tests to student performance; student performance to teacher performance; teacher performance to quantifiable goals; quantifiable goals to clear lines of authority and responsibility from the Commissioner of Education and the State Board of Education to local boards of education, superintendents, and principals; and clear lines of authority and responsibility to incentives and sanctions for accomplishing the goals. And even though the TVAAS provided the accountability that the business community demanded for increased education funding, a few legislators expressed deep reservations. Representative Phillip Pinion wondered out loud if the new management system based on business principles was really necessary and if the corporate model was a credible one for education:

> In accountability, I don't think good teachers mind being accountable, but it looks like to me we've proven in this state that we've got good teachers and if you've got a dud in the bunch, a good principal should be able to weed that teacher out. And I'm not sure we're going to have to go through all this process... I feel sort of strange that business is pushing all this, when I wish we could get as much out of some of our automobiles that we buy as we do out of our teachers that we have in the state already. (Legislative minutes, Tennessee House Education Committee, 4/8/91, Rep. Philip Pinion)

Commissioner Smith responded that there was a widespread perception that "we're not doing a good job and that we have a lot of bad teachers... This process will show differently—that the majority of the teachers in this state are doing an outstanding job." Pinion responded that the media was creating that perception (Legislative minutes, Tennessee House Education Committee, 4/8/91, Commissioner Smith).

A skeptical elementary school teacher, Carol Stinson brought a temporary hush to the debate when she addressed accountability and its wider implications, when she asked:

> How will parents' responsibilities be measured? How will a county commissioner's, a legislator's, the governor's responsibilities be measured in terms of value-added student achievement?... The business community is interested in hiring graduates who are competent in the basic academic skills yet who also possess the communication skills necessary to work cooperatively with coworkers. We ask how can an achievement test measure a teacher's effectiveness in the development of socialization skills and democratic principles which are vital to the workplace and society?... We question the latest idea that schools and school systems can be run as a business. We do not work with raw materials, assembly lines, production quotas, or final products. If our students miss school, we cannot put another student in his or her place. We must be sure that student receives the instruction that they missed... We cannot remove, dismiss, or fire a student that does not meet or maintain certain performance standards... We feel Tennessee teachers are doing an outstanding job with the resources they have. (Legislative minutes, Tennessee House Education Committee, 4/8/91, Carol Stinson)

Following a long silence in a venue that is rarely quiet, Chairman Gene Davidson finally said, "It takes something like this to bring it back home, to bring it to heart, to what we're all trying to do. Thank you." After another pause of a length appropriate for moment of silent meditation, Chairman Davis got right back to the business at hand: "Now I think Commissioner Smith, Dr. Poulton, and Dr. Sanders are going to address accountability."

Fire Under the Reform Pot: Tennessee Small School Systems Lawsuits

Running parallel to the investigations of CERA and the crafting of new accountability management and funding systems was the ongoing lawsuit filed by the Tennessee Small School Systems in July 1988. While educational funding in Tennessee had been under study for a number of years, the 1989 ruling by the Kentucky Supreme Court in *Rose v. The Council for Better Education, Inc.* (790 S.W. 2d 186) created an urgency to head off the same kind of expensive legal rendering in Tennessee. In ruling the entire state school system unconstitutional in a 3–2 decision on June 8, 1989, the Kentucky Supreme Court had determined that

> ...Kentucky's system of common schools is underfunded and inadequate; is fraught with inequalities and inequities throughout the 168 local school districts; is ranked nationally in the lower 20–25% in virtually every category that is used to evaluate educational performance; and is not uniform among the districts in educational opportunities. (p. 9)

At the request of the Tennessee General Assembly following the Kentucky decision, Dr. Brent Poulton, Executive Director of the Tennessee State Board of Education, reviewed the Kentucky case for the Education Oversight Committee. In his review, he compared the Kentucky case to the *Tennessee Small School Systems v. McWherter* (851 S.W. 2d 139) case, which had been filed on July 7, 1988. What Poulton highlighted for Tennessee legislators was that the Kentucky Supreme Court was now the education authority in the state of Kentucky, developing both the program and funding formula for all public schools. In response to a question from Committee members about why state mandates for personnel had not been adequately funded in the past, Poulton replied that both the State Board of Education and the General Assembly had increased the need for personnel without regard for local systems' capacity to fund those positions, thus amounting "to tinkering with an overwhelmingly archaic system." Poulton added, "if we're really serious about having good schools in the State then we ought to go to the heart of the problem and change the system" (Legislative minutes, Tennessee House Education Oversight Committee, 7/12/89, Brent Poulton).

Poulton then explained the data collected in past funding reports completed by the State Board of Education and sent to the governor and the General Assembly had "identified funding problems as the single greatest impediment to achieving the goal of having schools among the best in the nation" (Weeks, 1988, p. 1). One report (Weeks, 1988) included an examination of the Tennessee Foundation Program (TFP), which was set forth in 1924 "as a means for insuring adequate funding in Tennessee's public schools" (Weeks, 1988, p. 1). Citing Tennessee as 51st in per pupil spending for public schools in both 1984 and 1988, the report identified three problems with the TFP:

- There is no link between the changes in appropriations and changes in the costs of delivering programs and services at the local level.
- The amount of funding provided is too little to ensure adequate funding of a basic educational program in all systems.
- It does not ensure the children in Tennessee equal access to quality educational resources (pp. 3–4).

The study recommended a basic education program that would adequately address needs for professional and support personnel, transportation and textbooks, staffing ratios, and expenditure levels. While calling for a new formula to fund these essential elements equitably, the report was notably silent on learning programs.

Having failed since 1909 in repeated efforts to equalize state funding for education, the State Board of Education used the Weeks (1988) recommendations to develop a new funding formula for the Basic Education Plan (BEP), which was approved by the State Board of Education in November 1988. The new plan, which would not become law for another four years, sought to narrow the funding disparities across counties in the state by establishing the basic elements for school operation, by shifting more of the funding burden to the state, and by assigning the local funding share according to the local board's ability to raise revenue (Snodgrass, 1990, p. 69).

In spite of the State Board's new funding formula, the State took a defensive position in response to the plaintiffs in the Tennessee Small Schools Systems case. Aiming to minimize the State's financial obligations, State Attorney General, Charles W. Burson, expressed the State's position in a legal brief:

> There are no constitutional rights to any specific allocation of funds for public education. All that is constitutionally required is some legislative scheme for funding public education that has a rational basis. These requirements have

> clearly been met. Even if students do not have computers or new textbooks as the complainant alleges, there is no indication that they are denied access to the fundamentals of education. ("No guarantees for poor areas," 11/27/88)

Cavit Cheshier, Executive Director of the Tennessee Education Association (TEA), responded that the defense's brief

> reflects a narrow view of what is required for a basic level of education in today's society. Computers, up-to-date textbooks, modern vocational training equipment and reasonably sized classrooms are essentials for educating children and preparing them to live in an increasingly complex, technological society. ("No guarantees for poor areas," 11/27/88)

Almost two years later, *Tennessee Small School Systems v. McWherter* (851 S.W. 2d 139) finally came to trial in Chancery Court on October 29, 1990, and after six weeks of argument, Chancellor C. A. High sided with the plaintiffs. Noting that "the statutory funding scheme has produced a great disparity in the revenues available in the different school districts" (Keese & Huffman, 1998, p. 165), the Court ruled that "under a uniform system [as guaranteed under the Tennessee Constitution of 1835], a child living in a poor district should have the same opportunity to receive substantially the same education as a child living in a rich district" (p. 165). The State appealed the decision, which resulted in a 2–1 reversal by the State Court of Appeals in April 1992. The following year, however, all five justices of the Tennessee Supreme Court "endorsed the conclusions of the trial court and remanded the case for the trial judge to draft an order to correct the funding inequity problem" (p. 165). When Chancery Court held its hearing to begin drafting an order in July 1993, the State offered the 1992 passage of the EIA with a specific revised funding formula of the Basic Education Program (BEP) as new evidence that the State was making good on its responsibility to phase in an equitable funding formula. Chancellor High was impressed and ruled that he would allow for the BEP to take effect before any further orders would be rendered (p. 165).

The BEP formula was comprised of 43 separate funding components that included almost every aspect and category of school operations except the most expensive one: teachers. Another major exclusion of the new funding plan was a provision for "annual review of the actual costs of each component and for reviewing the formula each year to make adjustments for improving the system (*Tennessee Small School Systems, et al. v. Ned Ray McWherter, et al.* No. M2001-01957-SC-R3-CV, October 8, 2002, p. 5). Arguing that an equitable state system could not be achieved without an effort to equalize teacher salaries, the plaintiffs returned to court in what was known as Small Schools II. In February of 1995, the Tennessee Supreme Court handed down a decision (Green, Smith, & Hydorn, 1995) in favor of equalizing teachers' salaries across the state: "The Court ruled that omitting teachers' salaries from the BEP was a significant defect and had the potential to impair achieving the objectives of the BEP" (p. 9).

The State's solution was to pass new legislation that provided state funding to equalize teacher salaries in school systems where the average salary was below the state average of $28,094. Because the plan did not provide for annual reviews or determine the state's ongoing obligation in the same way that other funding components were reviewed and adjusted, the plaintiffs returned to court once again in Small Schools III. The trial judge ruled in favor of the State that it had met its obligations to equalize teacher salaries, but on appeal, the State Supreme Court ruled once again in favor of the plaintiffs on May 1, 2002: . . . the salary equity plan in Tennessee Code Annotated § 49-3-366 fails to comport with the State's constitutional obligation to formulate and maintain a system of public education that affords substantially equal educational opportunity to all students (*Tennessee Small School Systems, et al. v. Ned Ray McWherter, et al.* No. M2001-01957-SC-R3-CV, October 8, 2002, p. 7). In rendering their judgment, the High Court clearly noted the State's long-term resistance to establishing structures required for an equitable school finance system:

> . . . the record supports the plaintiffs' argument that for the most part, the same disparities in teachers' salaries that existed when Small Schools II was decided still exist today. For example, in 1995, the City of Alcoa paid teachers an average of $40,672, while Jackson County paid teachers an average of $23,934, a difference of $16,738. In 1997, Oak Ridge paid its teachers an average of $42,268, while in Monroe County the figure was $28,025, a disparity of $14,243. In 1998–1999, the disparity between Oak Ridge and Monroe County grew to $14,554. Thus, wide disparities still exist, and it takes little imagination to see how such disparities can lead to experienced and more educated teachers leaving the poorer school districts to teach in wealthier ones where they receive higher salaries. In the end, the rural districts continue to suffer the same type of constitutional inequities that were present fourteen years ago when this litigation began. (p. 13)

The BEP formula of the EIA offered a façade of deep-rooted education finance reform within the state funding structure for education when, in fact, the BEP proved ineffective in altering the long-standing inequities among the state school systems. Peevely and Ray (2001) found that even when the phased in Basic Education Plan (BEP) reached full funding five years after passage in 1997, those underfunded systems named as litigants in the 1988 lawsuit against the State had improved funding, on average, only 5% "in comparison to both non-litigant and state average expenditure during the five year phase in of full funding (pp. 467–468). In 1999, plaintiff districts' per pupil average funding stood at $4,577, while non-litigant average funding was $5,157 (88%), and state average funding was $5,077 (90%). In 2000, the funding gap began to open up once more, and by 2003, almost all the progress made in narrowing the spending gap after 1992 had been lost once again (Center for Business and Economic Research, 2007, p. 41). Tennessee's BEP formula did not adequately address the inequity in education funding between rich and poor districts.

While it is clear that both poor and rich school districts suffer from underfunding when compared to the national average or to most states in the Southeast, citizens of poorer districts pay an unfair proportion of the taxes to support their schools. Tennessee's schools are funded by property taxes and local sales tax options, creating an inherent inequity (Edmiston & Murray, 1998) in both the distribution of the tax burden across income levels and between businesses and individuals, with the greatest burden falling on the poor who can least afford it: "if one compares the tax burdens of households earning $25,000 per year and $100,000 per year across all states, Tennessee has the most regressive tax system in the nation" (p. 193). Based on 2012 calculations by the Tax Foundation (2012), Tennessee still has the most regressive tax system in the United States.

With a string of continuing reform "firsts," from value-added assessment implementation to being one of the first two states to win a Race to the Top grant to singular recognition from the Secretary of Education, Arne Duncan, for "making unprecedented progress in producing statewide reform and boosting student achievement" (U.S. Department of Education, 2012) a 2012 report by the Education Law Center (Baker, Sciarra, & Farrie, 2012) showed that Tennessee compared poorly on four dimensions of education funding: funding level, funding distribution, state effort, and coverage. Tennessee ranks 51st in the nation for funding level, which is described in the report as the "overall level of state and local revenue provided to school districts" in comparison to other states' average per-pupil revenue (p. 6, 12). When comparing the distribution of funding across local districts within a state to student poverty rates in those districts, Tennessee received a grade of C in comparison to other states (p. 7, 14). Tennessee's funding effort, or "the ratio of state spending to state per capita gross domestic product (GDP)" rated an F (p. 7, 22), while "coverage" or the funding for the proportion of school-age children that attend public school versus parochial or private school ranked 46th in the nation (p. 7, 24).

Even when faced with State Supreme Court rulings, low national educational rankings, and continuing inequities between rich and poor systems, the executive and legislative branches of Tennessee government continued inadequate funding of education in the EIA, despite the rhetorical commitment to exceed the national achievement levels in Commissioner Charles Smith's Twenty-first Century Challenge. Instead of the promised "comprehensive approach to funding schools" that would enable "accountability standards for quality and productivity" (Goal 10), the state offered poor school districts the high goals and accountability demands of the EIA without the needed funding to achieve goals or satisfy demands. At the same time, the state adopted new value-added accountability measures that served to mask the continuing disparities between rich and poor systems, while justifying the regressive tax increases that proved inadequate and as inequitable as the system they sought to remedy. Meanwhile, Tennessee's continuing rhetorical commitment allowed resources to be shifted without fanfare toward purposes other than education and the state's most vulnerable citizens.

Budget Priorities in Tennessee: Healthcare, Prisons, and Foreign Investment

During the years of most intense education reform under Governor Alexander and Governor McWherter, Tennessee education lost ground in terms of the percentage of the State budget that it garnered. Edmiston & Murray (1998) found that from 1977 to 1995, the percentage of state spending going to education was almost halved, as it dropped from 40% to 22.3% of state expenditures. During that same 18 year interim, the average growth rate for spending among all state departments averaged a compound annual growth rate of 4.0, while the growth rate for education spending was the lowest among all function areas of state spending at 0.6.

At the same time that education funding was experiencing minimal growth and garnering a smaller and smaller percentage of the state budget, other state functions were claiming larger chunks while doubling and tripling their budget allocations. The three areas experiencing the largest growth were Health Care and Social Services (HC&SS); Law, Justice, and Public Safety (LJ&PS); and foreign industrial incentives. Between 1977 and 1995, the HC&SS budget more than tripled, from $1.365 billion annually to over $5 billion. In 1994, McWherter implemented TennCare, a competitive, free-market initiative to shift Medicaid patients to managed care companies to avoid "a looming fiscal crisis posed by federal tightening of rules on the use of provider taxes to fund Medicaid" (Conover & Davis, 2000, p. 6). In effect, new federal regulations allowed more of Tennessee's poor to qualify for Medicaid, while at the same time cutting substantially the Disproportionate Share Hospital (DSP) allotment that Tennessee had depended upon to fund almost a one-fifth of Medicaid costs. With a projected annual increase of 17% in Medicaid costs and a loss of almost $500 million from reductions of DSP allotments, Tennessee quickly "developed a Medicaid waiver proposal that was approved by the federal government less than six weeks before TennCare was hastily implemented..." (p. 7). While TennCare saved the state and federal government $700 million in its first five years by moving Medicaid recipients to managed care, the program costs Tennesseans "$3.8 billion more than if the former Medicaid program had been retained" (Conover & Davies, p. 9). Tennesseans assumed these deferred costs in the form of provider, local government, and patient contributions (p. 9).

Some years after the hasty implementation, TennCare employees told researchers (Aizer, Gold, & Shcoen, 1999) that they believed after the first year of implementation TennCare was "more about managed costs than managed care, with limited change in the delivery system" (p. 14). Managing costs, however, did not seem to extend to the health management organizations (HMOs) that the State selected to run managed care organizations (MCOs). In a bow by legislators to "free market" principles, the State did not require HMOs to cap administrative fees or profits, and the State did not provide adequate personnel to provide proper oversight from the first year forward: "The speed of implementation required a primary focus on urgent administrative needs, with only limited work on generic systems. As a result, procedures for implementing and overseeing many MCO provisions were poorly developed after the first year" (p. 14).

By 1996, complaints by providers and patients, alike, regarding MCO performance led to an audit of the State's second largest provider, Access... MedPlus. Two independent audits from 1996 to 1998 reported to Governor Sundquist, who had succeeded Ned McWherter, and the General Assembly numerous improprieties and violations in regards to record keeping, reporting, and non-payment of providers. Almost three years later with a grand jury investigation looming, the state finally acted on October 31, 2001 to cancel its contract with Access... MedPlus, which immediately filed for bankruptcy with an estimated $100 million unpaid in claims. At the time of the Access... MedPlus collapse, the company had 279,000 of the State's 1.2 million enrollees and was collecting $39 million from the State each month. Of that amount, 11%, or $4.29 million per month, was taken off the top for management fees, and the rest was purportedly paid out in claims filed by health care providers (Wade, 2002).

As a result of new state rules put in place in 2003 following the Access... MedPlus meltdown, two other MCOs were found to be in serious non-compliance and financial trouble (The Bureau of TennCare, 2003). Universal Care of Tennessee, Inc. had its contract cancelled on June 1, 2003 and was forced to hand back to the State a recent receivable of $54,436,971. Xantus, Inc. had its contract terminated on July 31, 2003, after reporting a net worth deficiency of –$98,199,688 (p. 4).

During those early years of implementation, TennCare was able to provide both primary and preventive health care coverage for the 800,000 Medicaid patients and 500,000 additional uninsureds and uninsurables, those unable to participate in Medicaid due to preexisting conditions received (Chang, 2007, p. 46). After nine years of TennCare, however, the actual number of uninsured and uninsurable citizens was lower than earlier years:

1994	1,251,008	836,647 Medicaid	414,361 uninsured and uninsurable
1997	1,231,220	848,566 Medicaid	382,654 uninsured and uninsurable[7]
2003	1,273,732	1,014,192 Medicaid	259,540 uninsured and uninsurable[8]

Even though the total number of enrollees increased modestly over the first decade of TennCare, patients and providers, alike, expressed strong criticism of the system. The Tennessee Medical Association and the Tennessee Justice Center filed a string of lawsuits on behalf of TennCare enrollees, who felt they had not received "federally mandated" due process, benefits, and services. As a result, judges offered court decisions in favor of the plaintiffs in 1995, 1996, 1998, 1999, 2000, 2002 and 2005 (Chang & Steinberg, 2009). Sundquist, who had run as an anti-tax zealot, reportedly became interested in implementing a state income tax in 1999 to counter a large budget shortfall. As a result, the Governor endeavored to win the support for his plan from the powerful insurance and health industries by allowing HMOs to bill the State for patient services, rather than paying a flat fee for patient services as called for in the original TennCare plan. According to the Tennessee Justice Center and others ("Twenty-five percent of TennCare enrollees cut," 2005, p. 18), this change in the billing process essentially moved the insurance "risk" from the insurance companies back to the State:

> This is when costs began to rise drastically. The HMO's had no reason to take cost-controlling measures. When costs rose, the State was on the hook for the expense. The main scapegoat were the optional, newly insured populations of people, but these people had been covered for several years already without any significant jumps in cost. It was this change in "risk" policy that was the true reason for the program's problems. (Tennessee Justice Center, n.d.)

While Sundquist continued to support a state income tax to deal with budget shortfalls in healthcare, the General Assembly averted that political risk with a short-term solution by increasing TennCare funding by $190 million in May 1999, while freezing all new enrollment for the "uninsured" and the "uninsurable" (Conover & Davies, 2000, pp. 1–2).

While Sundquist's efforts to placate business interests paid off for the healthcare and insurance industries, the State was left with increased economic responsibility that was paid for by reducing the number of TennCare enrollees, along with quality and quantity of services. Despite earlier protestations against regressive taxes, during his last legislative session in 2002, Sundquist led the effort to raise the limit on the state sales tax to 9.75%, one of the highest in the United States (Baker, 2011, para. 29).

During his gubernatorial campaign to replace Sundquist at the end of his second term, Phil Bredesen vowed to fix TennCare. When he took office in 2003, TennCare was consuming 36% of total state appropriations (Chang & Steinberg, 2009). Bredesen had plenty of experience in the health care industry, having made his personal fortune with the creation in 1980 and subsequent sale six years later of HealthAmerica Corporation, a Nashville-based health care management company. Following HAC's sale in 1986, Bredesen cofounded Coventry Corporation, which was a Fortune 500 managed care provider until 2007 ("Phil Bredesen, Former Governor of Tennessee," n.d.).

Bredesen's efforts to reduce TennCare's share of state expenditures to 25% quickly ran into trouble. In September, 2004, Bredesen's administrative staff uncovered a large TennCare budgeting error of almost $200 million at the same time that news came that plans to reduce prescription drug coverage could be in trouble from the powerful pharmaceutical industry (Heher, 2004). Just two months later in November, Bredesen announced plans to cut hundreds of thousands of enrollees from TennCare and to return to "a traditional Medicaid program" (Ku & Wachino, 2004, para. 1). Bredesen's eventual "fix" resulted in the "disenrollment of 190,000 people from TennCare Standard" (Chang, 2008, p. 18), a curtailment of prescription benefits, and other reductions "based on a new, more restrictive definition of a reimbursable service that would be considered a medical necessity" (Chang, 2007, p. 48). According to Chang (2007), Tennessee's model healthcare reform was put in place much too quickly and without the oversight structures in place to rein in "'homegrown' MCOs that were not experienced in managing the care for the Medicaid and uninsured population that they were given responsibility for." To complicate matters, twelve TennCare directors in twelve years maintained a constant churn that led to programs and policies that "were inconsistent and contradictory" (p. 49).

Along with a modest increase in the number of Tennesseans receiving medical services, TennCare left Nashville transformed into a major center for the healthcare industry, with 17 major corporations employing 145,000 and generating annual revenue of $26 billion. According to a study released by the Nashville Health Care Council (2013), "Nashville's health care industry contributes nearly $30 billion and 210,000 jobs to the local economy... The industry also has a far global reach, with 56 health care company headquarters that generate nearly 400,000 jobs and more than $62 billion in revenues worldwide."

The Prison Business

Corrections Corporation of America (CCA) is the largest private prison management company in America, and it is headquartered in Nashville. According to their website, CCA controls over 80,000 inmates, approximately 90,000 bed, and more than 60 prisons in 16 states, 44 of which are owned by CCA. CCA and the American Exchange Legislative Council (ALEC) have partnered through the Criminal Justice/Public Safety & Elections Task Force to promote model bills in state legislatures "that lengthen sentences, which have dramatically increased incarceration rates... putting more of those inmates under the control of for-profit corporations" (Center for Media and Democracy, 2012, para. 12).

Tennessee's second leading area of growth in state expenditures from 1977 to 1995 was Law, Justice, and Public Safety (LJ&PS), with the largest portion going to corrections. Richard Chesteen (1998) points out that between 1985 and 1995, "Tennessee went from having an unconstitutional prison system to having the only fully accredited state prison system in the country" (p. 174). Under federal court order with 11 prisons in 1977, Tennessee was not under court order 20 years later, and it had 20 ACA-accredited prisons (Kyle, 1998). Between 1977 and 1995, state expenditures for LJ&PS more than tripled, from $222.3 million to $671.5 million. At the heart of the growing state commitment to corrections facilities was the emergence of the for-profit prison management industry led by CCA, whose founder and current CEO, Tom Beasley, was a friend and senior advisor to Governor Alexander when the new Tennessee commitment to prison expansion began in the late 1970s. As Chesteen (1998) recounts,

> Beasley and Alexander go way back. While a Vanderbilt University undergraduate, Beasley rented a garage apartment from the Alexanders. He was Tennessee Republican Party chairman from 1977 to 1980 and was one of the founders of Corrections Corporation of America (CCA). In 1985, CCA won

a contract from Governor Alexander to build and operate two new 500-bed facilities in Tennessee's prison system.

Chesteen also details how Alexander's wife, Honey, profited handsomely from buying and trading CCA stock during Alexander's two terms as Governor, but Governor Alexander's wife was not the only prominent Tennessean to profit from for-profit prisons. According to Wray (1986), CCA stockholders included former Alexander cabinet officers and Alexander's successor, Governor Ned McWherter. One CCA lobbyist also served as a Democratic state senator (p. 4).

During Alexander's second term in 1984, Tennessee became the first governmental body in the United States to award a contract to a private company for the "complete operation of a jail" (Cheung, 2004, p. 1). The jail was in Hamilton County, and the company was CCA. In 1985, CCA proposed "an unprecedented plan (Kyle, 1998, para. 5) to take over all of Tennessee's prisons, but the plan never reached a vote in the state legislature:

> The plan offered the state $100 million in cash for management rights and $250 million in up-front capital expenditures in exchange for CCA being paid a first-year management fee equal to Tennessee's adult correctional budget for the 1986–87 fiscal year (approximately $170 million). In his letter to the governor and the Legislature, CCA Founder and then-CEO Tom Beasley promised, "We will lock them up better, quicker and for less than you can." (Kyle, 1998, para. 5)

During their administrations, Governors Alexander, McWherter, Sundquist, and Haslam pursued legislation to advance privatization of state prisons, or else modified regulations and processes to give private prisons a larger role in housing state prisoners. By far, Governor Don Sundquist proved to be the most active Tennessee governor in pushing for privatized prisons during the last decades of the twentieth century, even though the evidence for associated cost savings was slim. The Fiscal Review Committee for the Legislature's Select Committee on Corrections (SOCC) issued a report in January 1995 that showed only "1% difference in the operational costs of the privately managed prison and the average of the costs for the two state prisons between July 1, 1993, and June 30, 1994" (Kyle, 1998, para. 18). Nonetheless, by 1998 Sundquist, who was also an advocate of returning the striped-clad chain gangs to Tennessee roadsides, (Chesteen, 1998, p. 180) was pushing hard for an expanded privatized prison system. In early 1998, Sundquist and his legislative allies presented a bill that called for the creation of a Department of Criminal Justice to "coordinate and administer public and private management of correctional facilities" (para. 26).

In reviewing the bill, the SOCC found serious flaws and responded with recommendations that would establish compliance with the Committee's earlier guidance, which crafters of the bill had largely ignored (Kyle, 1998). Among the shortcoming cited by the SOCC were these:

- The governor's emphasis was on privatizing, not on fair competition between the public and private sectors.
- The new governance structure lacked authority, accountability and continuity.
- The corrections commissioner was given sole authority over major state policy decisions, such as how many prisons to privatize and which prisons to privatize.
- Independent contract administration and monitoring (by an outside agency or body) were not included.

The committee did conclude that the language of the bill, which attempted to guarantee protection for state employees, was strong; however, state employees remained opposed to the bill (para. 24).

Ignoring the recommendations for changes, Governor Sundquist and his allies attempted, nonetheless, to push the bill through, but even with support by legislative leaders and the AFL-CIO, the bill failed to get beyond the "critical Senate and House committees" (para. 25). The bill was withdrawn late in the 1998 session.

According to CCA's website in 2012, the company now operates six correctional facilities in Tennessee with capacity for 8,238 inmates. Of the 20,236 adult inmates in Tennessee prisons, 5,594 are incarcerated in the private prisons of CCA. Near the end of his second and final term in 2010, Governor Bredesen, who succeeded Sundquist, proposed ending the State's contract with CCA to run one West Tennessee prison in Hardeman County, which Bredesen described as "not really justified." However, the new governor, Bill Haslam, intervened early in 2011 to stop the closure and to renew the CCA contract with the State worth $31 million a year. In order to come up with the money, Haslam cut $20 million from the higher education budget and $40 million from the expanded Medicaid program that replaced TennCare. When Haslam was questioned by reporters about his decision to keep the CCA prison open, he said, "We could have saved some money by closing that, but in the end we didn't think it was the right thing to do for the corrections system" (Schelzig, 2011).

Business Efficiencies in Public Schools and Public Money for Business

As Tennessee's governors and legislators sought free market solutions and opportunities over the past 30 years in the areas of health care and criminal justice, they sought to effect organizational and procedural changes in education that they hoped would have positive effects on student achievement as measured by test scores, teacher productivity, and spending for education. The formulation, advertising, enactment, implementation, and outcomes of CERA in 1984 and the EIA in 1992 provide examples of marginally funded short-term accountability plans that concentrated control of education into fewer hands, established a façade of ongoing and deep education reform, and effectively reduced the public share of spending on education while freeing up more public money for commercial interest and corporate priorities. The rhetoric of reform shifted the advertised purpose of schools toward economic ends, and the centralized control by closely aligned business and political interests focused on minimizing increases in education spending and avoiding tax reform that would require larger public investment by those better able to afford it.

By the late 1970s, Tennessee was prime real estate for attracting foreign business and industry investment due to its natural resources, new and efficient infrastructure, cheap electrical power provided by TVA, its "right to work" labor status, accessibility to U.S. markets, and its low state and local taxes. Tennessee placed "among the top four states" in a 1976 study on foreign investment (Livingston, 1998, pp. 204–205). Business interests in Tennessee needed a deal maker with political clout, and Lamar Alexander, as the newly elected governor in 1978 with deep political connections, was keenly interested and a quick study. Alexander was briefed on Nissan's interest in opening a large plant in Smyrna, Tennessee, and with a sales pitch of "sunshine and cheap labor," Alexander and 30 Tennessee businessmen traveled to Japan in 1979 to court 80 Japanese firms. Alexander received full backing of the Republican Senate majority leader and fellow East Tennessean, Howard Baker, whose influence provided "an estimable advantage when competing to recruit firms concerned about congressionally imposed protectionist measures" (p. 206).

Visiting Japan eight times during his tenure as Governor (1979–1987), Alexander knew how to sell Tennessee to the Japanese, and Alexander's public incentive of $66 million to Nissan for the Smyrna plant deal went a long way in getting the attention of Japanese corporations. From 1977 to 1993, "Japanese investment grew an astounding 23,000 percent" and the automotive industry became "one of the most vital parts of the Tennessee economy" (Livingston, 1998, p. 209). How did a $66 million incentive package impact Tennessee education budgets?

During the late 1970s and 1980s, Tennessee policymakers from business and industry were keen to impose corporate models and methods aimed to make schools and teachers more efficient, thus "wasting" less and, in turn, making more public financing available for business-friendly initiatives. In the example just above, we see sustained public efforts from Governor Alexander to attract business and industry to the state through tax incentives, high quality public infrastructure, and promises of a properly educated workforce. Citing the research of James O'Conner (1970), Martin, Overholt and Urban (1976), describe how curtailed public spending and tight state budgets provide the political and economic context for corporate-influenced education reform. Revenue lost in tax breaks to business and industry, state spending for highway systems and other infrastructure, and vocational education programs tailored to meet business and industry workforce needs leaves reduced funding to provide adequate and equitable education for all students in the state.

Another example of state subsidies to corporate capital were commonly termed "learning corporations" in the 1970s and 1980s, which were "corporate performance contractors to design and carry out accountability programs" (Martin et al, 1976, p. 46). Since those early days, the concept of business solutions in education has spawned a multi-billion dollar education industry, with testing, curriculum, and instructional materials increasingly concentrated within a small group of multinational corporations like Pearson and McGraw-Hill. In much the same way that President Eisenhower warned of the influence of the military-industrial complex, some education reform critics warn of a "testing-industrial complex" that views public education at all levels as an ongoing and reliable revenue stream that may be tapped by those who can offer more efficient solutions for low test scores than increasing poverty would, otherwise, demand. Tennessee has spent more than $326 million in accountability and assessment since 1992 (Smith, 2004; Tennessee State Department of Finance & Administration, 2012), and most recently the State has dedicated approximately $56 million of Race to the Top funds for accountability and assessment (U.S. Department of Education, 2010, January 18).

Just before Lamar Alexander was elected to his first term as Governor of Tennessee, scholars (Martin, Overholt, & Urban, 1976) were already warning of the effects the emerging accountability movement on schools, students, and teachers:

> The accountability movement attempts to apply mechanical solutions to a complex social institution. It constitutes an emerging power scheme designed to prespecify goals that are usually simplistic, irrelevant to the learner's developmental process and environment, inhibiting to his potential, empirically unverifiable, and logically indefensible. These prespecified goals function mainly to control what teachers will do in the classroom, and, even more important, to control the overall economic and political affairs of the school. (pp. 76–77)

Just over 30 years and many critiques later, Dorn (2007) notes that the current generation of accountabilists are more openly on the offensive, accusing teachers or anyone else who criticizes the current accountability agenda as being selfish or self-interested. Ironically, self-interest does not seem to matter if it is in pursuit of higher test scores, which reformers support with promises of pay bonuses for teachers who can produce higher scores. Those who do produce higher scores, then, provide evidence that resource inequalities or poverty is not an excuse for low achievement, thus providing reformers with enough evidence that accountability can work to allow another generation of reified inequality to remain unchallenged.

Educators Realize the Ruse: The TVAAS' Validity Challenged

Established by the EIA to monitor public schools' performance and to conduct studies the Governor, the General Assembly or the comptroller determined necessary, the Office of Education Accountability (OEA) prepared an evaluation study of the TVAAS, *The Measure of Education: A Review of the Tennessee Value Added Assessment System* (1995). The findings listed a number of concerns that included "unexplained variability in national norm gains across grade levels," questionable security of the system, a complexity of the system that made it difficult for non-statisticians to understand, and the attachment of high stakes to the TCAP achievement test in order to calculate TVAAS gain scores (Baker, Xu, & Detch, 1995). Sanders responded to the concerns expressed in the finding with an admonishment, "A report such as this with a high probability of widespread distribution should contain, at a minimum, acknowledgement of the previous and current validation efforts" (p. 41). Obviously unimpressed with Dr. Sanders' petulance, the OEA responded by noting that the "tremendous amount of validation that has already transpired" to which Sanders referred amounted to a single unpublished dissertation and conference papers that "are rarely subjected to the same level of scrutiny by acknowledged experts as are journal articles and replication studies" (p. 45). The final OEA recommendation called that all elements of the TVAAS undergo a thorough audit "by qualified experts knowledgeable of statistics, educational measurement, and testing (p. iv).

To conduct an independent audit of the TVAAS, the State hired a three-person evaluation team that included R. Darrell Bock, a distinguished professor in design and analysis of educational assessment and a professor at the University of Chicago; Richard Wolfe, head of computing for the Ontario Institute for Studies in Education; and Thomas H. Fisher, director of student assessment services for the Florida Department of Education. Bock and Wolfe (1996) agreed with the central concept of the assessment system, but made recommendations for the improvement of data collection, the quality of the test scores, and reporting gain scores. They recommended not reporting the school effects "until the year-to-year stability of estimated gains for schools can be improved," but they did support reporting teacher effects (with their recommended improvements) to "responsible authorities" (p. 34).

Fisher (1996) focused on the state testing program (TCAP) in his analysis. He found the basic structure of the testing program to be acceptable, but he recommended verifying the accuracy of the process and improving the management and oversight of the process. Unlike his colleagues, he recommended that the teacher effects not be reported until the data collection system could be improved and stabilized. All three evaluators questioned the use of national norm scores as the comparative standard for student performance progress. Bock and Wolfe (1996) had concerns about comparing the state gain scores to the national norm gain scores because of consistent patterns in the differences that would lead to misclassifying school performance as above or below the national norm. For example, in observing the performance of second and third graders at the fiftieth percentile for language, math, and science, second graders consistently performed above the national median and third graders performed consistently below the median: "as a result, there is a persistent tendency for third grade gains in Tennessee systems and schools to be classified undeservedly" below the norm by more than two standard errors (p. 29). The persistence, then, of this pattern that "may simply reflect different programs in reading instruction" could lead to the unjustifiable and persistent misclassification of third grade system or school performance as below the norm by more than two standard errors (p. 29). All commended Tennessee for its "bold steps" in working toward educational improvement, but Fisher offered this caveat: "There is no single way to foster educational accountability. The search for acceptable and understandable methodology should be seen as an open-ended quest" (p. ii).

An important area that the TVAAS audit did not deal with was any question or recurring concerns "bearing on the educational content of the [TCAP] tests or their alignment with the State of Tennessee curricular guidelines" (p. 1). Since TVAAS used norm-referenced test scores to determine value-added gains, the possible misalignment between norm-referenced tests and Tennessee curriculum standards would bring into question the continued use of TVAAS, particularly after the passage of the No Child Left Behind Act. NCLB required states to use criterion-referenced tests for improving alignment with their state curriculum standards. Additionally, in a 2004 legislative challenge to the continued use of TVAAS in light of the new NCLB regulations, Metro Nashville school officials reminded legislators of the Bock and Wolfe (1996) finding that "successive annual forms of the [CTB/McGraw-Hill] tests... show evidence of imperfect equating of difficulty between years in certain subjects," which made them "well-enough equated for low-stakes reporting of student score-level and school mean score levels." In short, the different grade level versions of the standardized tests used by the TVAAS were appropriate for diagnostic reporting but not appropriate for analysis and decision-making that involved the kinds of high-stakes sanctions or rewards connected with NCLB or its successor, Race to the Top.

No Child Left Behind: A Second TVAAS Challenged Again

Following questionable TVAAS results in Metro Nashville schools and the federal government's refusal to recognize value-added growth models for determining Adequate Yearly Progress as required by NCLB, Nashville legislators filed House Bill 2270 and Senate Bill 2542 in January 2004 calling for the abolishment of TVAAS. The fiscal note for this bill cited an annual savings of between four and five million dollars by no longer funding TVAAS, norm-referenced tests, and further development of high school end-of-course tests. Additionally, the fiscal note cited the possibility of jeopardizing federal funds if the state continued its use of norm-referenced tests.

Nashville school officials prepared a position paper, "Tennessee Accountability Concerns," in February (2/11/04) and presented their concerns to the full House Education Committee. Part of the problem appeared to be the test equating issues brought forward by Bock and Wolfe in their 1996 evaluation of TVAAS. Metro officials cited Bock and Wolfe's (1996) warning about the "imperfect equating" on successive forms of the CTB McGraw-Hill achievement tests contributing to unexplained discrepancies in reported value-added gain scores and the state reported achievement test scores as well as large changes in value-added scores from year to year. Tennessee state law requires non-redundant or new test forms each year, requiring testing companies to produce multiple forms of each grade level test. If the degree of test difficulty changes from grade level to grade level, which could occur due to the selection of test items for new tests each year, variations in achievement scores and their resulting value-added scores are a function of test construction and not teacher instruction. Based on an in-depth, two-year analysis of their achievement and value-added test scores, Metro officials felt that the unexplained discrepancies in their own estimated value-added gains and those reported by Sanders were the result of the "reestimation process" Sanders used to "smooth" the data when the testing scales were inconsistent from year to year. The reestimation process involved "readjusting gains based on the scores the students made in the following two grades with different teachers and perhaps in a different school" (p. 1). For example:

> the gains reported for a fifth grade math teacher are eventually changed based upon the math gains his/her former students make as sixth and seventh graders. If a fifth grade teacher is highly effective but is followed by less effective sixth and seventh grade math teachers, the TVAAS gains for the fifth grade teacher will likely be adjusted downward in future years. (Metro Nashville Public School, 2004, p. 7)

This reestimation process created a pattern in which "higher performing schools' [value-added] scores tend to decline while lower performing schools [value-added scores] tend to increase"(p. 1). The Metro report stated that there "currently appear to be test scaling disagreements between the TCAP publisher, CTB/McGraw-Hill, and the TVAAS contractor, Dr. William Sanders" and that as "a result, TCAP and TVAAS sometimes yield very different conclusions regarding the effectiveness of instruction" (p. 9).

Three years earlier in 2001, *The New York Times* (Steinberg & Henriques, 2001) discovered Sanders' dealings with CTB/McGraw-Hill while investigating errors in thousands of student test scores caused by the company's equating process in Indiana, New York, Nevada, Wisconsin, South Carolina and Tennessee. When Sanders found that "CTB's results broke patterns in individual student's scores that had been uninterrupted for years," he threatened the company with a "news conference to challenge the results." The company capitulated to Sanders' psychometric blackmail and "did something that it would not do in any other state: it simply raised the comparative rankings of many Tennessee students, and lowered some others, to conform to Mr. Sanders's statistical models." Satisfied that the veracity of his TVAAS system would not be challenged, Dr. Sanders settled for the imaginary McGraw-Hill numbers and chose to not go public, even as unknown numbers of students and teachers in other states were labeled as failures and as some administrators lost their jobs, most prominently among them New York City's Superintendent, Rudy Crew. Months later and only after 9,000 New York students were sent packing off to remedial summer school, the president of CBT/McGraw-Hill flew to New York to make the facts public:

> . . . the real shock came when school officials learned what the corrected test scores meant for the entire city. Instead of reading scores stagnating over all, the citywide average had actually risen five percentage points, a substantial jump, particularly for an urban school district.

At a hearing on March 3, 2004, the House Education Committee heard testimony from both Metro school officials and Dr. Sanders concerning the continued use of the TVAAS in Tennessee's education accountability model. In outlining problems emanating from Sanders' TVAAS reestimation process, former State Senator Andy Womack, a sponsor of the EIA in 1992, stated bluntly that the Tennessee General Assembly's had erred in giving "a monopoly to one model and one individual." With the new requirements of NCLB for criterion-referenced achievement tests, Womack argued the TVAAS had "run its course" and counseled the legislature to amend the EIA to introduce competition for the state testing contract in order to "allow for the results that you wish to have from a test of this nature and allow all sanctioned and qualified testing bureaus to compete for this contract." Paul Changas, Metro's Director of Assessment, reminded the House committee members that Wolfe and Bock (1996) had recommended elimination of the reestimation process because of its inconsistency with "good accountability process." As testimony continued, Metro officials presented specific examples of the inconsistencies found in Metro-Nashville and statewide testing data and TVAAS estimates to illustrate their concerns with the state's accountability system. In support of TVAAS, school officials from Grainger, Hamilton, Knox, and Tipton Counties offered testimony praising the TVAAS, but they gave no specific data examples to support how and why they used the data and how they accounted for any inconsistencies. For example, Vernon Coffey, Director of Grainger County Schools and former Tennessee Commissioner of Education, stated that he believed TVAAS to be as reliable and valid as SAT and ACT, while admitting that "I don't understand all the numbers, but I'm not supposed to."

In response to the concerns about the accuracy and reliability of TVAAS, Dr. Sanders complimented the Legislature's vision to found a "movement" with their enactment of his model, which signified a "major . . . paradigm shift," and he blamed the testing companies for any inconsistencies in the State's value-added data:

> With the enactment of the Education Improvement Act of 1992, this general assembly paved the way for a major, emphasize major, paradigm shift in educational accountability not only for this state, but for a movement that has taken root in other states. The accountability provision of the EIA was based on the idea that educators should be held accountable for the academic progress that children make, not attainment level at a specific time. Additionally, and this becomes very important, with the enactment of the EIA, the general assembly chose a different approach to the measurement of academic progress. It elected to use a statistical approach that required the measurement of progress of individual children over subjects and over grades rather than take a more simplistic approach to measurement of progress, that being just subtracting last year's scores from this year's scores. This primary approach, needless to say, has drawn much attention nationally and probably no other accountability system ever has received as much scrutiny as the Tennessee value-added assessment system has over the years. TVAAS... has been considered by most reviewers to be the most advanced, the fairest educational assessment system that has been developed in the country today. Independent reviews of TVAAS have been completed including a broad range of reviews from the educational policy community, educational measurement community and the statistical community... The TNDOE has put in our contract that we are to evaluate those scales and rotate them and to make sure that they are consistent over time. Most of the differences that was [were] reported by Changas are due not to the TVAAS process, but are due to the inconsistency of the scales as supplied by the test supplier. Mr. Chairman, our process is developed to be the most reliable estimates from any point of time. Now they are attempting to make a big issue of reestimation. What we do—what Changas said is a total misrepresentation—it is not based upon the gains 2 years later. What we do, in fact and any statistical, knowledgeable person would agree with this, we use all information on each kid each time and estimate those school effects because it's the professionally, ethically thing to do to give the most reliable information at any point in time. I submit to you that the issue they are trying to bring on reestimation would not be supported by the statistical community. (Tennessee House Education Committee minutes, 3/3/2004, William L. Sanders)

Sanders' testimony continued by enumerating other states interested in or experimenting with value-added assessment, whether with criterion-referenced or norm-referenced tests as the basis for value-added manipulations. In the follow-up question and answer session to testimony, Representative Les Winningham asked how many schools could come off the state list for failing to meet AYP as required by NCLB. Sanders responded that the federal department of education was planning to open the door for a value-added option, and if they did, then 380 schools would come off the list using value-added assessment. Sanders prediction was not borne out by facts, but it was too late to alter the Tennessee legislative decision in 2004 to keep the TVAAS and the Sanders VAM. When the U.S. Department of Education did conduct a pilot study to determine if "growth models show promise as fair, reliable and innovative methods of giving states credit for student improvement over time (U.S. Department of Education, 2/22/2006)" only 19 Tennessee schools in 2007 and 22 in 2008 made AYP using growth scores only, not the 380 as Sanders originally predicted.

Using the Sanders Model and eight different vertical scales for the same CTB/McGraw Hill tests at consecutive grade levels, researchers (Briggs, Weeks, & Wiley, 2008) later demonstrated the inherent problem in using value added classifications in high stakes situations like AYP designations:

> ...the number of schools that could be reliably classified as effective, average or ineffective was somewhat sensitive to the choice of the underlying vertical scale. When VAMs are being used for the purposes of high-stakes accountability decisions, this sensitivity is most likely to be problematic. (p. 26)

Other research since has examined more closely the reestimation effect, a process by which the gains reported for a fifth grade teacher can be changed based upon the gains his/her students subsequently make as sixth and seventh graders. UC Berkeley professor, Jesse Rothstein, chose a unique approach to examine assumptions about value-added methods, including one model using an equation for computing annual gain scores implied in the TVAAS model (2010, p. 182). Asking if a current fifth grade teacher's reading effect data could have predicted her students' achievement gains when those students were third and fourth graders, Rothstein's value-added calculations found, in fact, that they did, when the logical expectation would have been otherwise. Outside of Hollywood, anyway, future teachers cannot have an influence on their students' past scores. These findings are attributable to purposeful nonrandom assignment of students to fifth grade classrooms, leading to intentional or unintentional aggregation of specific student characteristics. Rothstein's research suggested that "classroom assignments are far from random" and that "even the best feasible value added models may be substantially biased, with the magnitude of the bias depending on the amount of information available for use in classroom assignments" (2009, p. 1). For anyone who has been a parent or a teacher, she knows that the teachers whose students score highest are the ones that the most influential parents demand for their children.

In 2004, the Office of Educational Accountability (OEA) of the Tennessee Comptroller's Office (Smith, 2004) presented a study of the EIA's educational influence by comparing the status of various educational realities before and after their implementation. One element under study in this report was the state accountability system before and after TVAAS. Prior to

EIA, Tennessee regularly assessed student learning in grades 2–8 and grade 10, but had no formal method of holding teachers, schools or districts accountable for the results. After passage of the EIA, TVAAS became the central strategy for measuring teacher, school, and district effects on student learning (p. C-59). The OEA found that the "accountability model itself has evolved into a very different system than conceived by the legislation's enactors" in 1992 (p. C-65). In effect, Sanders' advertised ability to isolate and measure teacher effects on test scores encouraged the kind of mission creep for the EIA itself. Working in conjunction with the "test and punish" (Ravitch, 2010) accountability measures of NCLB, which successfully replaced considerations for resource inputs with test score outputs, it is easy to see how the prominent goal within EIA of education funding equity became displaced by the permanent state of anxiety associated with making Adequate Yearly Progress.

A force shaping EIA's evolution was a federal Title I audit from 2002 (Cour, 2002) that found Tennessee in noncompliance with assessment requirements of the Title I statue. Specifically, the Title I audit report noted an absence of documentation for "how well the Terra Nova [CTB/McGraw-Hill] or any other part of the assessment system aligns with Tennessee's standards" (Cour, 2002, p. 32). NCLB did not allow for norm-referenced test data to determine adequate yearly progress toward achievement goals; NCLB, rather, required AYP to be based on criterion-referenced tests based on state academic standards. Having previously calculated effect data using norm-referenced tests, Sanders began in 2002 to move TVAAS toward merging its own accountability system with the one NCLB required for use in determining AYP. As part of that merger, TVAAS results were removed from the accountability system in 2003 and used for diagnostic purposes only (Smith, 2004, p. C-65).

In its recommendations the 2004 OEA study called for another outside evaluation of the state accountability system. In doing so, the OEA cited research of Carnoy and Loeb (2002) who compared state accountability models with NAEP results and rated Tennessee's accountability system as a 1.5 on a 5-point scale, with 5 being the highest mark (p. 325). The OEA (2004) further recommended the continued use of the TVAAS in the state accountability system for diagnostic purposes only, as intended by the legislature in 1992. While the TVAAS could not be used for placing schools on probationary status, teacher results could be used to help teachers document their "highly qualified" status as outlined in NCLB (p. D-6). The report noted, too, that Sanders was re-negotiating with the State to convert TVAAS for use with criterion-referenced test data (p. D-6).

While the 2004 challenge to the Sanders Model made public educators' simmering doubt and documented shortcomings, House Bill 2270 and Senate Bill 2542 never made it to the House and Senate floors for a vote. The resulting action of this legislative challenge to EIA was to amend the language of the 1992 EIA to further institutionalize the TVAAS by mandating "academic growth," as well as "achieving proficiency":

1. All public schools and local education agencies shall make adequate yearly progress (AYP) in achieving proficiency for all student subgroups in core academic subjects, as determined by the state board of education.
2. All public schools and local education agencies shall have academic growth for each measurable academic subject within each grade greater than or equal to standards for expected academic growth set by the commissioner with the approval of the state board. Growth shall be determined through the value added assessment provided for in §§ 49-1-603–49-1-608 [of the 1992 EIA] (Chapter No. 928, Section 2, b).

In a 1990 study specifically aimed to examine the factors that influence education policy decisions by the Tennessee State Legislature, Keese (1990) uncovered previously unacknowledged facts that provide contextual clues for understanding the reasoning behind these 2004 amendments. Keese found legislators minimally concerned with "knowing what effects a law will have and listening to expert information," and of least importance to Tennessee legislators was policymaking that was consistent "with existing law and procedure, maintaining established legal principles, or providing for orderly and manageable change" (Keese, 1990, p. 75).

In terms of influence groups on legislative policy, Keese found that "participants identified educational lobbyists as the most important outside decision-making resources. Least important outside resources were college and university representatives and governor" (p. 80). Legislators, though influenced by these outside groups, nonetheless, "see themselves working with fellow legislators and staff in negotiations and study of an issue rather than reacting to demands from education agencies, lobbyists, or constituents" (p. 106).

Research Findings Challenge High Stakes Use of the Sanders Model

If Tennessee legislators were tuned out to the growing body of empirical findings about VAM, educators were paying heed in growing numbers. In a review of TVAAS that included critiques by nationally respected university researchers, Kupermintz (2003) cited the conclusions of Millman and Schalock (1997), when he commented that "persistent substantive and methodological shortcomings [of VAM] have contributed to 'teacher skepticism and growing criticism of attempts to link learning gains to teacher work' (p. 7)" (p. 287). Had lawmakers been looking for criticism of Tennessee's homegrown version of VAM, the TVAAS, they could have found it in their own back yard at Vanderbilt's Peabody College.

In 2004, Professor Dale Ballou coauthored a value-added study with Dr. Sanders and fellow statistician at SAS, Dr. Paul Wright. Given that their study sample came from a "single, large diverse Tennessee district" (p. 47), which is even rarer in Tennessee than the remainder of the United States, the researchers were able to conclude that "controlling for SES and demographic factors at the student level makes very little difference to teacher effects estimated by the TVAAS" (p. 60). In the lengthy quote below from the concluding section of the article, the authors admit continuing uncertainty; however, with regards to the effects of "social and racial stratification" on student achievement in systems that are achieve less mixing, which is to say, most of America. Coming particularly from the source that it does, this important caveat raises unanswered questions related to high stakes outcomes involving both students and teachers in states that now depend upon the Sanders Model for determining value-added student score gains:

> This research does not resolve all questions about the TVAAS. In a Monte Carlo analysis of mixed models of the TVAAS type, McCaffrey et al. (2004) have shown that the extent to which the within-student covariance matrix can substitute for information on student demographics and SES depends on the extent to which the school system "mixes" students and teachers. In the district we have studied, there has been sufficient mixing, but we do not know whether this will be true of other school systems with greater social and racial stratification. It is also plausible that the make-up of the school influences achievement through peer effects. Because the covariance structure of the TVAAS does not capture the effects of student clustering (covariances across students, even those in the same class, are zero), we cannot be confident that the TVAAS controls for contextual variables in the same way that it controls for the influence of student-level SES and demographics. Several unresolved issues remain regarding the best way to control for peer influences, however, and our work in this area continues. (p. 61)

What this means, in essence, is that the Sanders Model does not measure or attempt to control for the peer effects on student achievement that result from student grouping patterns (i.e., "TVAAS does not capture the effects of student clustering"). We know from Coleman's findings in the 1960s and the mountain of confirming evidence accumulated since Coleman's study that the social capital that accumulates from certain "student clustering" patterns exerts powerful influences on achievement that may account for larger variations, even, than resource differentials between poor and rich schools. Indeed, the authors (Ballou, Sanders, & Wright, 2004) acknowledge that it is "plausible that the make-up of the school influences achievement through peer effects" (p. 61). Within the district site for this Ballou, Sanders, and Wright study, in fact, the absence of "social and racial stratification" provided the required contexts for high levels of social capital to be maximized. As such, we could surely expect that the SES and demographic factors to be minimized in the resulting value-added scores, which was, indeed, the case. This is what Coleman told us almost 50 years ago that we could expect (see Part 1).

If peer influence remains an "unresolved" factor in the Sanders Model, as the authors (Ballou, Sanders, & Wright, 2004) admit in the final sentence of the above quote, how may we place confidence in the resulting high stakes decisions that leave such a central question unanswered? May we, indeed, conclude that the site Sanders chose with low "social and racial stratification" and with high levels of shared social capital do, indeed, make "SES and demographics" less prominent factors in year to year gain scores for which his model does not control? If the choice of a system with high levels of social capital sharing is a coincidence, then with it comes the chance benefit, too, of depicting the Sanders Model so robust as to be able to control for poverty and discrimination in student gain scores.

If the Sanders Model may only reliably predict the weight of SES and demographics on scores in school systems where students are consciously integrated based on socieconomics or race, or both, then how are we to view the impact of SES and race on value-added results for the vast majority of school systems that use socioeconomic grouping practices and other less subtle segregating strategies? Are the Sanders Model measurements good enough to make high stakes decisions related to school closures, students' future academic opportunities, or teachers' career prospects?

In 2005, Ballou further elaborated his position on the racial and economic stratification issue that provided the tantalizing conclusion for the Ballou, Sanders, and Wright article in 2004. This time, Ballou wrote as sole author, and he did not wait until the final paragraph to bring up the subject again. Concerned with using TVAAS to compare teachers across school districts where diversity would be less than in schools of the large metropolitan school system studied in 2004, Ballou identified test measurement error and the impossibility of random placement of students in teachers' classrooms as contributors to bias and imprecision in teacher effect estimates:

> The luck of the draw and the luck of the test will confer advantages on some teachers . . . If we can observe a teacher over a sufficiently long time with sufficiently many students, we can reduce imprecision to any desired level. The same is not true of bias: year after year, a teacher might be disadvantaged by placement in a school serving a particular population, and her value-added estimate downwardly biased. (p. 5)

Using a modified TVAAS algorithm to control for variables of free and reduced lunch (F & R) eligibility, race, and gender, Ballou reexamined the 2004 data taken from classrooms that were "fairly well integrated" for these student characteristics. Ballou, then, compared the gain scores for an average-performing Black, male student eligible for F & R lunch in two different classroom scenarios: in one scenario, none of the student's schoolmates were eligible for the free lunch program, and in the other scenario, half of the school mates were eligible. Comparisons revealed that in reading, the non-privileged, Black, male student started behind and remained behind more privileged students, but in math, the student fell further behind over time when half of his classmates were poor as well:

> [The non-privileged Black male student] starts far below the district average: third grade reading scores are 30 scale score points below the district mean (50 points if half the student's classmates are also poor)" (p. 9) and remains about the same distance behind through the 8th grade. However, in mathematics this same student "falls farther back over time. The decline is especially pronounced when half of the student's classmates are also eligible for the free lunch program." (p. 9)

Unlike the "integrated" population that provided the sample in the 2004 Ballou, Sanders, & Wright study, schools across districts in Tennessee, generally, are not sufficiently mixed to eliminate bias in teacher effect scores. So, for example, teachers at Farragut Middle in Knox County Schools where there is a less than 1% chance of teaching a poor Black student, teachers have a distinct advantage over math teachers at Vine Middle/Magnet in Knox County, where a teacher has a 68.7% chance of teaching a poor Black student whose peers are predominantly Black and poor, with the tendency in scores to "fall farther back over time." The 2011 Tennessee Report Card shows that the math achievement grade for Farragut Middle is A with a 67 Normal Curve Equivalent (NCE) and their TVAAS rating is A with a 2.1 gain score. Vine Middle, on the other hand, rates an F/37 NCE and their value-added grade is D/-1.1 gain score. The range in African-American student populations across school districts in Tennessee is 0.1 to 83.0%, in Hispanic populations 0.0 to 23.8%, and in economically disadvantaged populations from 12.2 to 92.8%. Socioeconomic or racial mixing in schools is not one of Tennessee's strong suits, and to depend upon an assessment system with an unknown capacity to reliably account for lack of diversity and high levels of stratification presents troubling questions that have led the scientific community to look askance at VAM in general, and the Sanders Model in particular, for high stakes purposes.

In order to underscore his concern regarding the issue of "sufficient mixing," Ballou (2005) restated the finding of a RAND (McCaffrey et al, 2004) study from the previous year: "Longitudinal data on students can substitute for explicit controls for student characteristics only if there is sufficient mixing of students and teachers in the data" (p. 12). Ballou (2005) sums up his examination of imprecision in TVAAS scores, stating that

> ... like all estimates, value-added assessments of teachers are subject to imprecision. When there are ample numbers of observations, as shown by the pooled three-year estimates for seventh and eighth grade mathematics teachers [who have more students than self-contained elementary teachers], TVAAS attains an impressive degree of discriminatory power: 58% of such teachers are significantly different from average at the 10% level. However, due to turnover and frequent changes of teaching assignments, comparatively few instructors teach the same subject at the same grade level long enough to generate this much data. In addition, significant teacher effects are much rarer in some subjects than others, a circumstance that may lead to the perception of unfair treatment if value-added assessments are used for high-stakes personnel decisions. (pp. 18–19)

In Part 3, we will examine how "sufficient mixing" among students and the number of teacher observations impact bias and imprecision in teacher effects on test scores.

The Growth Model Pilot Project (GMPP) and Sanders' Testimony in Washington

Following a 2004 letter pleading for flexibility in NCLB accountability requirements from sixteen "state school chiefs" (Olsen, 2004), Secretary of Education, Margaret Spellings, announced the Growth Model Pilot Project in November 2005, as predicted by Dr. Sanders in his testimony in 2004 to the Tennessee House Education Committee. Under pressure from states and municipalities faced with increasingly impossible proficiency targets that NCLB required students from poorer districts where students were farther behind, the U.S. Department of Education developed a Peer Review Committee to evaluate state growth model proposals.

As indicated in Part 1, the potential effects of NCLB's unachievable proficiency targets were not a secret, even prior to passage. In her policy history of NCLB, Debray (2006) cites Dr. Joseph Johnson's comments in a public address prior to NCLB passage: "[P]eople are looking at the data and saying, 'This is going to be catastrophic because there are going to be so many low-performing schools and this isn't going to work'" (p. 138). Debray notes, however, that the Bush Administration, which had included a school voucher provision that was eventually struck from the final version of the Act, "had a political reason to want to see nonimproving schools identified so that NCLB's options to exit such schools for better ones or receive private supplemental instruction would produce visible results of Bush's educational innovations in the first term. There was political interest in identifying lots of failing schools" (p. 115). This would also be a boon for tutoring companies, canned remedial intervention programs, and other "learning corporations" to hawk their wares, including value added testing models for assessing test score improvement over time, in a mass market of desperate educators trying to achieve unrealistic testing targets.

Originally, NCLB disallowed states the use of value-added models and nationally norm-referenced tests to measure the effects of teachers, schools, and schools on student test performance. Instead, the USDOE directed states to use proficiency benchmarks based on criterion-referenced tests aligned with their own state standards. In a nod to growing criticism, however, the Spellings Growth Model Pilot Project allowed states to use "projection models" that could predict student performance on future assessments, thus answering the question: "Is the student on an academic trajectory to be proficient or advanced by 2014?" On May 17, 2006, Tennessee and North Carolina, the two states where the Sanders Model was in use, were approved to use their value-added projection models to track individual student progress in meeting NCLB academic goals. The GMPP allowed projection models as an acceptable "safe harbor" option in providing evidence that a state was making significant progress toward AYP proficiency targets.

During the implementation of the GMPP, Sanders testified to the U.S. House Committee on Education and Workforce on "No Child Left Behind: Can Growth Models Ensure Improved Education for All Students" (July 27, 2006). On March 6, 2007, Sanders presented at the U.S. Senate Committee on Health, Education, Labor, and Pensions as part of a roundtable discussion entitled "NCLB Reauthorization: Strategies for Attracting, Supporting, and Retaining High Quality Educators" (March 6, 2007). He called on Congress to replace the existing "safe harbor" options of NCLB with projection value-added models like his, promising that "effective schooling will trump socio-economic influences." Even though the focus of each hearing was different, Sanders used both opportunities to promote his own brand of value-added modeling that could separate educational influences from "exogenous factors (if not completely, then nearly so) allowing an objective measure of the influence of the district, school, and teacher on the rate of academic progress." Without naming any of them, Sanders described his growth model competitors as having "been shown to produce simplistic, potentially biased, and unreliable estimates." However, later in his testimony, he admitted that he "had to engineer the flexibility to accommodate other 'real world' situations encountered when providing effectiveness measures at the classroom level: the capability to accommodate different modes of instruction (i.e., self-contained classrooms, team teaching, etc.), 'fractured' student records, and data from a diversity of non-vertically scaled tests." Sanders expressed no doubt that his engineered flexibility was up to the task, even if other growth models on the market could not "and should be rejected because of serious biases."

Sanders provided the members of the U.S. Senate Committee on Health, Education, Labor, and Pensions a summary of the research finding that he attributed entirely to his "millions of longitudinal student records." According to Dr. Sanders, by "addressing research questions that heretofore were not easily addressed," queries of his databases had yielded that beginning teachers are less effective than veteran teachers, that inner city schools have a "disproportionate number of beginning teachers," that turnover rates were higher in inner city schools, that high poverty schools have a lower percentage of highly effective teachers as measured by test scores, that math teachers in inner city middle schools were less likely to have high school math certification, that high poverty students assigned to effective teachers "make comparable academic progress" with low poverty students. From talking to highly effective teachers across the country, Sanders said that he learned that these teachers knew how to "differentiate" instruction, how to use feedback from formative assessment to make instructional decisions, and how to maximize their instructional time. Never in his testimony did Dr. Sanders indicate that most of research questions had been asked and answered before his developing and marketing of value-added assessment took place.

Also known, were the obstacles teachers dealt with daily in applying teaching skills consistently across classrooms and schools, especially in high poverty classrooms and schools. This fact, however, is minimized by Dr. Sanders' misleading and obfuscating claims that "differences in teaching effectiveness is the dominant factor affecting student academic progress" and "the evidence is overwhelming that students within high poverty schools respond to highly effective teaching." Clearly, there are a couple of important qualifiers that Sanders fails to mention. First, the more obvious one: Sanders does not make explicit that his claim regarding the importance of teaching effectiveness is based solely on gauging academic progress of individuals on tests as measured by the Sanders algorithm. By omitting this most important point in his presentation to the senators and their staffs, Sanders allows the false impression to be drawn and/or perpetuated that teaching effectiveness is more important than all the other factors, whether in school or outside school, that determine the variability in student achievement across income levels, family education levels, diversity levels, social capital levels, or any of the other variables that researchers have demonstrated are more important than teacher quality in determining variability in levels of achievement among students. As noted earlier in Part 2, an impressive group of researchers (Nye, Konstantopoulos, & Hedges, 2004) just two years before Dr. Sanders' testimony noted in a most reputable peer-reviewed journal that, among 17 studies the researcher examined, "7% to 21% of the variance in achievement gains is associated with variation in teacher effectiveness" (p. 240).

The second point is not so easy to tease out or to discount, for there is commonsense and empirical veracity to claiming "the evidence is overwhelming that students within high poverty schools respond to highly effective teaching." When set atop the previous claim, however, the weight of potential misconception becomes too heavy to ignore. All sentient beings, we suggest, are more responsive to effective teaching than to ineffective teaching. Since Dr. Sanders never tells us what effective teaching is, we can only assume it is the kind that produces greater test score gains than would less effective teaching. Thus, higher test score gains are produced by more effective teachers, and we know they are more effective teachers because they have higher test score gains. We are not the first to point out the obvious circularity of this definition, but the resulting unquestioned tautology is worth keeping in mind when the term "effective teaching" is bandied about. The more serious difficulty with the Sanders claims about highly effective teaching in high poverty schools comes from the unstated conclusion to this unfinished syllogism that high-ranking politicians rush to, when given one thoroughly misleading premise and another that is full of emotional appeal and that can't be argued with: If teacher quality largely determines student achievement, and if poor and hungry children respond with higher achievement to good teaching, then teaching holds the key to closing that achievement gap left gaping from the last round of less than effective reforms.

This conclusion has proved appealing to both liberal political elites and conservative political elites: to the former because of a long-held suspicion that teachers are lazy and are just not trying hard enough, and to the latter because of the long-held suspicion that teachers are self-serving louts protected by their big unions. In either case, the political solution must be better teachers, and any policy to help advance that priority, then it must be a good policy. And if Dr. Sanders has a tool that can help tell us who is doing a good job and who is not, then we have an intervention worth investing in that is much less expensive and with a wider appeal, by the way, than trying to do something substantive about poverty, which has for a hundred years remained the inseparable shadow of the testing achievement gap, from whatever direction it is viewed.

Just days before Dr. Sanders offered his testimonial to the Senate Committee in March 2007, the U.S. Chamber of Commerce (2007) published a state-by-state assessment that compared state test results to achievement levels of NAEP. Tennessee did not fare well, earning an F for "truth in advertising about student proficiency" (p. 52). By Tennessee's own standards, however, and by Dr. Sanders' value-added calculations, the state seemed well on its way to meeting its NCLB benchmarks. The 2005 Tennessee Report Card, which provided one score for achievement proficiency and another score for value-added gains, showed 48% of 3–8th grade students proficient in Math and 40% advanced. In reading, Tennessee 3–8th grade students were 53% proficient and 38% advanced. Based on Tennessee's own scale and timeline for achieving NCLB targets,[9] the state gave itself a B for achievement and a B for value-added in both subjects.

For a state with 52% of its students economically disadvantaged, 25% African-American, and 16% with special needs, Tennessee's self-generated report card results looked respectable until set alongside results from the National Assessment of Educational Progress (NAEP), which showed Tennessee's proficiency rates dropping in 2005, rather than moving up as measured by state proficiency scores and value-added scores. In 2005, Tennessee claimed 87% of its 4th and 8th grade students were proficient in math, while NAEP proficiency levels for 4th and 8th graders were 27.7 and 20.6%, respectively. In reading the discrepancy was no less startling; state proficiency scores for fourth and eighth grade were 87%, and the NAEP proficiency scores were 26.7 and 26.2%, respectively.

In April 2010, The U.S. Department of Education issued an interim Growth Model Pilot Project (GMPP) Report that reviewed the approved growth models, including Tennessee's. In comparing the use of the NCLB's status model that measured the percentage of proficient students each year and the pilot states' growth model projections, the U.S. Department of Education came to the following conclusions:

1. Simply stated, "making AYP under growth," as defined by the GMPP, does not mean that all students are on-track to proficiency (p. 54).
2. There was little evidence that the type of model selected had an impact on the extent to which schools were identified as making AYP by growth within the GMPP framework (p. 54).
3. Schools enrolling higher proportions of low-income and minority students were more likely to make AYP under growth in the status-plus-growth framework than were schools enrolling higher proportions of more affluent and nonminority students. However, if growth were the sole criterion for determining AYP, schools enrolling higher proportions of low-income and minority students would be more likely to move from making AYP to not making AYP (p. 55).

In January 2011, the U.S. Department of Education published the final GMPP Report that analyzed two years of growth data from the participating states. The findings from the second year of the study were similar to those of the first. For Tennessee, that meant very few additional schools made AYP (22 in 2007–2008) using the projection growth model developed by Sanders. The 2011 Report also found that the type of model does make some difference in the number of students identified to be "on-track" to reach the 2014 NCLB target of 100% proficiency in math and reading, and with the Tennessee projection growth model, "relatively few students with records of low achievement but evidence of improvement are predicted to meet or exceed future proficiency standards, while students with records of high achievement but evidence of slipping are very likely to be predicted to meet or exceed future proficiency standards" (p. xix). In short, the Sanders projection model did little to address the essential unfairness perpetuated by NCLB proficiency requirements that required those further behind and with fewer resources to achieve more than privileged schools whose gains are required to be much smaller to reach the same proficiency point.

An interesting finding tucked away in Appendix A of the 2011 Report suggested how the parameters for using growth models could be adjusted to help identify more schools making AYP annual targets: "... results from growth measures used for state accountability purposes suggest that many more schools would make AYP if the first of the seven core principles of the *ESEA* project was relaxed" (p. 112). The first of the seven core principles "requires that the growth model, like the status model, be applied to each targeted subgroup as well as all students in the school." This means that growth outcomes are to be monitored separately, or "disaggregated," for major racial and ethnic groups, limited English proficient (LEP) students, special education students, and low-income students. To sacrifice or to "relax" the core principle of disaggregation so that the value-added estimates would identify more schools as making AYP would appear to neutralize NCLB's purported goal of bringing attention to those subpopulations of students who traditionally have not made adequate progress by any measure. It seems, too, that elimination of the core principle requiring disaggregation could serve to mask the amount of growth that low SES and minority students need to make in order to become proficient by means other than the relaxing of first principles.

Even though the U.S. Department of Education had approved the use of value-added projection models to demonstrate which schools and districts were making AYP, skepticism remains deep among highly respected statisticians, psychometricians, and economists when VAM is used for this and other high-stakes purposes. Some of those critical reviews will be examined in Part 3.

Tennessee in Position to Finish First or Last in the Race to the Top?

Following the hue and cry that went up in 2007 following the much-politicized "F" for "truth in advertising about student proficiency," Governor Bredesen's team set out to implement recommendations from the business community for more rigor in school curriculum and assessments. The release of Race to the Top guidelines in late 2009 lit the afterburners for that effort, and in the spring of 2010 something quite extraordinary happened to the high student proficiency rates on state tests. With hundreds of millions of federal dollars in Race to the Top grants available to states willing to toughen standards (just one of the favorability criteria), state officials, in conjunction with their test vendors, Pearson and ETS, came up with entirely new cut scores that presented a very different picture in regards to Tennessee student achievement. Between the time that Tennessee students took the 2010 Spring TCAP and the September 2010 announcement of scores, proficiency rates went from a majority of students that were labeled proficient to that same majority labeled failures (Roberts, 2010).

Beginning early in 2010, state officials initiated a concerted effort to forewarn school boards and parents of the coming changes and imminent freefall of state test scores. The campaign continued into the fall, and the release of test scores was delayed as state officials fanned out to put the best face on the new educational reality. The announcement in April, 2010 of over $500,000,000 in federal Race to the Top money helped to break the impact and import of the fall in test scores, and the State used the opportunity to implement additional reforms passed by the General Assembly during the Special Session of January 2010. These policy changes introduced a new generation of business-friendly reforms that (a) increased the frequency and number of standardized tests; (b) opened the door to unlimited expansion of charter schools; (c) consolidated the State data collection, storage, and retrieval system to include student data and teacher information; (d) committed Tennessee to adoption of the Common Core Curriculum Standards and accompanying assessments; and (e) began identification of the lowest performing schools (based on the new, harder tests) for turnaround or charter conversion.

As Tennessee students continued to lose ground when compared to students in other states, low-income student test performance continued to fall further behind middle class students than in 1992, when EIA and its Basic Education Program (BEP) and TVAAS were chosen to address educational inequity across Tennessee. In 2005, for instance, the test score performance gap between Tennessee's lowest and highest-performing districts, which is closely tied to income, local property taxes, and overall school funding, remained a whopping 60.2%: "the lowest performing district had a weighted average math score of 42.5 in 2005.... [t]he top performing system, on the other hand, produced a score of 68.1, a difference of 25.6 points or 60.2%" (Center for Business and Economic Research, 2007, p. 48).

By 2011, those disparities were more extreme. The 2011 Tennessee Report Card for Humbolt County, with the highest percentage of economically disadvantaged (92.8%), found 39% of its 3–8 grade students proficient and advanced in math and 39% proficient and advanced in reading/language arts. Humbolt County's 9–12 grade students were 33% proficient and advanced in math and 45% in reading/language arts. Williamson County, with the lowest economically disadvantaged percentage (12.2%), had 66% proficient and advanced in 3–8 grade math and 80% proficient and advanced in reading/language arts. In 9–12 grade math, 80% of Williamson County students tested scored proficient and advanced and in reading/language arts scored 89% were proficient and advanced.

The 2011 percentages of proficient and advanced student performance are derived from standardized test data two decades after the passage of the EIA with approval for the goals from the *Twenty-first Century Challenge* (Smith, 1990). We look now at progress made on each of the education goals since they were first offered, and in doing so, we respond to the implicit questions: are students better off? Are children the winners in the state's education race to be First to the Top? The answer is clearly no. The

Twenty-first Century Challenge included 12 goals (pp. 4–44) that were to be achieved "by no later than the first day of the Twenty-first Century:"

1. All entering first grade students—rich and poor, Black and White, urban and rural, gifted and disabled—shall be prepared to achieve at the first grade level.

Tennessee lawmakers made national headlines in 2012 with a number of controversial bills, including one that became law on April 10 that allowed teachers to challenge the science of evolution and climate change and another that Governor Haslam signed into law (TCA 49-6-201(8)(d)) that required kindergarten enrollees to be at least five years old, with the added stipulation that four-year olds could be considered if the school determined through "evaluation and testing that the child is sufficiently mature emotionally and academically." Like 40 other states, Tennessee's funding commitment does not provide for full-day kindergarten, even though half-day kindergarten was mandated by EIA in 1992. Importantly, retention rates dropped 5% per year between 1992 and 1996, and Tennessee educators have since confirmed that "kindergarten improved student readiness for first grade, both socially and academically" (Smith, 2004, p. C-42).

In 2005, Tennessee passed a Voluntary Pre-K (VPK) program funded by "excess lottery dollars," which is selectively implemented based on a competitive grant process. It was patterned after another EIA-inspired program that provided Family Resources Centers that coordinated $50,000 competitive grants to spawn parent involvement programs in elementary schools, early childhood programs, and programs for parents with preschool children considered at risk due to economic deprivation.

The EIA, focused mainly on class size to address K–3 at-risk students, made some strides in class size in the early grades, with the final approved pupil/teacher ratios for K–3 capped at 25 to 1. Left out of EIA discussion were the findings of the multi-million dollar state-funded Project STAR, which was commissioned by the Tennessee legislature in 1985. Project STAR found that students in primary grade classes with 13–17 pupils performed significantly better than those in classes with 22–25 pupils (Word et al., n.d.). Second and third phases of the study found that the positive academic benefits for smaller classes persisted into the later grades, and that children from the poorest seventeen districts in Tennessee improved from "well below average to above average in reading and mathematics" (Mosteller, 1995, p. 113).

Of course, there are other measures of first grade readiness that the EIA did not address. As a state, Tennessee ranked 39th (Gabe, 2012, p. 12) in the percentage of its population living in poverty, even though it ranked slightly ahead of most other Southern states. In terms of childhood poverty, Tennessee was tied with Texas at 44th in 2010, with 25.7% of children living in poverty (McCartney, 2011). The trend lines for homelessness in Tennessee appeared no less grim in recent years. An analyst for the State Comptroller's Office found that "the number of homeless students identified in K–12 public schools increased significantly between the 2006–07 and 2009–10 school years, both nationally (by 38%) and in Tennessee (by 74%) ... from 6,565 students in the 2006–07 school year to 11,458 in 2009–10" (Potts, 2012, pp 1–2).

2. Every child who completes the third grade shall be prepared to read and write and solve mathematical problems effectively at the fourth grade level. Children with identified disabilities shall be expected to progress in accord with their IEPs (Individualized Educational Program) established by their M-Teams.

While the average fourth grade NAEP math score improved between 1992 and 2011, from 211 to 233, the average fourth grade score was lower than the national average score of 240. Tennessee students scored lower in math than their peers in 43 states. When comparing the 39-point gap between students who ranked at the 75th percentile and the 25th percentile in 2011 to the 1992 performance gap of 41 points, the gap in NAEP math scores is basically unchanged. The academic performance gaps between Black and White students and between poor and non-poor students were not significantly different when comparing 1992 and 2011 NAEP scores in fourth grade math.

On 2011 state assessments, third through eighth graders received a C on the reading/language portion of their achievement tests and a D when assessing value-added; in mathematics, third through eighth graders received a B in both achievement and value-added performance (TN Report Card, 2011).

For fourth graders specifically, 32.1% were proficient and 12.6 advanced in reading/language and 25.7% were proficient and 13.0% advanced in mathematics. Their growth or value-added gain earned them a D in reading/language and a B in mathematics (TN Report Card, 2011).

3. Achievement levels of Tennessee students shall exceed the national average and be in the top one-third of the states in the Southeast.

The state's student achievement levels remain in the bottom quarter nationally (SCORE Report, 2010, p. 8). Tennessee received a D on K–12 Achievement when compared to other states on NAEP achievement levels, achievement gains, poverty gaps, graduation rates, and Advanced Placement test scores (*Quality Counts, 2011*, p. 46).

With the steady stream of high profile education reform initiatives coming out of Tennessee over the past 20 years, we might expect improved achievement test scores and value-added progress scores. What we find, rather, are consistent state gains as measured by the TVAAS after the passage of EIA, while educational progress stagnated or shrank when compared to other states or NAEP's averages. In the last 20 years of value-added accountability in Tennessee, students have lost, not gained, as indicated by NAEP comparisons to other states. Prior to the recalibration of testing norms in 2010, Tennessee was among the three states with the widest gap between proficiency on state tests and proficiency as measured by the National Assessment for Educational Progress (NAEP), considered by many as the Nation's Report Card. In Tennessee, the gap in 2005 was 54 percentage points (80% proficiency on TCAP compared to 26% proficiency on NAEP) for both 4th and 8th grade students (Center for Business and Economic Research, 2005, p. 51). The 20 year summary below, which begins with the new Tennessee era of EIA and the TVAAS, shows Tennessee students over the past quarter century losing ground slightly in three of four categories of measurement based on the national NAEP averages. Only 4th grade math scores registered a one-point gain for Tennessee students when compared to NAEP national average change over the 20-year span of intensifying accountability by testing.

TN Average NAEP Scores Compared to NAEP National Average

20-Year Span for TVAAS	1992/2011
TN 4th Grade Math	211/233
NAEP 4th Grade Math	219/240
Gap Status	8/7 = 1 point decrease in gap over 20 years
TN 8th Grade Math	259/274
NAEP 8th Grade Math	267/283
Gap Status	8/9 = 1 point increase in gap
TN 4th Grade Reading	212/215
NAEP 4th Grade Reading	215/220
Gap Status	3/5 = 2 point increase in gap
TN 8th Grade Reading	259/259
NAEP 8th Grade Reading	261/264
Gap Status	2/5 = 3 point increase in gap

When comparing Tennessee to other states' NAEP scores, we find a similar picture. From 1992 to 2011, NAEP results showed continuing slippage of Tennessee student test scores when compared to other states:

- From 36th/42 to 46th/52 in the nation in fourth-grade math[10]
- From 29th/42 to 42nd/52 in fourth-grade reading[11]
- From 35th/42 to 46th/52 in eighth-grade math
- From 25th/38 (1998) to 42nd/52 in eighth-grade reading

4. The statewide high school completion rate shall be at least 80%.

While the 2011 Tennessee Report Card records a graduation rate of 85.5%, the *Quality Counts 2011* Report (2011) has the graduation rate at 65.8%, which is based on diplomas issued and does not include students who receive certificates of completion (p.45). Another report (Balfanz, Bridgeland, Bruce, & Fox, 2012), *Building a Grad Nation*, puts Tennessee's four-year graduation rate at 77.4% in 2009, compared to 59.6% in 2002 (p. 85).

5. Teaching shall be a profession of choice for a significant portion of the best and brightest graduates of the state's colleges and universities.

The State Board of Education (2007) reported that "Tennessee los[t] 41% of new teachers within their first five years of employment." According to the Offices of Research and Education Accountability (2006), the state's recruitment efforts for high priority schools have been "limited" and are not adequately "combat[ing] Tennessee's teacher shortage problem" (p. ii). Additional strategies such as financial incentives to teach in high priority schools are part of the state's latest efforts to address the shortage. In examining teacher quality, CBER (2007) found that "while teachers in Tennessee are relatively well educated, many teach in classes outside their field of expertise" (p. 43). In 2008, Tennessee's ranking was 48th of 51 for "teachers with neither a major nor certification" (Almy & Theokas, 2010).

Between 2004 and 2011, the average teacher salary in Tennessee increased by 9.08%, while the average salary for directors (superintendents) increased by 15.3% (Tennessee Education Association, 2012). Tennessee's Basic Education Program (BEP) salary schedule for 2012 listed salary for a beginning teacher with a BA or BS at $30,420; for a teacher with a doctorate and 20 years of experience, the state salary was $54,105. Based on the state salary guarantees, the highest paid teachers in Tennessee in 2102 were paid less than the average U.S. teacher salary, which was $55,623 (NEA, 2011, p. 19). Even though Tennessee ranked 20th among states in total personal income (p. 26), the state ranked 45th in average teacher salary in 2012 ($45,891). With Tennessee ranked 47th in percentage change in average teacher salaries between 2000 and 2011 (p. 20), it is easy to see that financial hurdles remain in Tennessee's quest to attract the "best and brightest."

6. No less than 90% of the Tennessee adult population shall be literate.

In 2003, the National Center for Education Statistics estimated the percent for adults 16 and older lacking basic prose literacy skills to be 13%, based on the National Assessment of Adult Literacy (NAAL). These individuals were unable to do more than locate information "in short, commonplace prose text." The national estimated rate of illiteracy for adults 16 and older is 14.7%.

7. All students graduating with an emphasis in vocational education shall possess the competencies required to compete effectively in the job market within their geographical area of choice and/or to succeed in postsecondary technical education.

Tennessee students enrolled in Career and Technical Education classes in grades 9–12 make up 60.40% of the total 9–12 student enrollment. Of that 60%, 48.96% are economically disadvantaged, 51.23% are male, and 74.82% are White. In looking at the CTE student population academic performance, 92.33% met the reading/language arts target and 88.38% met the mathematics target. Graduation rate was 96.02% and technical skill performance targets were met by 90.18% of enrolled CTE students (Tennessee State Department of Education, 2011).

8. All local school districts shall be prepared to demonstrate conclusively improved performance and productivity.

Of Tennessee's 1,791 public schools, 282 were listed as "high priority schools," during the 2011–2012 school year, with 229 of those being Title I schools. In Memphis, where many schools remain intensely segregated by race and class, 94 of 282 schools were "high priority," or below minimal competency based on test scores. All 94 were Title I schools.

A review of the 2012 Tennessee Report Card data gives the Tennessee Comprehensive Assessment (TCAP) achievement test results for some of the groups mentioned above in grades 3 through 8. To meet the 2012 State benchmark for math, only 44.5% of the 3–8 grade students in each subgroup needed to reach the "proficient/advanced" level. The benchmark for reading only required 50.6% to be proficient/advanced. The percent of all students who scored as proficient and advanced in math was 47.20, and for reading 49.40% reached proficiency and advanced.

Of the 570,571 economically disadvantaged students tested, only 35.9% were proficient or advanced in 3–8th grade mathematics only 45.20% in 9–12th grade. Of the 230,556 African American students tested, only 28.9% of 3–8th graders and 38% of 9–12th graders were proficient or advanced, compared to 53.7% proficient or advanced 3–8th graders and 61.8% proficient or advanced 9–12th graders of the 662,045 White students tested. Of the 64,886 Hispanic students tested, 39.5% were proficient or advanced in 3–8th grade and in 9–12th grade 49.5% were proficient or advanced. Students with disabilities fared no better in 2012. Of the 141,781 tested, 31.4% scored at the proficient or advanced level in 3–8th and 25.2% in 9–12th grade.

Reading proficiency rates for White students across the state were 57.2 (3–8) and 68.5 (9–12) percent proficient or advanced. African-American students were rated 31(3–8) and 40.3 (9–12) percent proficient or advanced, and Hispanic students in reading were 38.9 (3–8) and 48.3 (9–12) percent proficient or advanced. For 3–8th grade economically disadvantaged students and special education students, they scored 37.5 and 32.8% proficient and advanced, respectively, and at the 9–12 grade level, 46.3 and 25%, respectively.

A review of the 2011 Tennessee 4th grade NAEP mathematics scores reveals that the performance gap between Black and White students is not significantly different from the gap in 1992. Nor is there a significant difference in the 2011 and 1996 performance gaps when comparing students who were eligible for free/reduced lunch with those who were not. The same is true for the 2011 8th grade NAEP mathematics scores—no significant difference in performance gap scores when compared to scores almost 20 years ago (National Center for Education Statistics, 2011, State Snapshot Report). When comparing performance gaps between Black and White, rich and poor, for both 4th and 8th grades on 2011 NAEP reading scores over 20 years, only the 8th grade performance gap between rich and poor showed a slight narrowing.

9. All students admitted to state universities shall be prepared to begin college-level work.

Based on educational attainment (Ryan & Siebens, 2012) of the residents 25 and over, Tennessee ranked 41st among states, in the percentage of high school graduates (83.1). Only 16% of 11th grade students in Tennessee were prepared to enter college without taking remedial coursework in 2010 (State Collaborative On Reforming Education, 2010, p. 12).

Demographic and socioeconomic disparities in Tennessee contribute to a wide college readiness gap, as measured by the ACT test scores of

African-American students (Center for Business and Economic Research, 2004) when compared to White students:

- 78% of White students meet the English benchmark while only 42% of African-American students meet the same benchmark.
- only 39% of White students and only 10% of African-American students meet the benchmark in mathematics (p. 54).

In terms of composite ACT scores, Tennessee did not make any sustained headway from 1994 to 2011 in closing the gap against the national ACT average scores. When the ACT started keeping state comparisons in 1994 (ACT, 1994), 14 other states and the District of Columbia had lower composite scores than Tennessee. In 2012, only Mississippi had a lower ACT composite score than Tennessee, even as Tennessee is one of seven states that require all students to take the ACT (Weider, 2012). The precipitous drop in 2010 scores can be partially accounted for by the fact that the ACT became mandatory for all high school juniors in 2010 (see Figure 3).

The continuing gaps in college readiness between Tennessee students and the other states are reflected in the national and state comparisons of college degree holders. In 2007, the University of Tennessee's Center for Business and Economic Research found that

> Tennessee continues to lag [behind] both the Southeast and the nation in the percentage of adult residents with at least a bachelor's degree and the disparity has actually grown over time....Only 16.0% of Tennesseans held at least a bachelor's degree in 1990 compared to a national average of over 20%, a dif-

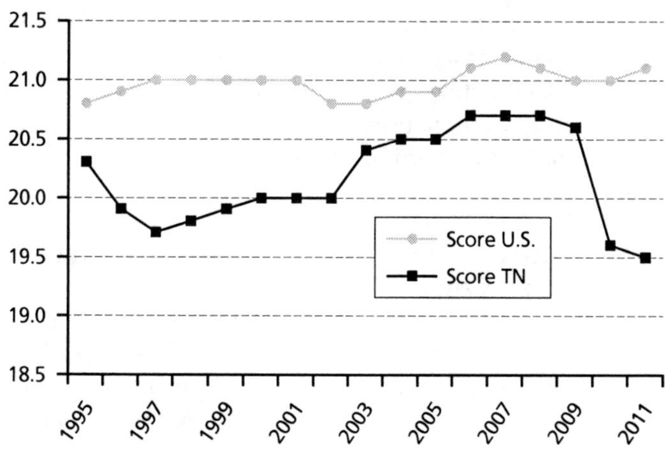

Figure 3 ACT scores: TN compared to national average.

> ference of 4.0 percentage points. By 2000, Tennessee's average rose to 19.6% while the national average climbed to 24.4%, a difference of 4.8 percentage points. (Center for Business and Economic Research, 2007, p. 57)

In 2010 (Ryan & Siebens, 2012), Tennessee ranked 41st in the nation in the percentage of four-year college graduates age 25 and older (23%), while the U.S. average was 27.9% and the average in Southern states was 25.8%. Between 1990 and 2010, Tennesseans had lost ground when compared to the national average by 0.9 percentage points.

10. A comprehensive approach to funding schools shall be in place and such an approach shall be linked directly to goals and tied to accountability standards for quality and productivity.

The 2008 McLoone Index, which gives the actual spending as a percent of the amount needed to bring all students to the median level, shows Tennessee with 89.8%. Additionally, the per-pupil spending levels weighted by the degree to which districts meet or approach the national average for expenditures shows Tennessee expenditures to be 78.3% of the national average (*Quality Counts 2011*, p. 52). This is not a significant change from 2006 data collected by the Center for Business and Economic Research (Center for Business and Economic Research, 2007) that indicated

> Tennessee is a relatively poor state by national standards, with per capita income at about 89% of the national average in 2006 (Center for Business and Economic Research, 2007). But Tennessee's per pupil spending is only about 75% of the national average, reflecting a choice we have made regarding our commitment to the future. (p. 57)

U.S. Census data (U.S. Census Bureau, 2009) showed Tennessee ranked 49th in public school funding based on the relation to personal income (p. 12). Table 2 shows year-to-year comparisons from 1995 to 2010 as a ratio between state and national per-pupil spending. The final number is for 2010, which shows a significant dip in spending when compared to the national average.

11. School-based decision making shall be the rule rather than the exception in all school districts of the state.

The Tennessee Comptroller's office (Smith, 2004) interviewed 10 systems concerning the implementation school-based decision-making and reported "what was to be the 'rule rather than the exception' for local district and school decision-making simply did not happen. Interviewees cited lack of requirement, lack of interest, and expense as reasons for nonparticipation" (p. C-46).

Table 2 15-Year Trend in Expenditures per Student, 1995 to 2010

School Year	U.S.	TN	Ratio
1994–95	$5,535	$4,076	0.74
1995–96	$5,699	$4,219	0.74
1996–97	$5,949	$4,372	0.73
1997–98	$6,214	$4,563	0.73
1998–99	$6,513	$4,853	0.75
1999–2000	$6,891	$5,103	0.74
2000–01	$7,324	$5,386	0.74
2001–02	$7,676	$5,570	0.73
2002–03	$8,064	$5,796	0.72
2003–04	$8,340	$6,107	0.73
2004–05	$8,661	$6,613	0.76
2009–2010	$12,250	$8,324	0.67

Source: Center for Business and Economic Research, 2007, p. 57; U.S. Census Bureau, 2009, p. 11

12. The Tennessee school curriculum shall be on the cutting edge of knowledge and fully responsive to the vocational, academic, and special education needs of all students as well as the employment needs of this state's businesses and industries.

In 1992, Commissioner Charles Smith worked diligently to convince legislators and the general public that the economic future of Tennessee depended on the quality of its schools, and that the quality of its schools depended upon more test-based accountability and alterations in the organization and control of schools in ways that aligned more with the operations and goals of business and industry. The state's accountability plan, mandated in the EIA, equated improved education to improved student tests scores and, like workers on the assembly line, teachers were to standardize their operations and adjust the scope and sequence of their work to the requirements of an unceasing stream of more tests. Sanders' value-added model claimed to objectively determine who was the most and least successful in the production line functions of the newly organized education industry.

Tennessee's commitment to this plan has diminished educational environments in Tennessee, while stunting the educational opportunities of children, particularly in urban areas, in ways that are likely to have lasting negative effects in adulthood. With the continuing need for changing workforce skill sets, both intellectual and applied, among ever-changing economic environments around the world, students enmeshed in testing protocols have not been provided with the education that they needed most to enable them to survive and thrive, or to prepare them as literate creators and innovators, responsible decision-makers, and collaborative problem-solvers. The capacity to assess high level cognitive and non-cognitive skills has been severely limited by the use of multiple-choice tests that became increasingly high stakes, for which teachers spent inordinate amounts of time preparing children to take and pass. The focus on the state tests and the results of the value-added manipulations has diminished students' access to learning environments that allow and encourage the development of high-level thinkers and doers. By no meaningful measure has Tennessee improved the education of its citizens. And yet, 20 years after the passage of EIA, the new generation of reformers supports more and tighter testing accountability with even higher stakes for those with the least power to alter the conditions that are responsible for the continued failure on the next generation of tests.

Measures of success not mentioned in Commissioner Charles Smith's list of unmet goals are the nonacademic and non-cognitive needs of health, safety, funding fairness, and economic equality that could help make his goals realizable. When combined with a neglect of these important considerations, what are the impacts of more behavioral strictures; scripted teaching practices, and repetitive test preparation in order to survive in high stakes testing environments? In 1992, the number of suspensions from school totaled 53,374, and the number of expulsions was 426. By 2012, the number of suspensions increased to 77,383 and expulsions to 7,079. The 1992 TN Report Card did not disaggregate these data, but in 2012 Black, male children were more likely to be banished from school that any other subgroup (Tennessee Department of Education, 2011). Nationwide in 2007 (Aud, Fox, & KewalRamini, 2010), 49.5% of Black male children were suspended between grades six and twelve, and 16.6% were expelled. Suspension and expulsion rates for White male children in the same grades were 21.3% and 1.3%, respectively. African-American children in 2007 were almost twice as likely (21 to 11%) to be retained than their White counterparts (pp. 92–93).

In considering Commissioner Smith's statement that "the educational system we have today is not significantly different from that in place in Tennessee at the midpoint of this century" (1990, p. 3), we can now say that the education system of 2012 was not significantly different from the one in place in Tennessee in 1992, despite the extension and hardening of accountability standards and business practices for determining and measuring the efficiencies of teaching and learning with high stakes value-added assessments.

TABLE 3 Comparison of TN Poverty and Crime Indicators From 1992 to 2010

Indicator	1992		2010	
Population under 18	1,216,604	24.9%	1,494,958	23.6%
Children in Poverty	251,529	21.0%	380,591	25.9%
Children Receiving AFDC	174,816	14.4%	NA	
Children Receiving Families First Grant	NA		119,929	8.0%
Children Receiving Food Stamps	681,581 (adults included)	14.0%	518,093 (adults not included)	34.6%
Free and Reduced Lunch	241,508	31.1%	439,795	47.8%
Under 21 Eligible for Medicaid	416,086	28.6%	NA	
Youth on TennCare	NA		740,633	42.0%
Referred to Juvenile Justice	47,782	3.9%	81,327	5.4%

The chart in Table 3 shows data comparisons from the 1992 and 2012 *Kids Count* reports on key indicators of poverty and crime. With the state's budget priorities of healthcare, prison construction, and foreign investment claiming more of the needed funding for education, academic performance fell while poverty and crime rose.

Even though Tennessee spent more than $326 million for accountability and assessment between 1992 and 2012 (Smith, 2004 and TN Budgets from 2005 to 2011), and the State has dedicated approximately $56 million of Race to the Top grant funds for accountability and assessment (U.S. Department of Education, 2010, January 18), *none* of the business-friendly goals established in Smith's Twenty-first Century Challenge plan were realized, even 12 years beyond the date they were to be accomplished. Perhaps, Tennessee should have focused on education as a "personal goal, meaningful and valued by the student and his or her family" (p. 4) rather than a mismeasured and miseducative ordeal that is impersonal, narrowly focused for test scores, and of little value for business and industry, higher education, or for taxpayers hoping to reduce the costs of welfare, the prison system, and education, too.

So even by Tennessee policymakers' own accountabilist standards for academic progress, the EIA, after 20 years, has been a failure. The long-term effect of education policy that has as its goal increased test scores and that is locked into a management and measurement system that maintains the status quo, cannot effectively or efficiently respond to the constantly changing needs of students, families, communities or states. The story of the EIA is instructive in terms of how policymakers' view of public schools as businesses leads to a marginalization of the public in the running of their schools and a weakening of public education in general. Some would argue that these are the most significant unintended consequences of the kinds of corporate education reform we see institutionalized in Tennessee. Whether intended or unintended we cannot say, but it is our contention that the effects of corporate management systems in education, increased accountability demands that require decreased autonomy of teachers, shrinkage of public oversight and regulatory structures for privately run schools at public expense, steady expansion of corporate education practices that ignore science and research, and the diminution of the social morality motive inherent in public institutions have served to narrow, rather than broaden, the adaptive capacity of our educational structures, to move the science and art of pedagogy further into the past, to further weaken our democratic institutions, and to concentrate and insulate power from the kind of probes and questions upon which open societies are based.

Until Tennessee's school assessments were re-normed in 2010 to align with the more compelling reality of NAEP and common sense, the State had presented a picture of continuing upward progress on the state tests that had coincided with unpublicized and continuing cuts in the percentage of the state budget going for public education. Between 1977 and 1995, the education budget commitment fell from 40% of total state expenditures to 22.3% (Edmiston & Murray, 1998, p. 198), and the higher percentages never returned to their previous levels. From 1995 to 2002, education spending got 21% of the state budget, and by 2010, that percentage had crept downward to 18% of state revenues spent on education (Chantrill, 2013).

When faced with the possibility of missing the cut in the 4.3 billion dollar Race to the Top, the exaggerated proficiency claims suddenly came into focus, and the long-delayed raising of state test standards finally occurred. While admitting the courageous role they played in adopting the higher standards in 2010, state politicians were universally silent on their involvement in the past 18 years of student testing achievement reports that they, themselves, were suddenly repudiating as fabrications. With no sense of perceptible irony, Superintendent Jim McIntyre from Knoxville called the announced increases to testing standards in early 2010 "a defining moment in public education in the state of Tennessee (Alapo, 2010)"; but, a defining moment for whom? Who gets over the finish line in a Race to the Top when, according to Douglas Massey (2007), the mechanisms of race, class and gender stratification in American society "increasingly operate through education, the ultimate scarce resource in a knowledge-based economy" (p. 259)?

A review of Tennessee's Race to the Top application tells the tale of winners and losers, a century-old tale of competitive business interests, competitive politicians and competitive vendors looking to control the outcomes in a $500 billion dollar education market, projected to be increased by 25% within the decade (Simon, 2012).

The TVAAS Become Law Redux

Signifying a significant shift in the rationale for the next generation of Tennessee education reforms, Governor Phil Bredesen did not extol the virtues of educators, as Commissioner Charles Smith had done in 1992 in his case to legislators for solving the educational shortcomings in organization and management. Bredesen had nothing to say, as Smith had, about the State's "outstanding and dedicated core of teachers and administrators," nor could he concede, as Smith had, that "the people are not the problem." On the contrary, Bredesen made it clear that the education problem was, indeed, what Smith had said that it was not: teachers. In a speech in 2007 at the U.S. Chamber of Commerce's Institute for Competitive Workforce Summit, Bredesen made his agenda clear:

> I believe with all my heart that the simplicity and focus that is needed in education is to refocus on the individual teacher; a commitment to getting the best possible people to teach in each and every classroom. The problem is not at its core about organization, or technology, or measurement; it's about human capital and how to maximize it. Once that is in place, everything else will fall in line." (Governor's Communication Office, 2007)

By 2010, Tennessee was ready to initiate a plan based on the Bredesen vision, if only the state could land a large chunk of the $4.3 billion in federal grant money from RTTT.

Defining from the outset the purpose of education as an improved economic future with a "refocus" on teachers, rather than organization, management, or even students, Tennessee's 1,063-page RTTT application (U.S. Department of Education, 2010) effectively placed evaluation, assessment, and technology between teachers and their students. Sounding much the note heard by legislators and state officials in 1992, the theme running through the proposed reform package of the RTTT application centered on increased efficiencies, but in this round of reform, the focus had shifted from organizational efficiencies to increasing the productivity of teachers. As in 1992, the measurements to assure that productivity were to be taken once again by Dr. Sanders:

> ...as Governor Bredesen articulated, the power of human capital: recruiting, developing, evaluating, and compensating the best talent Tennessee can find for its schools; equipping them with the tools they need to succeed, such as standards and data; defining expectations and setting the bar high for student, teacher, and principal success; rethinking old and out-of-date practices that keep great teachers and leaders from succeeding; and harnessing the power of external organizations, foundations, and committed partners to help Tennessee achieve its specific goals and targets... [and] Underlying all of our human capital reforms is a data system that is second-to-none—the largest student- and teacher-level database ever assembled, permitting value-added analysis and examinations of teacher effectiveness—which we will expand to new frontiers in this application. (p. 13)

The application extolled the reforms efforts of Governor Bredesen up to and during the development of the application. Adopting the strategies used by Alexander and McWherter before him, Bredesen had traveled the state in 2007 to consult with CEOs and business groups. He visited with over 130 leaders in business representing 114 companies. Bredesen's key objectives were focused almost entirely on satisfying the needs of the business community, with key objectives that included "understanding which skills business leaders want in potential employees; identifying gaps between business needs and workforce skills; and taking inventory of suggestions for closing the gaps" (p. 14). By gaps, the application writers were not talking about academic gaps among groups differentiated by race, class, or gender, nor were they referring to gaps in funding between poor and wealthy school systems in Tennessee, which remained even after numerous rulings by every level of the state judiciary. They were referring, rather, to gaps between current and future workforce needs for vocational and technical skills.

The application was a strong advertisement for the continued and expanded use of TVAAS for any school, system, or state that was "forward-thinking" enough or exhibiting the "political will" to "make bold changes around teacher and principal evaluation" (p. 84). Presumably, TVAAS could do everything from streamlining a system's personnel processes, including placement, retention, compensation, promotion, tenure, interventions and dismissal, to closing the teacher equity gap between high-poverty/high-minority schools and low-poverty/low-minority schools to evaluating teacher preparation programs and their effectiveness in workforce placement:

> Tennessee has the most sophisticated value-added assessment system in the United States. For tested grades and subjects, our state can track each child's achievement, link it back to his or her teachers, and measure not just the absolute performance of a school, but the actual academic growth that the school and its teachers are making or not making, as measured by standard-

> ized tests. The richness of our data allows Tennessee to perform unique and statistically significant predictive analyses of every child—predicted trajectories of students all the way up to graduation, ACT scores, and even success in STEM majors. With this information, we can address resource allocation, early intervention, and professional development in a radically different and intensive approach. In this application, we describe the ways in which we will use the data to create a dashboard-style early warning system for teachers, train teachers and principals on its use, and leverage other federal funds to create a P-20 [Pre-K through college] statewide longitudinal database that encompasses data from education and social service sectors. We seek to organize our efforts and interventions around this data, enabling it to be used from the Capitol to the classroom. (p.14–15)

TVAAS could do all that, and it could even research its own effectiveness. The new plan called for the creation of the Tennessee Consortium on Research, Evaluation and Development (TN CRED), a consortium to "place a series of investigator led initiatives to assess the success of Tennessee's innovative reform efforts and identify areas of greatest opportunity and challenge. The plan further called for $3,240,000 of RTTT grant money for TN CRED to "provide the intellectual and organizational capacity to inform policies, programs, and practices with research-based evidence; provisions that the state currently could not provide on its own" (C-46). With no perceptible irony noted or intended, the RTTT plan prominently placed the TVAAS vendor and his wife, Dr. Sanders and June Rivers, second and third on the list of luminaries that were to comprise the brain trust of TN CRED:

Matthew G. Springer, Chair, *Vanderbilt University; National Center on Performance Incentives; National Center on School Choice*
William Sanders, *SAS/University of North Carolina*
June Rivers, *SAS/University of North Carolina*
David Wright, *Tennessee Higher Education Commission*
William F. Fox, *University of Tennessee; Center for Business and Economic Development*
Bryan C. Hassel, *Public Impact*
Keel Hunt, *The Strategy Group*
Tony Bagshaw, *Battelle for Kids*
Melissa Brown, *Tennessee Education Association*
Susanna Loeb, *Stanford University; Center for Education Policy Analysis*
Steve Elliot, *Vanderbilt University; Learning Sciences Institute*
J.R. Lockwood, *RAND Corporation*
Brian Jacob, *University of Michigan*
Ellen Goldring, *Vanderbilt University* (C-52, 53)

Since 2010 TVAAS has become an element of *Tennessee's Longitudinal Data System 360 Degree View of the Student System (TLDS)* (Appendix C-1), which serves as "an early warning system" when any part of the system moves off the trajectory to 100% proficiency in math and reading from grades K through 12. *TLDS* is a partnership combining databases from SAS, Inc. (TVAAS), the Tennessee Department of Education, the Center for Business and Economic Research, the Department of Labor and Workforce Development and "will incorporate data elements from other child-serving departments and will facilitate more robust characterizations of health, social welfare and behavioral conditions that influence students' progress from earliest child care, through P12 and higher education, and into the workforce" (p. C-1).

Here the application differs from the State's 1990 *Twenty-first Century Challenge* and the State Board of Education's 1990 Master Plan, both of which embraced Dr. Sanders' notoriously incorrect claim that a teacher's influence is the most important factor in determining student achievement. The RTTT application states that teachers are "perhaps the most influential factor affecting student growth performance," and that

> in reality a child's personal and social circumstances are subject to ongoing change. For example, a third grader's parents might go on welfare, a parent might be imprisoned or the child might be placed in the custody of the state and then a foster home. Certainly these changing individual circumstances can be expected to affect a child's performance in school. (C-15)

Thus, the need to collect more information and

> provide principals and teachers with an early warning when situations that might impede student performance occur and activate a monitoring of a student's indicators of academic engagement (e.g., grades, discipline, and attendance). This would allow for additional intervention, should evidence accumulate to warrant it. (C-6)

The *TDLS,* including contracts with CBER and SAS, Inc., required spending $47,853,774 or 9.5% of the total grant. The question, here, is why not spend the $48 million on actual interventions rather than an expensive monitoring system that tells the teachers and parents what they already knew from grades, discipline and attendance? So far, then, Bredesen wins; CBER wins; SAS wins; Sanders wins and Vanderbilt wins. Who else wins?

What could not have been foreseen in 1992 when EIA became law was the emergence ten years later and ten years after that of an increasingly interconnected group of corporate and government insiders moving back and forth through a revolving door of continuing economic opportunity based on advancing more business solutions to education problems. What evolved by 2012 constituted a number of interlocking networks made up of a top level of think-tankers, venture philanthropists, hedge fund experts, corporate foundation heads, and CEOs; and a second level of hardware, software, consulting, and management companies, came to constitute a new and expanding education industry, most of them shared a common disdain for public schools and public school teachers and an uncontained confidence that contracting as much of public school operations to corporations was as socially responsible as it was economically lucrative.

Tracing out these webs of corporate and government back-scratching is beyond the present project, but a tiny slice from a single example may serve to give some idea of the situation.

As governor in 2008, Bredesen launched new, tougher curriculum standards, partly in response to a report by the U.S. Chamber of Commerce in 2007 that assigned an "F" to Tennessee for "truth in advertising" in regards to student proficiency. Bredesen's Tennessee Diploma Project worked in partnership with Achieve, Inc., a non-profit corporation responsible for placing business and workforce-friendly curriculums in 35 states. As a result of "his powerful commitment and Tennessee's extraordinary progress," Governor Bredesen was selected as national co-chair of Achieve, Inc. in 2009(U.S. Department of Education, RTTT Application, 2010, p. 11). Under Bredesen's leadership, Tennessee became a winner in April 2010 of the Race to the Top grant worth $501 million. As Tennessee's governor and co-chair of Achieve, Inc., Bredesen helped land in September 2010 a federal grant of more than $170 million for Tennessee and other states within the PARCC consortium "to develop an assessment system aligned to the national Common Core standards, called the Partnership for the Assessments of Readiness for College and Careers (PARCC)" (Partnership for the Assessments of Readiness for College and Careers, n.d.). At the time, PARCC was managed by Achieve, Inc. and remained at press time a subsidiary.)

High Stakes Get Higher

Appendix E of Tennessee's RTTT application contained "accountability" documents explaining the hierarchy of sanctions against schools that failed to meet AYP targets. It also outlined the requisite lines of authority in meting out those sanctions, which would come to mean closure, charter conversion and loss of local control in educational decision-making to something new called the Achievement School District. Senate Bill 5 or the "Tennessee First to the Top Act of 2010" offered an additional strategy to the continuum of state sanctions begun as a result of NCLB, and that was the creation of an "achievement school district," a trans-geographic entity controlled from Nashville by a single director with far-reaching authority:

> The commissioner shall have the authority to contract with one or more individuals, governmental entities or nonprofit entities to manage the day-to-day operations of any or all schools or LEAs placed in the achievement school district, including but not limited to, providing direct services to students TCA 49-1-614 (c) (E-18).

With oversight by the Commissioner of Education, the Achievement School District (ASD) was intended to comprise a collection of the "persistently lowest achieving schools" not meeting state performance standards for four consecutive years. The state claimed that the ASD would "mov[e] the bottom 5% of schools in the state to the top 25% in five years" (Jones, 2012). Reality set in, however, in October 2012 when the first results (Roberts, 2012) came in that showed ASD students at the 16th percentile nationally in both math and reading. The entity taking control of these lowest performing schools or districts was given the authority by the ASD "to determine whether any teacher who was previously assigned to such school shall have the option of continuing to teach at that school as an employee of the managing entity TCA 49-1-614 (d)(1)" (E-18).

While the small, underfunded public school districts of Tennessee continued to struggle for needed funds to operate, the new ASD was flush with cash as a result of RTTT to pay charter operators and private management companies to run the converted public schools, whose buildings were also turned over to the ASD without any stipulation to require charter operators to lease or to pay rent for those public properties. The state and local funding that would normally have been distributed to the failing school was turned over as part of the "turn around" strategies under the managing entity chosen by the Achievement School District. In order to harness "the power of external organizations, foundations, and committed partners" to be First to the Top (p. 164), $49,168,869 in RTTT grant funding was set aside for the ASD, with "$30.6 million invested in The New Teacher Project and Teach for America" (p. 164) to recruit minimally trained beginning teachers to teach in schools with severest need for experienced professional teachers. The superintendent, or director, of the ASD was to be paid $1,379,761 in salary, fringe benefits, and travel over the four years of RTTT grant implementation (pp. 237–238). Teachers in the new ASD were subject to the same evaluation as all Tennessee teachers, with 50% of the evaluation based on student performance, 15% on achievement measures and 35% based on student growth measured by TVAAS. Missing, however, were due process protections of tenure and a salary schedule. In the ASD schools, teacher pay was to be determined by student "progress rates."

In preparation for the RTTT grant application (2010), Tennessee lifted its cap on charter school growth in 2009, while "easing restrictions in an effort to attract national charter management organizations to provide additional options for students and families" (pp. 11–12). Under an agreement to merge Memphis and Shelby County Schools in 2012, the plan called for 26 charter schools by FY16, to be comprised of a mix of local charter schools and ASD schools (principally charters). The new consolidated school system was projected to lose 19% of its school population during that interim, which the state-approved Transition Team Plan (2012) acknowledged would cost the new system $212 million between FY12 and FY16:

> To date, the districts have found creative ways to manage the increased costs of the existing multi-operator system (e.g., cutting or shifting 400+ positions out of the General Fund to right-size staff). However, with the projected share of students in non-district operated schools expanding rapidly in the next few years—from approximately 4% in FY2012 to 19% by FY2016 (equivalent to approximately $212M of revenues shifted to charter schools and the ASD in FY2016)—it is critical to implement strategic cost management to ensure each pathway in the Multiple Achievement Paths model is financially equitable to students. (p. 168)

The Transition Team suggested that $58 million could be recovered if the new system "aggressively implements a set of management practices to manage its school and staffing fooprint" (p. 171). In short, the plan called for big personnel cuts:

> ...with an estimated decline or shift of 9,500 students from FY2012 to Fy2014, the district will have to make the following types of approximate reductions—390 general education teachers, 60 elective and vocational teachers, 50 clerks, and 15 central office positions—keeping in mind that new teaching and other employment opportunities would be created in the ASD and charter schools. (p. 171)

In November 2012, Shelby County voters rejected by almost 2 to 1 a half-cent increase to already record-high sales tax that was intended to help pay down the large debt incurred from the big charter expansion and the ASD takeover (Moore, 2012).

Tennessee's RTTT application budget produced an impressive list of financial commitments to outside consultants, vendors, contractors, and NGOs to help "turn around" Tennessee's failing schools. One intervention listed in the budget stands out, and that is the Rural Literacy Program, a contract with Save the Children for $1,673,835. Given the state's poor adult literacy rate and a long trail of unimpressive NAEP results, it would seem appropriate that reading would be a top priority. Inexplicably, Tennessee placed 0.3% of RTTT funds toward reading intervention programs, even as 49.3% of 3–8 grade students were below proficient on state reading tests while the application was being drafted. Clearly, the Race to the Top application signals the perpetuation of corporate practices that lead to the increased opportunity for corporate profit, the targeting of schools and teachers for "hostile take-over" and the perpetuation of inequality.

The Perpetuation of Inequality and the Targeting of Teachers

In his comprehensive analysis of the American stratification system during the last decades of the twentieth century, Douglas Massey (2007) explains the mechanisms of power that policymakers, whether social or political, wield to "exploit or hoard" market opportunities with little concern for the "categorical inequalities" that are left in the wake of their economic progress. Examining the "infrastructure of the social institutions, cultural practices, and conceptual understandings upon which markets rest," Massey shows how the political economy benefits the rich over the poor, one race over other races and the male over the female in American society (p. xvi). His definition of stratification is "the unequal distribution of people across social categories that are characterized by differential access to scarce resources" (p. 1) and he describes, as one example, how real estate laws deny certain groups access to housing they could afford if they were only of the right race or social status. This real estate segregating of groups geographically, then, leads to higher or lower community capacities to raise taxes for needed social services such as funding for excellent jobs, schools, healthcare, housing and other community services.

Massey divides population groups along the perceptual axes of warmth and competence forming four quadrants of groups that evoke specific emotional responses contributing to prejudices. The quadrant of people who are most like the perceiver are considered warm and competent, the "just like me" group. The people who are perceived as lacking warmth, but competent, are envied for their perceived advantages, "such as Jews in medieval Europe" (p. 12). Those who are warm, but incompetent, are pitied such as the "disabled or elderly" (p.12), and those perceived as lacking warmth and competence evoke disgust "such as drug dealers and lazy welfare recipients" (p. 13). When prejudices against groups less and least like our own develop from these emotional foundations, strategies for exercising individual privilege over the common good are more easily justified, especially when we are not aware of the political, social and economic mechanisms that are put in place by policymakers looking out after members of their own group (Massey, 2007; Johnson, 2001). When groups must compete for scarce resources, subconscious prejudices emerge to influence the rules designed to give one group an advantage over another group, defined by the cultural fine-tuning of the human brain's natural propensity to distinguish differences (Massey, 2007; Johnson, 2001).

According to Johnson (2001), as corporate profit is the prime motivator in a capitalist society, the value associated with an individual or group is determined by usefulness in making profit, often referred to as labor. When strategies are put in place by corporations to reduce the cost of labor, such as the use of technology, foreign labor pools, or historically embedded exclusionary practices, workers whose skills and knowledge are no longer needed are economically marginalized, thereby diminishing their income, wealth, and power. These workers are seldom members of the corporate elite's social group. The corporate elites and the policymakers who curry their favor are in positions to influence the inclusiveness or exclusiveness through laws and policies and regulations that "perpetuate a class system based on widening gaps in income, wealth, and power between those on top and everyone below them" (p. 45), and they feel justified in doing so.

Martin, Overholt and Urban (1976) outlined the process whereby state policymakers, in deference to corporate leaders' profit-seeking, use accountability measurement schemes to diminish the income, wealth and power of workers. In the case of professional educators, this process diminishes both educators and the education of students. While state government subsidizes capital formation through corporate tax breaks, improved infrastructure, updated and expanded vocational curricula, corporate reform charter schools, and the privatization of public services, the money available to improve public education that is controlled by the public is significantly lessened, as we outlined in Tennessee's budget from 1977 to 1995. While the proportion of Tennessee's budget increased for attracting foreign investment, privatizing prisons, and creating a bonanza for healthcare and insurance corporations, the portion of the total state education budget for education was cut almost by half. When faced with federally mandated or corporate-motivated education reform, state governments have three options (O'Connor cited in Martin, Overholt, & Urban, 1976) to raise revenue for "needed" education reform: "(1) by engaging in profit making enterprises itself, (2) by expanding the number of state loans (thereby increasing the state debt), or (3) by increasing taxes" (pp. 46–47). Though controversial and discouraged in the past, state governments responding to federal incentives have embraced partnerships with "learning corporations" to privatize the operation of public education with public tax dollars via charter school expansion.

State governments are reluctant to take on more debt or to raise taxes, even as deficits loom as a result, as in Memphis, of charter school expansion. Policymakers find themselves in crisis mode as the cost of education continues to rise, and the pressure for increased productivity continues to escalate, even as unmet productivity expectations are blamed on teachers. This media-reinforced scenario places teachers into Massey's (2007) category of warm but incompetent group, in need of assistance to become more effective or to be counseled out of teaching. If teachers advocate for children and themselves aggressively, however, as in the case of Chicago Teacher' Union in 2012, teachers risk the designated label as not only incompetent but also greedy (lack of warmth), thus provoking strong reactions among policymakers and a sense of disgust. When teachers "fail" the state's accountability measures, then, policymakers attribute the failure to teachers' incompetence, apathy, or greed, while presenting to the general public[12] this "failure" as unacceptable from adults who "care for children."

Already in partnership with, or ingratiated to, corporate interests, state policymakers in Tennessee adopted more corporate efficiency processes and measures through the EIA (and RTTT) that they hoped would improve productivity, even as history offered no little evidence to warrant that hope. Martin, Overholt, and Urban (1976) explain that by applying business models for evaluating educational productivity, the state's authority for educational expenditures is co-opted by "corporate financial interests which can increasingly be served indirectly if a state apparatus does the evaluating, or more directly by private evaluation process" (p. 48). Tennessee's adoption of business management concepts and practices and value-added modeling as the central pillars of education reform, funded by only an additional half-cent increase in sales tax, continued to serve corporate interests. This was accomplished in an indirect fashion by reserving budget funds for corporate investments, and directly by contracting with elements of the education industry to run charter schools, develop curriculum, provide standardized achievement tests, and operate and expand the TVAAS to evaluate the educational productivity of teachers and students. Just as the Bush Administration was politically motivated to identify lots of failing schools "so that NCLB's options to exit such schools for better ones or receive private supplemental instruction would produce visible results of Bush's educational innovations..." (p. 115), observers may ask about the motivations of Tennessee's last iteration of business-induced education reform codified in Tennessee's First to the Top plan that began with its Race to the Top application.

In NCLB and in the Tennessee education initiatives emanating from the Race to the Top grant, the use of student test scores to determine the effectiveness of teachers and schools was reinforced with incentives for compliance and sanctions for noncompliance with the education goals. The legislative tradition of using mandated assessment for compliance with performance standards began with the "compliance-assistance" policy of ESEA in 1965, and it evolved to the "compliance-dominant" policy of P. L. 94-142 in 1975. A similar pattern occurred in Tennessee. Signed into law in 1984 by Lamar Alexander, CERA was designed to be a compliance-assistance policy with evaluation tied to the use of an instructional model and merit pay for outstanding performance, that is, improvement on criterion-referenced tests. With the 1988 lawsuit in state courts (*Tennessee Small School Systems v. McWherter*) seeking a fair state funding policy, what began as a fine-tuning process of CERA's Career Ladder component became a compliance-dominant policy in the EIA in 1992. When faced with a potential system overhaul like Kentucky and having achieved only nominal success with the compliance-assistive policies of CERA, Tennessee policymakers decided a more stringent compliance policy was in order. CERA was not specific or efficient enough in its goals, expectations, lines of authority, or accountability.

The EIA became more compliance-dominant as a result of the increased role legislators played in developing evaluation, management, and curriculum components of educational policy. The State Board of Education was charged with developing an equitable education funding formula. The trade-off was more money for more accountability, and more accountability meant a greater involvement by the legislature in designing the command system and operational structure for the state public school system and, in particular, setting specific assessment parameters into state statute with a sole source vendor. The tradition of mandated assessment policy had the effect, over three decades, of increased specificity in the design, purpose, and use of assessment, while minimizing variations in or exploration of other assessment practices available to educators.

The process of making assessment practices more specific over time had the effect, too, of pushing state accountability demands that had first been focused at the system and school levels down to the student and teacher levels. This shift, particularly with regard to teachers, took on a new energy after the Tennessee courts intervened in Small Schools II and III to include teachers and teacher pay in the parameters for establishing the equitable state funding system demanded by Small Schools I. As Small Schools III coincided in 2002 with the implementation of the unprecedented accountability demands of NCLB, Tennessee legislators became re-energized once more to make sure the State was getting its money's worth. Encouraged by the Bush Administration, business principles and practices became even more prominent than in 1992. As a result, teachers were more apt to be viewed as human capital, and teaching as a production function of measurable productivity. If ups and downs in production could be accurately monitored and measured in ways that could influence personnel and payroll patterns in favor of the greater producers, then it stood to reason, as far as the reasoning went, that the goals of equitable education and ending the achievement gap could be folded into the goal of accountability, which is where the goal of equity became lodged with the passage of NCLB. With the coming RTTT and its expanded role for data collection, monitoring, and high stakes decisions based on student "progress rates," the disappearing of equity behind the accountability wall was completed. Education was said to be the civil rights issue of the time by Secretary of Education, Arne Duncan, and a dispirited, harassed, and stressed corps of teachers was under threat to make the testing gaps go away, which would signify the arrival of the civil rights train at the mountain top and the end of lawsuits about funding disparities.

In Tennessee and in Washington, the underlying rationale for the Sanders Model to separate higher and lower producing crops of teachers could finally be fully appreciated by legislators and USDOE bureaucrats looking for a way to do just that. No one in Tennessee seemed to notice that the rationale for reform from 1992 to 2012 had changed from organizational re-engineering to allow Tennessee's good teachers and students to shine. Taken up, rather, by the new generation of reformers with re-packaged versions of previous reform strategies was the mantra of "no excuses" for students and ramped up teacher evaluations based largely on student test scores. For corporate education reformers, the new generation of accountability held an added possibility, or at least it was thought until the Chicago Teachers' Union strike of 2012 indicated a new level of organized resistance, that if teachers did not increase "progress rates," they could simply be replaced. The earlier value placed on the Sanders Model as a diagnostic tool to identify points for intervention was put in the background by a summative intent for which there was no scientific basis upon which to proceed. New York principal, Carol Burris, who initiated a statewide petition that garnered the support of over 1,500 New York principals against use of VAM for teacher evaluations, wrote

> Teachers object to VAM because they know its limitations and flaws. It was never designed to evaluate individual teachers; it was designed by researchers to be a tool to assess systems and programs. Using VAM to evaluate teach-

ers is akin to using Lysol as a mouthwash because it does a good job killing germs on your kitchen counter". (Strauss, 2012)

The use of a single academic performance measure to achieve multiple objectives, as in Tennessee's case of accountability for both expenditure justification and student performance, offers a powerful example of a macro-measurement instrument—in this case a standardized achievement test of dubious quality—applied indiscriminately to micro-manage the entire system. The results of the state test were used, then, to monitor the system for variation from the pre-set standard and then to enforce the adjustment back to the standard. As a result, the potential loss in diversity of thought, creativity in teaching and learning, and the cultivation of adaptive capacities to change could have incalculable consequences, not to mention the potential costs of defending the use and spread of a system that has been shown to lack scientific credibility, common sense feasibility, and basic fairness.

For policymakers in Tennessee, the goal of achieving a system for accurately measuring results moved to the level of fixation that essentially displaced the original intent of creating an efficient and equitable state funding system. The trade-off of "equitable" funding for increased accountability had the effect of lowering the political risk for policymakers by (a) focusing public attention away from expensive actions that would be required of legislators, and toward more acceptable interventions in schools whose outcomes, if negative, could place responsibility at the feet of teachers; and (b) neutralizing the public's perception of an ineffectual legislature lacking political courage to act. What began with the Alexander Administration's assisted compliance education reform plan eventually became, through EIA, NCLB, and RTTT, a corporate-inspired strategy that unapologetically placed demands for total compliance squarely on the teacher's desk.

Senator Shockley's concern back in 1987, as Senator Dunavant presented his resolution for accountability based on test scores, that creative thinking and problem solving could be lost in a swamp of tests was washed away in the political tsunami of "accountabilist" rhetoric. While they effectively explain the political and economic incentives for accountability among corporate education reformers, Martin, Overholt, and Urban (1976) also warned almost 50 years ago of more profound outcomes of "accountabilist" management and measurement techniques—the elimination of student thinking:

By definition, a student who is just sitting and thinking is engaging in no measurable form of learning. Therefore, he is doing nothing relevant to the educational process. And if his thinking results in behavior incompatible with the objectives which have been prespecified, then he must be stopped. The teacher's responsibility in such a situation would be to interrupt this

> thinker, to call him back to his appointed task of the moment, and to get him (literally) moving again. Only at their own risk could teachers tolerate, let alone encourage, this pondering and reflecting. (p. 79)

Students can be trained to perform on achievement tests without gaining the requisite knowledge or capacity to understand what it means, other than for more tests later on. Whether or not teachers can be trained to ignore that lack of understanding remains to be seen.

Perhaps the EIA, after 20 years, has been a limited failure. We use the word "limited," for there is room for more damage still to accrue if the policy remains on its present course. The story of the EIA may be instructive of how policymakers' thinking in regards to public schools as businesses leads to a marginalization of the public in the running of their schools and a weakening of public education in general. Some would argue that these are the most significant unintended consequences of corporate education reform. Whether intended or unintended we cannot say, but it is our contention that the effects of corporate management systems in education, increased accountability demands combined with decreased autonomy of teachers, shrinkage of public oversight and regulatory structures, steady expansion of corporate education practices that ignore and seek to marginalize science and research, and the diminution of the social morality motive inherent in public institutions, have all served to narrow, rather than broaden, the adaptive and growth capacity of our public education processes and outcomes. The implementation of these systems has moved the science and art of pedagogy further into a discounted past, and it has served to weaken our democratic institutions now and in that uncertain future that so many miseducated children will help shape. By concentrating and insulating education power brokers, directors, and reform school CEOs from the kinds of probes, questions, public scrutiny, and debate upon which open societies depend, democratic aspirations are frustrated and demands for public power sharing are proportionately more adamant with less and less reserve or restraint.

3

From the TVAAS to the EVAAS

Is it Desirable?

When the right thing can only be measured poorly, it tends to cause the wrong thing to be measured, only because it can be measured well. And it is often much worse to have a good measurement of the wrong thing—especially when, as is so often the case, the wrong thing will in fact be used as an indicator of the right thing—than to have poor measurements of the right thing.

—John Tukey, mathematician
Bell Labs and Princeton University

In following Flyvbjerg's (2001) framework for analyzing social policy, this section of the book examines the desirability of using high-stakes standardized tests, in this case the Tennessee Value-Added Assessment System (TVAAS), to measure student learning and teacher effectiveness for diagnostic accountability, and control purposes. According to its developer, William L. Sanders,

> The Tennessee Value-Added Assessment System is a statistical method of determining the effectiveness of school systems, schools, and teachers. TVAAS uses statistical mixed model theory and methodology to enable a multivariate, longitudinal analysis of student achievement data. These data include

The Mismeasure of Education, pages 147–191

> student scores on (a) the Tennessee Comprehensive Assessment Program (TCAP), a group of tests in five subject areas (math, science, social studies, reading, and language arts) administered annually to all Tennessee students in grades three through eight; and (b) end-of-course tests in high school subjects. (Sanders & Horn, 1998, p. 2)

Since 1992 when TVAAS was written into state law in Tennessee, Sanders has successfully marketed his statistical method, SAS® EVAAS,® to school systems in at least 13 other states (SAS, 2011, p. 2) [http://www.sas.com/resources/product-brief/SAS_EVAAS_for_K–12.pdf].

In 1997, Jason Millman, a nationally recognized expert in educational measurement and teacher evaluation, edited what proved to be his final book on assessment, *Grading Teachers, Grading Schools: Is Student Achievement a Valid Evaluation Measure?* The book reviewed four large-scale accountability plans that were designed to sort out how schools and teachers affected academic performance of students, and one of those was Sanders' TVAAS model in use in Tennessee. Millman did not contribute directly to the section devoted to the TVAAS, but in a chapter of the "Synthesis and Perspectives" section of the book, Millman (1997) concluded that "the real value of TVAAS lies in its ability to serve as a data source for formative assessment" (p. 247). Speaking in general terms about all four methods examined (Oregon, Dallas, Kentucky, and Tennessee), Millman spoke from a lifetime of professional experience, stating "that when an assessment system tries to serve two purposes, the accountability and improvement functions, the system is less than optimum for accomplishing either purpose" (p. 247). Notwithstanding Millman's clear observations and James Popham's (1997) more pointed insight in that same volume that "humans are so confoundingly complicated that I fear our aspirations for evaluative precision almost always exceed our evaluative capabilities" (p. 273), the Sanders Model has expanded its terrain and its uses beyond what Millman, Popham, or anyone else besides Dr. Sanders, perhaps, could have imagined at the end of the twentieth century.

And with the spread of TVAAS and other product lines within the value-added modeling (VAM) catalog, politicians armed with what they accept as empirical truth about the "cause" of students' poor academic performance enact harsher forms of the same testing reform strategies that further remove teachers from educational decision-making and further embed production-function models borrowed from industry to run schools. Production function models use production function measurement to determine the relationship between inputs (funding for labor and materials) and outputs (products and services). The measurement is designed to help the producers minimize inputs for maximized outputs, thereby making profit for the producers when goods and services are sold. TVAAS and other VAMs are examples of production function measurements that, when used diagnostically, may help determine how students are and are not responding to instruction aimed to increase production of standardized test scores or to identify which classrooms or schools are making more or less gain than others in particular grade levels or subject areas. This use may help direct targeted observations by principals and others to observe and further assess classrooms that differ from the mean performance. However, when VAMs are extended for evaluation purposes, as Sanders has done, to isolate and examine the relationship of two variables, teacher effect and student academic achievement, from the very complex and context-dependent process of education, the probability of mismeasurement increases as context-dependent variables such as student characteristics, instructional contexts, peer interaction, or student placement decisions are not easily quantified. In using input-output analyses like TVAAS, the focus on teacher effect is substituted for education funding and resource allocation as the educational input and student test scores are substituted for student learning as educational outputs. The locus of control, then, is further insulated from the point where accountability measures are applied, which allows failure to meet production targets to be attributed to worker shortcomings, whereas high levels of production become celebrated as evidence of sound policies in practice. This deployment and parsing of variables is problematic, for the TVAAS production function model ignores the fact (Alexander & Salmon, 1995) that student and teacher serve both as inputs (active participants) and ouputs (more sophisticated learners) (p. 355) within a complex ecology that is not so amenable to statistical treatments designed for systems without social and communicative domains. In short, the statistical underpinnings of TVAAS may provide effective tools in parsing out variables that influence the growth of corn crops, but classrooms are not simply comprised of biological subjects but, rather, of biological, social, and language beings who constitute interacting histories of transformations whose interwoven influences defy linear approaches to measure them. This confounds the results of any model attributing a direct causal relationship of teacher effect and student learning, even as measured by standardized tests, for the variability in the inputs and outputs of educational contexts are too numerous "to capture the behaviors that produce achievement" (p. 356).

Alexander and Salmon (1995) make a compelling argument that the application of production-function measurement in its current state to educational settings "can be accurate only by chance" and that "its explanatory power is problematic [and] its predictive ability is without validation" (p. 352). Alexander & Salmon argue against the continued use of current production-function models, as the analysis from such models "is based on a standardized process derived from fully articulated and detailed production inputs and techniques that allow very little variation... [while on the other hand] education inputs and techniques gradually evolve as teachers reshape and modify instruction" (p. 356), thus creating a great deal of variance in inputs and techniques. As we shall see, this is not the only issue that calls into question the validity of a model based on linear, causal relationships between inputs and outputs. Since exact measures are lacking for other educational inputs such as family background, peer influence, initial endowments, school factors, and other achievement measures, variance in student achievement based on change in one or more of these inputs does not "represent causal relationships in education" (p. 359). There are many impacts on student achievement test results with the "standardized achievement" test being a proxy for actual student learning and a very limited proxy for higher cognitive skill development. While the achievement test may offer a limited measure of students' recall powers and problem solving abilities within a small set of options, it does not adequately measure powers of judgment and reasoning or how well students are prepared intellectually for mature and fruitful lives. And as VAMs are dependent on achievement tests in calculating teacher effect on student learning, researchers and educational measurement experts have many questions about the validity, reliability, and fairness of using such models in high stakes decision making.

Since the late 1980s, state courts across the country have examined state education funding strategies for equitable distribution of resources among school districts and adequacy in supporting needed educational services across districts. And since the early 1990s, educators, psychometricians, statisticians and economists have expressed deep skepticism of a measurement model that minimizes vast social, economic, and learning opportunity differences among various populations, while singularly attributing the influence of teachers to the learning outcome variations that are measured by test scores. It seems only a matter of time before the courts will be faced with challenges to educational measurement models that displace the importance of more tangible assets in order to afford children the equal opportunity to have their progress rates measured by standardized tests. The likelihood of court challenges is magnified by the intense focus and increasing high stakes that value-added modeling exhibits by attributing teacher effect to student test scores for high stakes decisions related to teacher pay and job security.

In examining the evidence related to the desirability of these policy developments, we begin this section with a brief review of the legal challenge that spurred the Tennessee General Assembly to (a) direct the State Board of Education to revise the state's education funding formula, resulting in the Better Education Program (BEP) of the Education Improvement Act (EIA); and (b) require the Tennessee Department of Education to revise the management structure and accountability mechanisms in the state's education policy, resulting in the appointed superintendent and the Tennessee Value Added Assessment System.

In 1988, 77 Tennessee small school systems filed a lawsuit (*Tennessee Small School Systems v. McWherter*) to challenge the constitutionality of the state's education funding system, claiming the distribution of state money to local districts was "inequitable" (Meyers, Valesky, & Hirth, 1995, p. 394). It was filed too early to benefit from other state high court decisions focused on the "inadequacy" of educational services, rather than the "inequity" of educational funding. One such case was decided next door in Kentucky in 1989, and in a ruling for the plaintiffs in *Rose v. Council for Better Education*, the Court declared the entire system of education unconstitutional because it was "inadequate and well below the national effort" (Rebell, 2002, p. 234). The Kentucky case benefitted from the judicial use of the National Education Summit's academic goals to measure the state's effort to provide an adequate education to *all* students so that each might have "sufficient knowledge of economic, social and political systems to enable the student to make informed choices" and "sufficient levels of academic or vocational skills to enable public school students to compete favorably with their counterparts in surrounding states, in academics or in the job market" (Rebell, 2002, p. 234).[1]

Following Kentucky's precedent setting case, other state courts in the 1990s began to base judgments (Rebell, 2002) on students' *educational opportunity* to develop higher cognitive skills necessary to achieve the goals of political activism and economic competitiveness, rather than more traditional educational outcome measures like standardized achievement test results: "Output measures are considered important guideposts for determining whether an education system is functioning well and whether further scrutiny is warranted, but they are not seen as constituent elements of a constitutional definition of adequacy" (p. 242). In other words, it is more appropriate to use outcome measures for low stakes than high stakes. This distinction in determining the constitutionality of a state's education system by equal opportunity rather than performance on educational outcome measures is significant, and it could provide the foundation for a fourth appeal to the Tennessee Supreme Court by poor school districts still seeking equal opportunity for all students to engage in the higher cognitive skills necessary to achieve civic responsibilities and decent, meaningful employment. The Tennessee Supreme Court established the foundation for such an appeal when it defined "education" for the state in the first small school systems appeal:

> [T]he word "education" has a definite meaning and needs no modifiers in order to describe the precise duty imposed upon the legislature. Indeed, modifiers would detract from the eloquence and certainty of the constitutional mandate—that the General Assembly shall maintain and support a system of free public schools that provides, at least, the opportunity to acquire general knowledge, develop the powers of reasoning and judgment, and generally prepare students intellectually for a mature life. (TSSS v. McWherter, p. 27 as quoted in Meyers et al., 1995, p. 404)

While the Better Schools Program (BEP) within the Education Improvement Act (EIA) temporarily addressed the plaintiff's claim of *inequitable* distribution of educational funds[2] in 1993, a compelling case may be made that the State continues to fall short of the Tennessee Supreme Court's *adequacy* test of *equal opportunity* for all Tennessee students to acquire these components of education. The focus of education reform in Tennessee for the past quarter century has not been on the adequacy of resources to provide equal opportunity for all children. Rather, reformers have turned to more accountability measures that gauge a narrowing portion of the curriculum focused on recall and basic comprehension of factual material. Twenty years after the implementation of the EIA's accountability-based education reform, Tennessee's average 2012 ACT composite score for general knowledge and reasoning skills was 19.7, ranking Tennessee 48th among 50 states and the District of Columbia (http://www.act.org/newsroom/data/2012/states.html). Tennessee was ranked 50th in ACT math with a score of 19.1.[3] At a time when math and science competencies are at a premium for citizens to be prepared "intellectually for a mature life," the general knowledge gap between advantaged and disadvantaged students widened as seen in Table 3. Predictably, ACT math scores for districts with higher percentages of economically disadvantaged (% ED) students are significantly lower. Likewise, the percentage of economically disadvantaged students who are proficient on the state math achievement test or who graduate with a high school diploma is lower than more economically advantaged districts. However, most poor districts' value-added scores are above the state average, sometimes exceeding the growth of wealthier districts. For state legislators looking to convince constituents that a third decade of the same accountability plan is what is needed, it is easy to see that Dr. Sanders' growth numbers offer the only evidence that could be used for such a purpose.

The "Mean Gain" in Table 3 is a gain score that reflects the school district's progress in relation to the state's growth standard, which was zero

TABLE 3 2012 Tennessee Math Scores for Economically Disadvantaged (ED) Students for Select Districts

	Per Pupil Expenditure	% ED	TVAAS 3-8 Grade Mean Gain	% Prof/Adv for 3-8 Grade ED Tested	ACT Math Scores	% ED Graduation Rate
State	$9,123	58.6	1.7	35.90	19.1	87.2
Highest % Econonically Disadvantaged						
Memphis	$11,250	85.1	0.8	23.50	16.3	70.3
Humboldt	$10,410	84.6	5.3	44.10	16.6	80.0
Scott	$8,388	84.5	1.9	35.70	16.6	87.8
Grundy	$9,394	81.5	2.2	29.70	17.6	90.0
Bledsoe	$9,383	80.0	2.9	40.20	19.0	81.0
Hancock	$9,822	79.9	3.6	28.20	17.2	74.7
Cocke	$8,837	79.3	3.2	52.90	17.6	93.6
Hardeman	$9,874	79.3	1.8	33.20	17.2	82.3
Haywood	$9,133	78.0	2.5	32.60	17.3	84.5
Lauderdale	$8,722	77.2	1.0	25.40	17.3	93.4
Madison	$9,813	77.0	0.6	30.40	17.5	95.1
Lowest % Economically Disadvantaged						
Montgomery	$8,639	46.9	1.0	40.30	18.9	95.2
Rogersville	$8,448	45.1	2.9	49.00	NA	NA
Gibson C. Special District	$6,836	43.9	2.9	49.60	18.3	93.0
Rutherford	$8,098	43.5	2.2	46.90	19.3	90.7
Greeneville	$10,356	43.0	3.5	43.10	21.3	97.4
Franklin SSD	$12,466	41.5	1.6	49.70	NA	NA
Sumner	$7,947	39.6	0.8	39.40	19.8	91.2
Shelby	$9,318	38.6	1.8	38.50	20.2	90.5
Maryville	$9,477	32.2	1.3	46.40	23.0	91.7
Wilson	$7,803	28.8	2.6	45.60	19.2	95.5
Williamson	$8,436	12.4	1.9	53.10	22.3	92.2

for 2012. If the score is greater than zero, the district's progress is greater than the state's growth standard. If the score is less than zero, the district's progress is less than the state's growth standard.

While Humboldt Schools, with 84.6% of its students economically disadvantaged, made the most growth in mathematics among the ten most disadvantaged and the ten least disadvantaged districts in 2012, it would be fanciful to believe that Humboldt students could progress from 44.10%

proficient to the No Child Left Behind goal of 100% proficiency by 2014; if not 2014, then when? Do TVAAS growth scores mask students' proficiency levels for parents, the media, and politicians alike? If Humboldt is making more growth than more advantaged districts like Williamson County, then can parents and politicians agree that the BEP is adequate for providing an equal educational opportunity for all students across the state?

A great hazard in using the value-added manipulation of test scores to determine a student's projected academic gain is the annual recalculation of the student's value-added score to include all of his previous test scores. This recalculation has the potential to mask the distinct possibility of a student never reaching proficiency. In a 2009 Carnegie-funded report, Charles Barone (2009) refers to this danger as Zeno's paradox and he ably uses fractions and a frog to illustrate what he means:

> Let's say a frog very much wants to get to a lily pad that is 100 meters away. He knows he can't make it all the way, but judges he can make it a third of the way (he's a championship frog). So on his first try, he jumps 33 1/3rd meters. He decides to jump a third of the way to his goal from where he stands each time, until he gets there. When does he get there? On first glance, most of us would say in three jumps. In fact, in strict mathematical terms, he *never* gets there. After three tries, he is actually only 19/27ths (71%) of the way there. (p. 8)

After 20 years of using an accountability system based on value-added assessment to measure the success of the Tennessee's K–12 education system, though making greater gain than wealthier districts only 80% of Humboldt students are crossing the finish line to graduation while Williamson County students are 92.2% of the way there.

Barone (2009) points out, too, that focus on value-added gains in predicting proficiency may downplay the need for interventions to address low proficiency rates: "Due to the projection toward proficiency being recalculated annually [in the TVAAS model], there is not necessarily a significant progression, over time toward proficiency... causing a delay of needed intervention at appropriate developmental times" (p. 8). Effective interventions are expensive and could require another review of the state's BEP formula for adequacy of resources to provide equal educational opportunity to disadvantaged students. And, for example, that would require an examination of Memphis' taxing capacity in a state that still has one of the most regressive tax systems in the nation.

While the Tennessee Supreme Court established a qualitative education standard "*for* assessing the educational opportunities provided in the several districts throughout the state" (Meyers, Valesky, & Hirth, 1995,

p. 404) in the *Tennessee Small School Systems v. McWherter* case, the Tennessee General Assembly used a quantitative and reductive measurement, TVAAS, as the enforceable standard for assessing educational progress. The opportunity for significant change in the state's education system was lost when the Tennessee Supreme Court remanded the case back to the Chancery Court, which accepted the newly formulated BEP of the EIA[4] as a remedy to the constitutionally impermissible disparities in educational opportunities "caused principally by the statutory funding scheme" (Meyers et al., p. 405). If the Tennessee Supreme Court had examined the TVAAS as the *quantitative* standard for academic progress, what would have become figural was TVAAS's masking effect, that is, while showing growth it may also mask the fact that minority and poor children are far below their well-heeled peers in becoming "generally prepared intellectually for a mature life." And in masking the actual academic progress of the poor and minority students, the state is let off the hook for maintaining and supporting an *adequate* system of public education for all students in the state. At the same time, it can celebrate higher "progress rates."

In 1983, William Sanders was a station statistician at the UT Agricultural Campus and an adjunct professor in UT's College of Business. Based on his own experimentation with modeling the growth of farm animals and crops, Sanders proposed a hypothetical and reductive question: Can student achievement growth data be used to determine teacher effectiveness? He then built a statistical model, ran the data of 6,890 Knox County students through his model and answered his own question with an unequivocal affirmative. Proceeding from this single study, Sanders' claims went beyond the customary correlational relationship between or among variables that statisticians find as patterns or trends in data. He pronounced that teachers not only contributed to the rate of student growth, but that teacher effectiveness was in fact the most important variable in the rate of student growth:

> If the purpose of educational evaluation is to improve the educational process, and if such improvement is characterized by improved academic growth of students, then the inclusion of measures of the effectiveness of schools, schools systems, and teachers in facilitating such growth is essential if the purpose is to be realized. Of these three, determining the effectiveness of individual teachers holds the most promise because, again and again, findings from TVAAS research show teacher effectiveness to be the most important factor in the academic growth of students. (Sanders & Horn, 1998, p. 3)

This provocative pronouncement sent other statisticians, psychometricians, mathematicians, economists, and educational researchers into a bustle of activity to examine the Sanders' statistical model and his various claims based on that model, which became the Tennessee Value-Added Assessment System (TVAAS), and which is now marketed by SAS as Education Value Added Assessment System SAS® EVAAS®. In sharing the findings of that body of research, it becomes clear that using TVAAS to advance education policy is (a) undesirable when examined for high standards of reliability, validity and fairness; and (b) counterproductive in reaching high levels of academic achievement.

At first glance, Sanders' question seems reasonable and his answer logical. Why entrust students to teachers for seven or more hours a day and expect children to grow academically, if teachers do not contribute significantly to student learning? In the Aristotelian tradition of logical conclusions "if a = b and b = c, then c = a," Sanders' argument goes something like this: (a) if student test scores are indicative of academic growth; and (b) academic growth is indicative of teacher effectiveness; then (c) test scores are indicative of teacher effectiveness; and therefore, they should be used in teacher evaluation.

If test scores are improving, then, academic growth has increased and teacher effectiveness is greater. On the contrary, if test scores are not improving, academic growth has decreased and teacher effectiveness is diminished.

When Sanders made his causal pronouncements, he made assumptions that, in turn, made the teaching and learning context largely irrelevant. Using complex statistical methods previously applied to business and agriculture to study inputs and outputs of systems, Sanders developed formulae that eliminated student background, educational resources, district curricula and adopted instructional practices, and the learning environment of the classroom as variables that impact student learning. Sanders (1994) expressed his rationale for attempting to isolate teacher effect from the myriad effects on student learning at an online listserv discussion with Gene Glass and others in 1994:

> The advantage of following growth over time is that the child serves as his or her own "control." Ability, race, and many other factors that have been impossible to partition from educational effects in the past are stable throughout the life of the child.

What we know, of course, is that a child's economic, social, and familial conditions can and do change depending on the larger contexts of national recessions, mobility, divorce, crime, and changing education policies. It stands to reason, then, that the high stakes claims made while using statistical models such as TVAAS must be held to higher standards of proof when making high-stakes declarations of causation that simultaneously render contexts irrelevant. These standards are shaped by the following questions: Are the value-added assessment findings reliable? Are the findings valid? Are the findings fair? Based on critical reviews of leading statisticians, mathematicians, psychometricians, economists, and education researchers, the Sanders Model does not meet these standards of proof when used for high-stakes purposes, with the most egregious shortcomings apparent when used for the dual purposes of diagnostics and evaluation. Briefly, there are three reasons the Sanders Model falls short: Sanders assumes (a) that tests and test scores are a reliable measure of student learning; (b) that characteristics of students, classrooms, schools, school systems, and neighborhoods can be made irrelevant by comparing a student's test scores from year to year; (c) that value-added modeling can capture the expertise of teachers fairly—just as fairly as Harrington Emerson thought he could apply Frederick Taylor's (1911) *Principles of Scientific Management* to the inefficiency of American high schools in 1912 (Callahan, 1962). As explained in Part 2, the TVAAS is simply the latest iteration of business efficiency formulas misapplied to educational settings in hopes of producing a standard product in a cost effective fashion. Sanders made this clear in 1994 while distinguishing TVAAS from other teacher evaluation formats,

> TVAAS is product oriented. We look at whether the child learns—not at everything s/he learns, but at a portion that is assessed along the articulated curriculum, a portion each parent is entitled to expect an adequately instructed child will learn in the course of a year. ([http://gvglass.info/TVAAS/])

This quote is even more telling for what remains implicit, rather than expressed: "the portion that is assessed" is the portion that can be reduced to the standardized test format, which is required for Dr. Sanders to be able to perform his statistical alchemy to begin with. Not only does Dr. Sanders claim to speak here for the millions of parents who may have greater expectations for their children's learning than those reflected in Dr. Sanders' minimalist expectations, but he also tips his hand as to a deeper accountability and efficiency motive that is exposed by his concern for the "adequately instructed child." Once the other contextual factors (resources, poverty levels, parenting, social and cultural capital, leadership, etc.) have been excised from Dr. Sanders' formulae, the only remaining contextual factor (the teacher) must absorb the full weight of any causative change. Such contextual cleansing may make for beautiful statistical results, but it performs a devastating reduction to what is considered learning in schools, all the while acknowledging to not care a whit for either what is taught or how it is taught. All these basic shortcomings are reinforced by assuming that learning is linear, a demonstrably false assumption that will be discussed later in this section.

While there were distinct statistical and psychometric challenges to the efficacy of TVAAS in the educational measurement and evaluation research literature from 1994 to 2012, one overarching theme ran through them all: value-added modeling at the teacher-effect level is not stable enough to determine individual teacher contributions to student academic performance, especially as it is related to personnel decisions (i.e., evaluation, performance pay, tenure, hiring, or dismissal decisions). As early as 1995, scholars (Baker, Xu, & Detch, 1995) offered a strong warning that the use of TVAAS for high-stakes might create unintended consequences for both teachers and students, such as teaching the test (thus narrowing the curriculum), teaching test skills instead of academic skills, over-enrolling students in special education since special education scores were not counted in TVAAS calculations, cheating to raise test scores, and using poor test performance to hurt teachers professionally. By 2011, researchers (Corcoran, Jennings, & Beveridge, 2011) offered empirical evidence that all teachers do not teach to the test, but when they do, student learning depreciates more quickly than when teachers teach to general knowledge domains and expect students to master concepts and apply skills.

In the following examination of these three standards of proof (reliability, validity, and fairness), we summarize the findings of national experts in statistical modeling, value-added assessment, education policy, and accountability practices. Taken together, they provide irrefutable evidence that Sanders fails to meet these standards by using TVAAS for high-stakes decision-making such as reducing resources to schools, closing low-scoring schools, or sanctioning and/or rewarding teachers. Most importantly, however, is the Sanders-sanctioned myth that if students are making some yearly growth on tests that were constructed for diagnostic rather than evaluative purposes, then those students will have received an education sufficient for a successful life, economically, socially, and personally.

The Tennessee Value-Added Assessment Model—Reliability Issues

The Tennessee Comprehensive Assessment Program (TCAP) achievement test is a standardized, multiple-choice test composed of criterion-referenced items administered to 3–8th grades. It is purported to measure student mastery of the general academic concepts and skills as well as specific Tennessee learning standard objectives. Controversy surrounding the use of achievement tests stems from the degree of test reliability needed for the high stakes purposes for which they are used. To achieve reliability, achievement test scores must be consistent over repeated test measurements and free of errors of measurement (RAND, 2010). The degree of reliability is biased by test construction such as vertical scales or test equating and test use such as diagnostic versus evaluative.

As early as 1995, the Tennessee Office of Education Accountability (OEA) reported "unexplained variability" in the value-added scores and called for an outside evaluation of all components of the TVAAS that included the tests used in calculating the value-added scores (p. iv). A three-person outside evaluation team included R. Darrell Bock, a distinguished professor in design and analysis of educational assessment and professor at the University of Chicago; Richard Wolfe, head of computing for the Ontario Institute for Studies in Education; and Thomas H. Fisher, Director of Student Assessment Services for the Florida Department of Education. The outside evaluation team investigated the 1995 OEA concern over the achievement tests used by TVAAS. Of particular interest to TVAAS evaluators were the test constructions of equal interval and vertical scales and the process of test equating [needs layman's terms or explanation].

Bock and Wolfe found the scaling properties acceptable for the purpose of determining student academic gain scores from year to year, but unacceptable for determining district, school, and teacher effect scores (p. 32). All three evaluators had concerns about test equating. Fisher's (1996) concerns focused on the testing contractor, CTB/McGraw-Hill, having the sole responsibility for developing multiple test forms of equal difficulty at each grade level, stating that "[t]est equating is a procedure in which there are many decisions not only about initial test content but also about the statistical procedure used. If care is not exercised, the content design will change over time and the equating linkages will drift" (p. 23). And indeed, Bock and Wolfe found in their examination of Tennessee's equated tests forms that test form difficulty (due to item selection) created unexpected variation in gain scores at some grade levels. Bock and Wolfe also emphasized the importance of how the scale scores, used in calculating value-added gain scores, are derived (pp. 12–13). Why are the scaling properties of tests important?

Achievement tests are measurement tools designed to determine at which point on a continuum of learning a student's performance falls. The equal interval scale of a test is the continuum of knowledge and skills divided into equal units of "learning" value. If one thinks of measuring learning along a number line ranging from 1 to 100, the assumption of equal intervals of learning would be that the same "amount" of learning occurs whether the student's scores move from 1 to 2 or from 50 to 51 or from 98 to 99 on the number line or measurement scale. The leap of faith here is that the student who scores 1 to 10 at the less difficult end of the testing continuum has learned a greater amount than the student who increases his or her score by fewer intervals, say 95 to 99, and at the most difficult end of the continuum. Dale Ballou (2002), an economics professor at Vanderbilt University who collaborated with Sanders during the 1990s, has maintained that the equal intervals used to measure student ability are really measuring the ordered difficulty of test items, with the ordering of difficulty determined by the test constructor (p. 15). If, for example, a statistics and probably question requiring students make a prediction based on various representations is placed on a third grade test, it is considered more difficult than an item requiring the student to simply add or subtract. It is difficult to say who has learned more, the third grade gifted student who answers the statistical question correctly but makes less progress than the student who answers all the calculation questions correctly and appears from the test score to make more progress. Therefore, student ability is inferred from test scores and not truly observed, thus making value-added teacher effect estimates better or worse depending on how these equal interval scales are designed for consistently measuring units of "learning" at every grade level over time. Differences in units of measurement from scale to scale yield differences in teacher effect scores, even though the selection and use of the scales are beyond the control of any teacher. Ballou has concluded that a built-in imprecision in scales leads to quite arbitrary results, and that "our efforts to determine which students gain more than others—and thus which teachers and schools are more effective—turn out to depend on conventions (arbitrary choices) that make some educators look better than others" (p. 15).

The vertical scaling of an achievement test is based on the measurement of increasingly difficult test items from year to year on the same academic content and skills. Vertical scaling is important to Sanders' TVAAS model because he uses student test scores over multiple years in estimating teacher effectiveness. Therefore, the content and skills at one grade level must be linked to the content and skills at the next grade level in order to measure changes in student performance on increasingly difficult or more complex concepts and skills from third grade through eighth grade. Problems arise, however, when there is a shift in the learning progression of content and skills. For example, third grade reading may focus on types and characteristics of words and the retelling of narratives, fifth grade on types and characteristics of literary genres and interpretation of non-fiction texts, and eighth grade on evaluation of texts for symbolic meaning, bias, and connections to other academic subjects such as history or science. While the content and skills are related from grade to grade, there may not be sufficient linkage between content and skills or consistency in the degree of difficulty across grades and subjects to render accurate performance portraits of student and the resulting teacher effect estimates, even if one has faith that test results can mirror teacher efforts in the best of all possible worlds: "Shifts in the mix of constructs across grades can distort test score gains, invalidate assumptions of perfect persistence of teacher effects and the use of gain scores to measure growth, and bias VAM [value-added model] estimates" (McCaffrey & Lockwood, 2008, p. 9).

The same kinds of inconsistencies can occur when using the same tests for other high stakes measure such as school effectiveness. Using the Sanders Model and eight different vertical scales for the same CTB/McGraw Hill tests at consecutive grade levels, Briggs, Weeks, and Wiley (2008) found that

> the numbers of schools that could be reliably classified as effective, average or ineffective was somewhat sensitive to the choice of the underlying vertical scale. When VAMs are being used for the purposes of high-stakes accountability decisions, this sensitivity is most likely to be problematic. (p. 26)

Lockwood (2006) and his colleagues at RAND found that variation within teachers' effect scores persisted, even when the internal consistency reliability between the procedures subtest and the problem-solving subtest from the same mathematics test was high. In fact, there was greater variation from one subtest to the next than there was in the overall variation among teachers (p. 14). The authors cited the source of this variation as "the content mix of the test" (p. 17), which simply means that test construction and scaling are imperfect enough to warrant great care and prudence when applying even the most perfect statistical treatments under the most controlled conditions.

In order for students to show progress in a specific academic subject (low-stakes) and for Sanders to isolate the teacher effect based on student progress (high-stakes), tests require higher degrees of reliability in equal interval, vertical scaling, and test equating. Tests are designed and constructed to do a number of things, from linking concepts and skills for annual diagnostic purposes to determining student mastery of assigned standards of learning. They are not, however, designed or constructed to reliably fulfill the value-added modeling demands placed on them. Though teachers cannot control the reliability of test scaling or the test item selection that represents what they teach, they can control their teaching to the learning objectives of the standards most likely to be on tests at their grade levels—those learning objectives that lend themselves easily to multiple-choice tests. For example, an eighth grade teacher might have students identify bias in different reading selections, easily tested in a multiple choice format, instead of studying the effect of reporting bias in the news and research literature on current political issues and policy decisions in the students' community. Or, if she does teach the later lesson, she and her students get no credit on a multiple-choice test for their true level of expertise in teaching and understanding the concept of bias. In fact, if she spends the time to examine reporting bias as part of the student's social and political environment at the expense of another test objective, student scores and her resulting value-added effect designation may suffer. This is an unintended consequence of high-stakes testing and a survival strategy for teachers whose position and salary are bound to policies and practices that focus on high test scores. As an invited speaker to the National Research Council workshop on value-added methodology and accountability, Ballou pointedly went to the heart of the matter when he acknowledged the "most neglected" question among economists concerned with accountability measures:

> The question of what achievement tests measure and how they measure it is probably the [issue] most neglected by economists.... If tests do not cover enough of what teachers actually teach (a common complaint), the most sophisticated statistical analysis in the world still will not yield good estimates of value-added unless it is appropriate to attach zero weight to learning that is not covered by the test. (National Research Council and National Academy of Education, 2010, p. 27)

In addition to these scaling issues, the reliability of the teacher effect estimates is a problem in high-stakes applications when compromised by the timing of the test administration, summer learning loss, missing student data, and inadequate sample size of students due to classroom arrangements or other school logistical and demographic issues.

Achievement tests used for value-added modeling are generally administered once a year. Scores from these tests are then compared in one of three ways:

1. From spring to spring
2. From spring to fall
3. From fall to fall

Spring to spring and fall to fall schedules introduce what has become known as summer learning loss—what students forget during summer vacation. This loss is different for different students depending on what learning opportunities they have or do not have during the summer (e.g., summer tutoring programs, camps, family vacations, access to books and computers). What John Papay (2011) found in comparing different test administration schedules was that "summer learning loss (or gain) may produce important differences in teacher effect" and that even "using the same test but varying the timing of the baseline and outcome measure introduces a great deal of instability to teacher rankings" (p. 187). Papay warned policymakers and practitioners wishing to use value-added estimates for high-stakes decision making that they "must think carefully about the consequences of these differences, recognizing that even decisions seemingly as arbitrary as when to schedule the test within the school year will likely produce variation in teacher effectiveness estimates" (p. 188).

In addition to the test schedule problem for pre/post test administration, achievement tests are usually administered before an entire school year is completed, meaning the students' achievement test scores impact two teachers' effect scores each year instead of just one. By using multiple years of student data to estimate teacher effect scores, Sanders has remained unconcerned with this issue by assuming the persistence of teacher effect on student performance is an assumption of his model. Ballou (2005) described Sanders' assumption in the following way "... teacher effects are layered over time (the effect of the fourth grade teacher persists into fifth grade, the effects of the fourth and fifth grade teachers persist into sixth grade, etc.)" (p. 6). However, the possible "contamination" of other teachers' influence on an individual teacher's effect estimate was noted in the first outside evaluation of TVAAS by Bock and Wolfe (1996), who questioned the three years of data that Sanders used in his model. Bock and Wolfe agreed that three years of data would help stabilize the estimated gain scores, but they were concerned, nonetheless, that "the sensitivity of the estimate as an indicator of a specific teacher's performance would be blunted" (p. 21). Fourteen years after Bock and Wolfe's neglected warning, the empirical research presented in a study completed for the U.S. Department of Education's Institute of Education Sciences (Schochet & Chiang, 2010) found that the sensitivity of the estimate of a specific teacher's effect was, indeed, blunted. They found, in fact, that the error rates for distinguishing teachers from the average teaching performance using three years of data was about 26%. They concluded

> more than 1 in 4 teachers who are truly average in performance will be erroneously identified for special treatment, and more than 1 in 4 teachers who differ from average performance by 3 months of student learning in math or 4 months in reading will be overlooked. (p. 35)

Schochet and Chiang (2010) also found that to reduce the effect of test measurement errors to 12% of the variance in teachers' effect scores would take 10 years of data for each teacher (p. 35), an utter impracticality when using value-added modeling for high-stakes decisions that alter school communities and students' and teachers' lives.

McCaffrey, Lockwood, Koretz, Louis, & Hamilton (2004) challenged Sanders' assumption of the persistence of a teacher's effect on future student performance. In noting the "decaying effects" that are common in social science research, they concluded the Sanders claim of teacher effect immutability over time "is not empirically or theoretically justified and seems on its face not to be entirely plausible (p. 94). In fact, in earlier research, McCaffrey and his colleagues at RAND (2003) developed a value-added model that allowed for the "estimation of the strength of the persistence of teacher effects in later years" (p. 59) and found that "teacher effects dampen [decay] very quickly" (p. 81). As a result, they called for more research concerning the assumption of persistence. Mariano, McCaffrey and Lockwood (as cited in Lipscomb et al., 2010) research concerning the persistence of teacher effect showed that "complete persistence of teacher effects across future years is not supported by data" (p. A14). Using statistical methods to measure teacher persistence effect on student performance across multiple years in math and reading, Jacob, Lefgren and Sim (2008) determined that "only about one-fifth of the test score gain from a high value-added teacher remains after a single year.... After two years, about one-eighth of the original gain persists" (p. 33). They went on to say that "if value-added test score gains do not persist over time, adding up consecutive gains [over multiple years] does not correctly account for the benefits of higher value-added teachers" (p. 33). In light of these more recent research studies, Sanders' unwavering claims have proven more persistent than the teacher effect persistence that he claims. In light of the mounting body of research that, at a minimum, acknowledges deep uncertainty regarding the persistence of teacher effect, the claim by Sanders and Rivers (1996) that the "residual effects of both very effective and ineffective teachers were measurable two years later, regardless of the effectiveness of teachers in later grades," (p. 6) clearly needs to be reexamined and explicated further.

By claiming the persistence of a teacher's influence on student performance, Sanders is able to assume that access to three years of data lessens the statistical noise created by missing student test scores, socioeconomic status, or other factors that affect teacher effect scores (Sanders, Wright, Rivers, & Leandro, 2009). Missing data was a primary issue in the 1996 evaluation of TVAAS by Bock, Wolfe and Fisher. Their examination of the data quality showed that missing data could cause distortion to the TVAAS results and the "linkage from students to teachers is never higher than about 85%, and worse in grades 7–8, especially in reading" (p.18). It is important, of course, that test scores of every student in every classroom in every school are accounted for and attached or linked to the correct teacher when computing teacher effect scores. Poor linking commonly occurs in schools, however, due to student absences, students being pulled out of class for special education, student mobility, and team teaching arrangements, just to name a few (Baker et al., 2010). Missing or faulty data contributes to teachers having incomplete sets of data points (student test scores) and "can have a negative impact on the precision and stability of value-added estimates and can contribute to bias" (National Research Council and National Academy of Education, 2010, p. 46). A small set of student test scores, for example, can be impacted by an overrepresentation of a subgroup of students (i.e., socioeconomic status or disabilities), or that same set of scores may be significantly impacted by a single student with very different scores, high or low, from the other students in a class.

In addition to assuming multiple years of data will increase the number of data points per teacher sufficiently, Sanders assumes that missing data are random, but this is doubtful as students whose test data are missing are most often low-scoring students (McCaffrey et al., 2003, p. 83) who missed school or moved, entered personal data incorrectly, or took the test under irregular circumstances (i.e., special education modifications, make-up exams) and may have been improperly matched to teachers (Dunn, Kadane, & Garrow, 2003). Sanders attempts to capture all available data for teacher effect estimates by recalculating those estimates to include missing data from previous years that is eventually matched properly to the correct teacher (Eckert & Dabrowski, 2010).[5] This causes variability in past effect scores for the same teacher and increases skepticism about TVAAS accuracy, especially when such retrospective conversions come too late to alter teacher evaluation decisions based on the earlier version of scores. In his primer on value-added modeling, Braun (2005) pointed out that the Sanders claim that multiple years of data can resolve the impact of missing data, "required empirical validation" (p. 13). No such validation has been forthcoming from the Sanders Team.

Ballou (2005) explained that imprecision arises when teacher effect scores are based on too few data points (student test scores linked to a particular teacher). The number of data points can be too few based on the number of years the data are collected, whether one, two, or three years. The number of data points can be reduced, too, by small class size, missing student data, classes with a large percentage of special education students whose scores do not count in teacher effect data, or students who have not attended a teacher's class for at least 150 days of instruction, and by shifting teaching assignments for either grade level and subject area. Data points may be reduced, too, by team teaching situations whereby only one teacher on the team is linked to student data. Ballou's (2005) research indicated further that the "imprecision in estimated effectiveness due to a changing mix of students would still produce considerable instability in the rank-ordering of teachers [from least effective to most effective]" (p. 18). Ballou recommended adjusting TVAAS to account for all of a teacher's grade level and subject area data, as too few teachers teach the same grade level and same subject over a three-year period (p. 23). Ballou concluded, too, that only one year of student test data makes teacher effect data too imprecise to be meaningful or fair for its use in teacher evaluation.

In 2009, McCaffrey, Sass, Lockwood and Mihaly published their research concerning the year-to-year variability in value-added measures applied to teachers that were assigned small numbers of students such as special education teachers since special education students are often exempted from taking the tests. The small number of student scores are impacted by extremely high or extremely low scores resulting in extremes in teacher value-added scores, "so rewarding or penalizing the top or bottom performers would emphasize these teachers and limit the efficacy of polices designed to identify teachers whose performance is truly exceptional" (p. 601). Even though using multiple years of data helps reduce the variability in teacher effect scores, "one must recognize that even when multiyear estimates of teacher effectiveness are derived from samples of teachers with large numbers of students per year, there will still be considerable variability over time" (p. 601).

With these unresolved issues and deep skepticism related to test reliability, Sanders' logic in justifying the use of value-added modeling for teacher accountability weakens, as in our slightly modified syllogism: (a) if student test scores are unreliable measures of student growth; and (b) unreliable measures of student growth are the basis for calculating teacher effectiveness; then (c) test scores are unreliable measures for calculating teacher effectiveness, at least for high-stakes decisions concerning teachers' livelihoods and schools' existence.

The Tennessee Value Added Assessment Model—Validity Issues

No one should be deluded and believe that unambiguous inferences can be made from a nonrandom sample.

—Howard Wainer, Wharton School, University of Pennsylvania

The second question that must be answered in the affirmative for TVAAS to be desirable for high-stakes educational decision-making centers on validity: Are value-added assessment findings valid? Are the inferences Sanders makes from the TVAAS calculations accurate? And are the inferences strong enough to support policies for high-stakes accountability? Three of Sanders' assumptions impact the validity of value-added models and must be sustained for the model to claim any credible level of validity: (a) the assumption that students and teachers are randomly assigned to classrooms; (b) the assumption that student characteristics can be "blocked" from the teacher and school effect scores; and (c) the assumption that achievement tests are a valid measure of student learning.

Stated simply, the method the Sanders Model uses to distinguish one teacher's effect from any other teacher's effect is to compare each teacher's student gains in the year that she taught them to the average gain in the district. If the students' growth is above the district mean, the teacher has a positive effect; if student growth is below the district mean, the result is a negative effect. If student growth is equal to the district mean, the teacher effect is zero. By comparing a student's test scores from year to year, Sanders assumes that each student serves as his or her own control, blocking other factors outside of teacher effect that might impact student learning.

Concerns about TVAAS validity were among the findings of the first review of TVAAS completed in 1995 by the Tennessee Office of Education Accountability (OEA). Particular validity questions arose from the curious case of the Scotts Hill School, which is situated on a county line between Henderson and Decatur counties and served students from both counties.[6] Based on previous test scores, students from both counties were placed in classrooms with equal numbers of girls, boys, high-achievers, and low-achievers. The OEA expected to find the achievement gain estimates from each county would be similar, since students from both counties attended the same school and had the same teachers. After all, if Sander's claim that teachers account for the differences in TVAAS scores, then one would expect students, regardless of home county would do equally well or not well in the same class with the same teacher. TVAAS, however, showed different results, with Decatur County students making greater gains in third, fifth, sixth and seventh grades than Henderson County students. Sanders addressed the OEA's surprise in finding quite different gain scores by explaining that the school "tailored its curriculum to lower-achieving students" and since Decatur County had more of the lower-achieving students than Henderson County, "it follows (according to Sanders) that the larger gains will come from the lower achieving students in Decatur County (p. 52). The OEA disagreed, saying that Sanders gave no evidence to support his hypothesis and suggested that the difference in the separate county scores was dependent on student characteristics and not on school effects since "the school [was] the same for both groups of students" (p. 18). This particular case simulates experimental conditions in which each teacher appears to have an equal chance of receiving male, female, high-performing and low-performing students in his or her classroom, and yet, depending on which county their students' homes were in determined the value-added scores. From the beginning of the TVAAS implementation, the on-going argument between Sanders and other researchers concerning Sanders' claim of being able to isolate teacher and school effect on student achievement has been most contentious around the issue of randomization of students and teachers and the accounting for the effect of student characteristics on test score gains. Subsequent studies to the OEA's report (examined below) have been conducted to tease out how value-added scores behave in conditions of random and nonrandom placement of students and teachers to classrooms, and how these conditions, particularly the aggregated student effects in nonrandom placements, impact teacher effect scores.

In a study entitled *Teacher Effects and Teacher Effectiveness: A Validity Investigation of the Tennessee Value Added Assessment System*, Kupermintz (2003) found "several logical and empirical weaknesses of the system, [which] underscore the need for a strong validation research program on TVAAS" (p. 287). Specifically, Kupermintz examined the TVAAS definition of teacher effectiveness, how teacher effectiveness is calculated using TVAAS, and the relationship between TVAAS teacher effect scores, student ability, and socioeconomic status. Through the reexamination of Sanders' logic concerning the assumption that teacher effectiveness *causes* improved student learning, without demonstrating that other factors are less causal, Kupermintz discovered logic constrained by and limited to its own assumptions, thus making it circular and non-referential. As described by Kupermintz (2003):

> The statement appears to imply that there are two distinct variables—teacher effectiveness and differences in student learning—and that the former causes the latter. Unfortunately, such causal interpretation is faulty because teacher effectiveness is *defined and measured* by the magnitude of student gains. In other words, differences in student learning *determine*—by definition—teacher effectiveness: a teacher whose students achieve larger gains is the "effective teacher." TVAAS divides teachers into five "effectiveness" groups according to their ranking among their peers in terms of average gains. To turn full circle and claim that teacher effectiveness is the *cause* of student score gains is at best a necessary, trivial truth similar to the observation that "all bachelors are unmarried."(p. 289)

Kupermintz (2003) found, too, that the Sanders formula for isolating teacher effect from the complex process of teaching and learning was not discerning enough to formally evaluate teachers. He explained that the "blocking" strategy Sanders uses to minimize student background characteristics was developed as a result of a controlled experiment that Sanders fully controlled, a situation unlike the thousands of schools where the strategy is applied. Kupermintz notes importantly that the integrity of Sanders' design strategy depends upon two conditions, neither of which is commonly found in Tennessee schools: "(1) random assignment of students to teachers, or (2) a careful, systematically balanced allocation of students to teachers" (p. 292). In Tennessee, no educational policy or administrative rule exists that requires schools to randomly assign teachers or students to classrooms. Therefore, principals may assign students to teachers based on course descriptions, teacher strengths, student needs, teacher favoritism, or other nonrandom factors. Additionally, if a school has a large representation of minority, special education, immigrant, or lower socioeconomic students, the school population is not a representative sample of the state student population, bringing into question the comparison of a school or district's value-added gain with the state's gain. The effect of nonrandom placement of students from classroom to classroom, school to school within a district, or from system to system further erodes Sanders' causal claims of teacher effect, as well as his claims as to the irrelevant impact of student characteristics on student achievement.

Kupermintz (2003) reexamined the TVAAS data from an unpublished report circulated by the University of Tennessee Value-Added Research and Assessment Center (1997) that claimed to "show that the effectiveness of a school cannot be predicted from a knowledge of the racial composition" (p. 295). Kupermintz's analysis of the graphical data showed "schools with more than 90% minority enrollment tend to exhibit lower cumulative average gains" and school systems' data showed "even stronger relations between average gains and the percentage of students eligible for free or reduced-price lunch" (p. 295). Kupermintz (2003) cited data from the 1996 Sanders and Rivers (1996) report to support this previously acknowledged impact of minority and economic status on average gains by noting that Sanders' own data from 1996 showed "[w]hite students were more often associated with more effective teachers than were Black students" (p. 295). Kupermintz also cited Ballou (2002) regarding the impact of student characteristics on teacher effect data, stating "about a third of the teachers who deserved to be rewarded for superior performance could be denied recognition because the calculation of their effects did not take into account factors [like demographic variables] beyond their control and potently affected their students' achievement" (p. 296). Kupermintz's reexamination of the Sanders Model raises the question: Does TVAAS judge teacher effectiveness by inferior or superior teaching ability or by the learning ability, economic status, and racial and class privilege status of the students placed in their classrooms? Kupermintz called for a "proper validity investigation" to include not only the model's design but also the TVAAS data (p. 296). Kupermintz concluded his review by noting that his requests for TVAAS data were rebuffed, as had at least one other request for data by Robert Linn, former President of AERA and distinguished researcher at the University of Colorado and the Carnegie Foundation (p. 297).

The RAND Corporation, a nonprofit institution supporting research for improved policy and decision-making since 1948, conducted several research analyses of value-added modeling that included the TVAAS model. In 2003, the RAND Report, *Evaluating Value-Added Models for Teacher Accountabilty,* reinforced Kupermintz's conclusion that "the research base is currently insufficient to support the use of VAM for high-stakes decisions" (McCaffrey, Lockwood, Koretz, & Hamilton, 2003, p. xx), and the RAND researchers directly challenged the Sanders (Wright, Horn, & Sanders, 1997) claim that the "teacher is the most important factor in student learning" (p. xiii). Reexamining this claim through a simulation study of Sanders' value-added calculations, the RAND team found Sanders' results not strong enough to "imply that teacher effects explain more variance than all the other predictors" (p. xiii). In other words, the Sanders Model was not strong enough to imply, much less to conclude, that teacher effect is more important than all other variables known to impact student learning, such as poverty, teacher selection, classroom resources, or the district's adopted curriculum. The only way to prove Sanders' causal claim with a high level of certainty would be to apply the Sanders Model in experimental conditions in which students and teachers are placed randomly in classroom within schools, across schools within districts, and across districts within states. Only in doing so could teacher effects be distinguished from classroom, school or district effects. Validation of TVAAS, however, presents the classic "compared to what" conundrum, for "[u]nlike a new curriculum or program where there is often a well-defined single alternative such as the current curriculum, there is no single plausible alternative for a specific teacher's effect" (McCaffrey et al., 2003, p. 10).

There are other value-added assessment models that include the variables known to impact student learning. When McCaffrey et al. (2003) applied such a model[7] to education achievement and compared the results with other well-known models like TVAAS, they found "the risk of bias from omitted student characteristics depends on the characteristics of educational systems—specifically, the extent to which teachers or students with different characteristics are clustered in schools within and across years of testing" (p. 4). Simply stated, the more clustered or aggregated the characteristic the more difficult it is to truly distinguish teacher effect from the effect of a particular characteristic (p. 113).

Ballou (2005), who completed a study with Wright and Sanders in 2004, returned to the examination of TVAAS and the model's design to use "no explicit controls for any factors that might influence student progress" (p. 1) such as socioeconomic status, parent involvement, peer influence, school resources. Ballou explained that bias is introduced into the TVAAS due to the impossibility of "teachers having an equal chance of being assigned any of the students in the district of the appropriate grade and subject" and that "a teacher might be disadvantaged [her scores might be biased] by placement in a school serving a particular population" year after year (p. 5). This finding is especially important as new Tennessee charter school legislation creates the potential for a changing demographic in existing public schools. If students leave their home school to attend a charter school in the same district because their home school is designated as a failing school, the students remaining in the home school may over-represent students with special needs, economically disadvantaged students, or minority students. Also, public schools' resources for needed learning interventions will be reduced as tax dollars move with the students who enroll in charter schools. Teachers remaining in the home school are disadvantaged in this situation due to an imposed bias caused by aggregated student or teacher characteristics (those left behind), resulting in an invalid and unfair situation for high-stakes personnel decisions when teachers are compared within districts. While TVAAS uses multiple years of data to counteract the effect of student assignment to a teacher's classroom, teachers' value-added scores will reflect student characteristics on academic achievement, whether placed year after year in classroom that aggregate, or cluster, students of poverty and minorities or in classes dominated by middle class top flyers.

Using value-added methods similar to those used in TVAAS, Betebenner (2004) examined student data from a large school district in California. The main purpose of the analysis was to study the relationship between free and reduced lunch percentages and value-added scores. Findings from this research point to the potential unfairness of ignoring student background and teacher characteristics in arriving at value-added scores (p. 19). Betebenner found teachers had an important impact on student scores, the socio-economic/racial makeup of a class and elementary teacher certification "impacted the value-added estimates derived for teachers" (p. 20). Teachers teaching in schools with high percentages of poor or minority children where recruitment of certified personnel is difficult and certification waivers are common "would be at a relative disadvantage in comparison to their peers who teach White students from higher socio-economic backgrounds if value-added estimates ignored these student characteristics" (p. 18). If models like TVAAS, which are designed to use a student's own previous scores to block the impact of student poverty or teachers' lack of proper certification, are insensitive to conditions where these characteristics are aggregated in individual classrooms or schools, then they negatively impact the accuracy of value-added estimates, thus making them unreliable, invalid, and unfair influences on high-stakes personnel decisions.

In research aimed at examining assumptions made by value-added methods, Jesse Rothstein (2008, 2009, 2010) offers a unique reverse engineered approach to checking the validity of reported annual gain scores implied by the TVAAS model (2008, p. 10; 2010, p. 182). With so much attention given to the likelihood of bias in teacher effect data that results from a lack of randomization of student and teacher placement in classrooms, Rothstein played the models backwards to determine if bias was present and could lead to the misidentification of a teacher as above or below average. Asking if a fifth grade teacher's reading effect data could predict her students' achievement gains when those students were third and fourth graders, Rothstein's value-added calculations answered "yes" when the logical answer should have been "no," given the existential fact that future teachers cannot have an influence on their students' past scores. Rothstein's findings are attributable to purposeful nonrandom assignment of students to fifth grade classrooms, leading to intentional or unintentional aggregation of specific student characteristics. Rothstein's (2009) research indicated that "classroom assignments are far from random" and that "even the best feasible value added models may be substantially biased, with the magnitude of the bias depending on the amount of information available for use in classroom assignments" (p. 1) [www.nber.org/papers/w14666]. Principals assign students and teachers to classrooms for a variety of reasons: teacher instructional strengths with particular groups of students, interpersonal strengths of teachers with particular groups of students, parent requests, and favoritism resulting from institutional politics. Rothstein's research brings into question again the validity of teacher effect scores when teachers do not have an equal chance of having any students in the school from his or her grade level and subject area. Value-added models like TVAAS that assume random assignment of students to teachers' classrooms "yield misleading [teacher effect] estimates, and policies that use these estimates in hiring, firing, and compensation decisions may reward and punish teachers for the students they are assigned as much as for their actual effectiveness in the classroom" (Rothstein, 2010, p. 177).

Koedel and Betts (2009) conducted a study to extend the analysis of the Rothstein test as well as to determine the feasibility of using value-added for teacher merit pay. Using data from San Diego students, they repeated the test that Rothstein ran on North Carolina data to determine if fifth grade teachers' effect data could predict fourth grade achievement gains. They confirmed Rothstein's findings on the lack of randomization in teacher assignments and student placement, "suggest[ing] that student-teacher sorting bias is a significant complication to value-added modeling" (p. 11). Koedel and Betts extended the Rothstein test by using three years of student performance data instead of one, and their sample of teachers taught in all three years of their data set. While they still found bias in the estimates of teacher effect, they were smaller with three years of data. In summarizing their findings, the authors conclude that a single year of value-added data should not be used to determine retention of novice teachers and that

> [t]o the extent that our results corroborate Rothstein's findings, they highlight an important issue with incorporating value-added measures of teacher effectiveness into high-stakes teacher evaluations. Namely, value-added is manipulable by administrators who determine students' classroom assignments. Our entire analysis is based on a low-stakes measure of teacher effectiveness. If high stakes were assigned to value-added measures of teacher effectiveness, sufficient safeguards would need to be put in place to ensure that the system could not be gamed through purposeful sorting of students to teachers for the benefit of altering value-added measures of teacher effectiveness. (p. 26)

For novice Tennessee teachers who have less than three years of VAM data and whose retention from 2012 forward was based significantly (35–50%) on value-added teacher effect data, these research findings are significant and troubling. For new teachers with no input on the assignment of students to their classes in schools that regularly assign the most challenging students to novice teachers, these findings will be significant as evidence in grievance hearings or in courts of law. In states like Tennessee that have laid out ambitious plans for VAM that gained favor from federal education authorities, all teachers without tenure have one-year contracts that allow for dismissal to occur based significantly (up to 50%) on a single year of data: "When necessary it [the teacher evaluation] will also provide useful data, analysis and documentation needed to determine what teachers shall be dismissed during the contract year" (TN RTTT Application, p. 94).

In their working paper for the Center for Education Data and Research, Goldhaber and Chaplin (2011) created simulations using North Carolina data that confirmed and extended Rothstein's findings by modifying his original experimental test. Their results showed that while the Rothstein's test for bias in value-added scores was not "definitive" in detecting bias (p. i), it "does provide evidence of tracking and that tracking *could* cause VAM misspecification" (p. 8) or bias in the teacher effect estimates, creating further doubt about value-added application for high stakes purposes.[8] The research of Rothstein, Koedel and Betts, as well as Goldhaber and Chaplin, point to the need for randomizing students and teachers in classroom placements for existing value-added model estimates to be valid. In Tennessee as elsewhere, this is rarely the case.

In Henry Braun's (2005) value-added primer for laypersons, he stated clearly and in bold print that the "**fundamental concern is that, if making causal attributions is the goal, then no statistical model, however complex, and no method of analysis, however sophisticated, can fully compensate for the lack of randomization**" (p. 8). This concern for students being randomly placed in teachers' classes and teachers being randomly assigned to classrooms of students appears again and again in the reviews of value-added methodology. Braun highlighted the diagnostic uses of value-added modeling in identifying teachers who might benefit from targeted professional development or schools in need of targeted assistance, but he did not support the use of value-added results "as the sole or principal basis for making consequential decisions about teachers," citing the "lack of sufficient understanding of how seriously the different technical problems threaten the validity of such interpretations" (p. 15).

Causal claims about teacher effectiveness are dependent on randomization of student assignments. As it is related to educational settings, randomization cannot be a plausible assumption; therefore, causal claims of teacher effectiveness are highly suspect. As the research demonstrates that non-randomization and bias due to aggregated student, teacher, school, or system characteristics bring into question the validity of the underlying assumptions of VAM, it becomes clearer that learning and teaching contexts deeply influence both student achievement and teacher effectiveness, realities that can only be ignored by assessment systems at the peril of their validity. Teacher quality doubtless affects student performance in many ways, but what is it about that quality that makes a difference in student learning, and how is that quality tied to what is known about the learning/teaching process? Many who ask these questions do so with an added urgency after looking to see how VAM does not offer answers to them, even as its viral spread across the assessment landscape would seem to outrun any efforts to inoculate its hosts from what may prove to be extremely damaging side effects.

It was with the threat of massive school failure resulting from NCLB's impossible 2014 AYP performance targets that more and more states early on began to actively consider value-added models for the evaluation of schools and teachers for accountability purposes. Dr. Sanders was in Chicago in early 2003 promoting his value-added model at the national conference of the AERA, warning researchers and scholars in attendance that, without a value-added dimension, which NCLB did not have, states would have "no latitude as to how AYP is calculated," and as a result they could suffer "serious sanctions." He concluded what may be fairly described as scholarly sales presentation with the claim that "[s]tudents in states that add a value-added dimension to their state accountability system will have greater protection from educational practices that result in inequitable student opportunities" (Sanders, 2003, p. 3).

The Spellings decision in 2006 to allow a pilot project for growth models opened the door for VAMs, and Tennessee (home of TVAAS) and North Carolina (home of EVAAS) became two of the states approved by the U.S. Department of Education for piloting the use of value-added models to demonstrate AYP. From that modest introduction in 2006 that led to the strong encouragement of VAMs in Race to the Top, the VAM business exploded. By 2012, Tennessee was one of 18 states that required teacher evaluation to be "significantly informed" by student achievement and value-added gain scores (http://www.nctq.org/p/publications/docs/nctq_stateOfTheStates.pdf). In that brief interim, almost none of the serious concerns by VAM critics and evaluators were addressed to correct the serious shortcomings previously identified. Many testing experts, scholars, and lay educators agreed by 2010 that VAM advanced too far much too fast to credibly achieve the high stakes accountability purposes for which it was hurriedly deployed.

An outspoken critic of the Sanders Model, Arizona State University professor, Aubrey Amrein-Beardsley, offered testimony with other scholars[9] from major universities and the National Research Council before the U.S. Education Senate Committee on September 14, 2011 on the intended and unintended effects of value-added modeling. The presentation was entitled "Getting Teacher Evaluation Right: A Challenge for Policy Makers" http://legacy.aera.net/uploadedFiles/Gov_Relations/AERA%20-%20NAE%20briefing%20_%20Combined%20Slides%20(9-20).pdf. Based on research (http://epaa.asu.edu/ojs/article/view/1096/982) on how multiple measures of teacher effectiveness compare. Amrein-Beardsley presented to the committee the EVAAS data for three teachers whose recent terminations from the Houston Independent School District were "largely due to a significant lack of progress attributable to the educator and insufficient student academic growth reflected by [EVAAS] value-added score" (Amrein-Beardsley & Collins, 2012, p. 6). Each teacher provided a representative case of many teachers across the country in similar scenarios, and the three cases from Houston were only three of more than 100 in which teachers were fired from HISD in 2011 based on their value-added scores (p. 6).

Teacher A, an elementary school teacher, had 10 years of experience, showed positive value-added gains 50% or more of the time between 2006 and 2007 and 2009 and 2010, and received strong evaluations from her supervisor as well as the superlative awards of Teacher of the Month and Teacher of the Year. Teacher B, teaching middle and high school math, was a "career-changer" with a bachelor's and master's degree in mathematics, certified by HISD's alternate certification program. Only year three of Teacher B's last three years experience showed positive value-added gains. Receiving proficient ratings from her supervisor, she shared the teaching responsibility of her students with another math teacher. Teacher C taught multiple subjects under her alternate teaching certificate, receiving positive value-added gains 50% of the time until she was assigned a large number of English language learners. Her supervisor rated her as "exceeded expectations" or "proficient." Careful analyses of multiple measurements of teacher effectiveness, including EVAAS scores, were examined within the school and district contexts of these teachers. Findings challenged the claims of Sanders and the EVAAS advertisements on the SAS website for a reliable and unbiased measure of teacher effectiveness that doubles as a diagnostic tool to help teachers improve their instruction (Amrein-Beardley & Collins, 2012, p. 20). Amrein-Beardsley and Collins concluded in a research article that was published after her testimony that it appears "the district is inappropriately using inconsistent data within and across subject areas to make high stakes decisions about teachers and in this case teacher termination" (p. 20).

While the use of these teachers' value-added scores present important validity and reliability issues, an even more disturbing pattern emerged. Much like Tennessee, where principals whose observations did not match up with value-added scores were assigned to retraining (Gonzalez, 2012) [http://www.wbir.com/news/article/226990/0/TN-education-reform-hits-bump-in-teacher-evaluation], the Houston teachers felt there was external pressure on principals in HISD to align their observational evaluations with annual TVAAS/EVAAS scores; If scores were low, then HISD officials exerted pressure to make observational data reflect "below expectations" as well (Slide 65). Amrein-Beardsley concluded her presentation for the U.S. Senate Committee by listing the unintended consequences that resulted from the use of evaluation schemes that include value-added models like TVAAS/EVAAS, and she called into question the inclusion of value-added assessment in proposed federal revisions to ESEA legislation, and she outlined how these measures lead to unintended consequences:

- Large variations in scores unconnected to changes in practice
- Confusion and demoralization of teachers
- Distortion of other evaluation information
- Disincentives to teach newly mainstreamed English learners, special education students, gifted students, and those in certain grade levels
- Disincentives to remain in teaching (Slide 67).

To validate the initial findings from his proposed value-added model, Sanders (McLean & Sanders, 1983) invited county school supervisors to rank teachers within their district relative to effectiveness. The supervisors were in 100% agreement on top-ranked teachers and "about" 90% in agreement for those with the lowest value-added scores. All of the supervisors agreed that Sanders' "objective estimates of teacher effects could be invaluable for formative evaluation" of teachers (p. 12). More current research comparing value-added gains to other measures of teacher quality continues to show that principals have sufficient capacity to effectively determine who is and is not teaching children well. Sass (2008) offered research that showed consistent effectiveness among principals in identifying those teachers who will have the greatest affect on student achievement (Sass, 2008, p. 6). While studying the persistence of teacher effect on student performance, Jacob, Lefgren, and Sim (2008) found that value-added measures of teacher quality were not statistically different from principal ratings or national board certification measures and that "contemporaneous value-added measures are a poor indicator of long-term value-added" (p. 30). Comparing the ability of past teacher value-added scores and principal ratings to predict future teacher value-added, Harris & Sass (2009) found that "teacher value-added and principals' subjective ratings are positively correlated and principals' evaluations are better predictors of a teacher's value added than traditional approaches... based on "experience and formal education"(p. iv). With research consistently supporting principals' capacity to observe, assess, and predict who in the building will be successful in engaging students in learning activities, it would appear to be more cost effective to improve the observational skills of principals, already in place, than to invest in additional testing and value-added assessment products and services that operate under darkening clouds of doubt. If the goal is to lead teachers in best practice for learning at higher cognitive levels and not specifically for test performance, principals' administrative education will need to include a deeper examination of how students learn and the most effective instructional practices to engage students at higher thinking levels. If teacher practice requires changes in order to help students learn more and more effectively, then it follows that principals will need to focus their observations on instructional practices that support those levels and to be responsive to teachers' need to support their practice. If principals focus on high test scores, so will teachers to the detriment of higher cognitive skills as shown by Corcoran, Jennings, & Beveridge (2011).

Looking at the difference in how value-added results affect "teachers' own stake in the test outcome" (p. 1), Corcoran, Jennings, & Beveridge (2011) compared high-stakes testing results of the state achievement test in Texas (TAAS/TAKS) and low-stakes testing results of the Stanford Achievement Test (SAT) for the 165,000 students tested every year in the Houston Independent School District between 1998 and 2006 (p. 14). Distribution of rewards and sanctions for schools and teachers in the district were based on the TAAS/TAKS results, while Houston officials used SAT results which were for diagnostic purposes only. The research found that teacher effectiveness as measured by test scores on the low stakes SAT improves gradually and over a longer stretch of their careers, as opposed to the high stakes state test results that showed big increases in the first few years, followed by a "sharp depreciation in effectiveness." Researchers attribute the big increase followed by this decaying effect to the pressure, sanctions, and rewards that the high-stakes assessment system uses to get immediate, though short term, results (p. 5).

McCaffrey, Sass, Lockwood, & Mihaly (2009) found "very little of the variation in a teacher's performance over time can be explained by observable teacher characteristics like experience, attainment of advanced degrees, or in-service training."[10] However, they also found systems that adopt VAM as the sole accountability vehicle may expect that "approximately one-third to one-half of the variation in teacher effects is simply due to sampling error or noise in student achievement," thus leading to "considerable variation in who is rewarded across time" (pp. 599–601). What is not clear from the McCaffrey, et al. (2009) study is how much weight *can* be given to the value-added estimates in accurately or validly assessing teacher influence on test scores. Where is the evidence from the Sanders research, or elsewhere, to offer evidence that 35–50% of a teacher's evaluation may be based on value-added scores without contributing to bias, whether for good or ill, in the final outcome of a teacher's evaluation?

Kupermintz, Shepard, and Linn (2001) warned over a decade ago of the instructional distortions that may go unacknowledged when student test score gains are equated with teacher effectiveness, so that "it becomes impossible to distinguish between instructional practices that narrowly teach to the test or genuinely promote student skill and knowledge in the broad domains reflected in the curriculum" (pp. 17–18). With the added stress on principals to match up their observations with the testing data, or else undergo mandatory re-training in their observation techniques, the likelihood increases that bad teaching, as measured by any other measure other than test scores, may be rewarded, rather than corrected. At the National Council on Measurement in Education Annual Meeting in 2001, these authors presented their research examining the construct validity of the TVAAS model by asking the question: does TVAAS truly measure the quality of schools and teachers? In attempting to isolate teacher effects, their concerns were with the challenge of measuring "(a) the dynamic and interactive nature of the learning process, and (b) the inevitable confounding of many of the formal and informal influences on the process" (p. 6). They argued that prior achievement scores were poor substitutes when used as a "proxy" for formal and informal influences on student achievement, especially if students are not randomly assigned to teachers in a school. The dangers of equating teacher effectiveness with test score gains, as Kupermintz, Shepard, and Linn saw it, were two-fold: the educational experience was diminished for students as the curriculum narrowed, and the opportunity to identify effective practice was lost.

Using a novel analogy to contextualize the arcane world of value-added projection modeling, Reckase (2004) compared the practice of using lower grade test items in predicting performance on upper grade items (as in the TVAAS projection model) to the practice of predicting the future height of a fully grown adult from his or her weight as a young child, aptly noting the "relationship between the variables is not the same for the different age groups" (p. 118). In the example of mathematics, if the testing focus is predominantly arithmetic skills in third grade and the focus shifts to problem-solving, pre-algebra, and algebra skills by eighth grade, the math score is not measuring the same constructs from 3rd to 8th grade, which brings into question Sanders' use of past scores for predicting future math scores.[11] Reckase makes a compelling case that student academic growth does not happen in neat increments from year to year, but "may take a circuitous path through many domains of test content" and that tests "may or may not reflect the actual path of change in knowledge and skills" (pp. 118–119). If a teacher uses his or her professional judgment and screening to focus on the skills and knowledge that students need that are not aligned entirely with the grade-level standards and/or the summative grade-level assessment used at that level, Reckase states that a "mismatch between instruction and the assessment will result in an underestimate in students' change in performance." For such complex, though common, learning situations wherein student needs remain more important than testing need, Reckase suggests that "nonlinear multivariate models may be needed to track changes in educational performances" that would take into account the "actual path of growth" in students' academic performance (pp. 119–120).

In citing the research of statistician, William Schmidt, who studied the changes in Michigan's math curriculum from second to eighth grade, Wainer (2011) indicated that what is measured when the test's content or constructs change over time is "some general underlying ability to do math" (p. 135). This ability, Wainer suggests, is related to factors other than schooling that are not conducive to pedagogical alteration, thus making it "a poor characteristic by which to weigh the efficacy of schooling" (p. 136). Both genetic and environmental in character, intelligence is highly correlated with student characteristics that are beyond the control of the classroom teacher. The irony of VAM, says Wainer, is that it lead us away from substantive judgments about the quality of teaching and schools: "... by focusing attention on the gain score over a multiyear period, VAM directs us away from those aspects of a child's performance that are most likely to inform us about the efficacy of that child's schooling" (p. 136). The potential harm of using assessments purported to measure one thing when, in fact, they measure another remains as real today as it was a hundred years ago.

Calling into question the content-validity of standardized tests, J. R. Lockwood and his colleagues at RAND (2006) compared teacher effect data for math subtests (one for computation and one for problem solving), and their finding was that there was "more variability in effectiveness within teachers [between math subtests given by the same teacher] than across teachers" and that these "results suggest that conclusions about individual teachers' performance based on value-added models can be sensitive to the ways in which student achievement is measured" (p. 1). This variation could indicate that the curriculum taught is misaligned with the test (which can occur when available classroom resources are not updated as state curriculum standards and tests change), that the teacher's instructional approach is more effective for teaching some skills over others, or that the test maker gives more or a different emphasis to particular concepts and skills than the teacher does to assess grade level standards. If there is a difference in the teacher effect scores for the same teacher on different subtests of a math achievement test, what is the real contributing factor to student performance? Is the teacher's instruction or the test design responsible for the gain or loss; or something else? When value-added scores are reported only on composite scores versus subtests in evaluating teachers and schools, does that value-added score conceal students' learning growth in a major content area that the composite score does not capture? Researchers have demonstrated with certainty that these kinds of assessment practices narrow focus to test content in order to boost skills that are more easily tested than applied problem-solving abilities, but as for the accurate attribution of gain scores and what the scores represent, researchers who are unwilling to accept Dr. Sanders' assurances must wait for more compelling evidence.

Lockwood, McCaffrey, Hamilton, Stecher, Le and Martinez (2006) "indicate that value-added teacher effect estimates calculated from total scores may be sensitive to the relative contributions of each construct to the total scores" (pp. 16–17) and proposed a possible scenario for appreciating how teacher effect differences across these math subscores may play out when one test objective is given more emphasis by the test designer by the number or type of items selected for the test and does not match up with the emphasis given by the teacher(s) for that same test objective. If students were taking more than one math course in the same year with different curricular emphases, their performance on the math subtests might vary based on what each teacher emphasized in his or her math class (p. 18). If, for example, an eighth grade student were taking a general mathematics course and an Algebra I course, the overlap of algebraic concepts might boost student performance on the math problem-solving subtest. Lockwood and his colleagues recommended that "[u]sers of VAM must resist the temptation to interpret estimates as pure, stable measures of teacher effectiveness" (p. 21).

Other researchers have looked at the stability of value-added measures for the same teachers across different value-added models, across different courses, and across years (Newton, Darling-Hammond, Haertel, & Thomas, 2010). As part of a larger study for the Teachers for a New Era (TNE) research initiative at Stanford University, Newton and fellow researchers examined the correlation between the teacher effect estimates generated by five different value-added models for math and English language arts teachers from six San Francisco Bay Area high schools. They used only one prior year of student data to mimic what would be the most likely conditions in other districts and states to collect data to satisfy the requirements for value-added models currently in use (p. 8). The five value-added models they used to calculate teacher effect estimates used different variables to predict estimates (prior achievement, student characteristics, school characteristics and combinations of characteristics). They found that teacher effect estimates were significantly related to: (a) student racial /ethnic background; (b) student socioeconomic status; and (c) regular or advanced course placement (p. 10):

> Even though three of the five models controlled for student demographics as well as students' prior test scores, teachers rankings were nonetheless significantly and negatively correlated with the proportions of students they had who were English learners, free lunch recipients, or Hispanic, and were positively correlated with the proportions of students they had who were Asian or whose parents were more highly educated. (p. 10)

Next, Newton et al. (2010) examined the impact of different types of courses on teacher effect data for the same teacher (e.g., a math teacher teaching algebra and geometry or an English teacher teaching regular and honors English). According to their findings, the value-added estimates were more sensitive to the course taught than to the teacher teaching it, with effectiveness for teachers teaching "high track" or advanced classes higher than for untracked classes (p. 13). This finding once again introduces the question as to what effects are being measured, those of teachers or other variables that remain unacknowledged by VAM.

Using the five value-added models to examine the correlations of teacher effect estimates over two years, Newton, et al. (2010) found that all of the correlations failed to reach "the level of reliability customarily demanded as a basis for consequential decisions affecting individuals" (p. 14). In summary, the authors made a case for the "context specific rather than the context free" nature of teacher effectiveness, and their findings

> suggest that we simply cannot measure precisely how much individual teachers contribute to student learning, given the other factors involved in the learning process, the current limitations of tests and methods, and the current state of our educational system. (p. 20)

Whether tests are for high stakes or low stakes impacts teacher value-added scores; whether tests are properly scaled impacts teacher value-added scores; the random or nonrandom placement of students in teachers classrooms impacts teacher value-added scores; high percentages of poor or minority, special education or English Language Learners, gifted and talented students in teachers classroom over multiple years, all impact teacher value-added scores; the purpose, content, and construction of the student test impacts teacher value-added scores; and the value-added model used to assess teacher effectiveness impacts value-added scores. As Jason Millman (1997) so wisely said 15 years ago, "when an assessment system tries to serve two purposes, the accountability and improvement functions, the system is less than optimum for accomplishing either purpose" (Millman & Schalock, 1997, p. 247).

Since 1992, when TVAAS was established, scholars have established a growing body of research literature that provides evidence to seriously challenge the validity claims of value-added modeling based on current multiple-choice assessments with linear scales to assess all levels of student learning. As a result, Dr. Sanders' claims for isolating teacher effectiveness weakens further: (a) if student test scores are unreliable and invalid measures of student growth; and (b) unreliable and invalid measures of student growth are the basis for calculating teacher effectiveness; then (c) test scores are unreliable and invalid measures for calculating teacher effectiveness, at least for high-stakes decisions concerning teachers' livelihoods, schools' existence, and meaningful student learning gains.

The Tennessee Value Added Assessment System—Fairness

> Given that the ability of the [value-added] models and estimators we examine to produce accurate teacher performance measures is context-dependent and that the potential for misclassification is nontrivial, we conclude that it is premature to attach stakes to such measures at this time.
>
> —Guarino, Reckase, Wooldrigde, 2011, p. 1.

An explication of the careful academic research language from the quote just above might yield this translation: Because teaching is a contextually embedded, nonlinear activity that cannot be accurately assessed by using a linear, context-independent value-added model, it is unfair to use such a model at this time. Any system of assessment that claims to measure teacher and school effectiveness must be fair in its application to all teachers and to all schools. Some researchers deem value-added models to have beneficial low stakes uses such as screening and diagnostics (Ballou, 2002; McCaffrey et al., 2003; Braun, 2005), program evaluation (Harris, 2010; Papay, 2011), or student and teacher assignments (Glazerman & Max, 2011). However, consensus among VAM researchers recommends against its use for high stakes purposes. Any assessment system that can misidentify 25% or more of the teachers as above or below average when they are neither is unfair when used for decisions of dismissal, merit pay, granting or revoking tenure, closing a school, retaining students, or withholding resources for poor performance. When almost two-thirds of teachers who do not teach subjects where standardized tests are administered will be rated based on the test-score gains of other teachers in their schools, then the assessment system has led to unfair and unequal treatment [Gonzalez, *The Tennessean*, 7/17, 2012]. When the assessment system intensifies teaching to the test, narrowing of curriculum, avoidance of the neediest students, reduction of teacher collaboration, or the widespread demoralization of teachers (Baker, E. et al., 2010), then it has unfair and regressive effects. Any assessment system whose proprietary status limits access by the scholarly community to validate its findings and interpretations is antithetical to the review process upon which knowledge claims are based. An unfair assessment system is unacceptable for high stakes decision-making.

On January 19, 2010, the Center for K–12 Assessment and Performance Management at the Educational Testing Service (ETS) convened a meeting with 17 national experts and leading practitioners to discuss the "new opportunities and old challenges in measuring growth and informing instruction" (ETS, 2010). Pellegrino's (2010) paper was figural among those papers presented during the seminar as he presented a *learning* sciences perspective, rather than a statistical or economic perspective, on issues of growth and measurement in assessment systems. Coming from a cognitive psychology and education background, Pellegrino attributed problems with the current high-stakes accountability assessment models, including VAM and other growth models, to a design problem arising from "implicit and highly limited conceptions of cognition and learning" that tend to be "fragmented, outdated, and poorly delineated for domains of subject matter knowledge" (p. 5). This, he said, sets the stage for decontextualized teaching to the test, narrowing of the curriculum, and limiting of the learning repertoire. According to Pellegrino, if assessment took into account how students learn based on accepted scientific theory, "teachers should place more emphasis on the conditions for applying the facts or procedures being taught, and that assessment should address whether students know when, where, and how to use their knowledge" (p. 8). In other words, the use of assessments that are consistent with how humans learn would push teachers to focus on growth in student learning at the highest levels, rather than the growth of student achievement test scores that measure learning at its most rudimentary levels. The work of Dreyfus and Dreyfus (1986) is instructive here to briefly outline a definition of learning that includes learning at the highest levels.

Learning

One of the most unfortunate and miseducative consequences of the early twenty-first century's "orgy of tabulation" in schools continues to be the constriction of what is taught and how it is taught so that both match more closely the way that learning is assessed by thoroughly inadequate models. A scan of the educational literature relevant to assessment, in fact, finds the word "learning" often replaced by the psychometrically correct "achievement," or the more theatrical "student performance," as is evident in all the critiques above. Sadly, the value of every sort of educational experience, concept, technique, or intervention gets regularly weighed against its capacity for increasing achievement or raising student performance, rather than the more expansive and pragmatic goal of improving student learning. Where "learning" remains as part of the educational lexicon, it is most often an imprisoned half of a marginalized compound term such as "constructivist learning" or "cooperative learning." If we were able to operationalize something called constructivist achievement, then learning, perhaps, may have a prominent future, even though its meaning would have been exorcised in the process of making it relevant to stimulate or satisfy a stubborn testing fixation.

There are many models that adequately capture the multiple levels or domains of learning. For teachers who have been through teacher preparation programs, whose value is increasingly measured by whether or not their graduates increase student achievement or raise student performance levels, there is the familiar Bloom's Taxonomy (1956). Bloom acknowledged a layered process to acquiring knowledge and developing understanding in multiple domains of increasing complexity, and these domains ranged from simple recall to comprehension, application, analysis, synthesis, and evaluation.

The Dreyfus and Dreyfus novice-to-expert learning model has been put to good use by Flyvbjerg (2000) in making a case for understanding and appreciating social inquiry as an interpretive, or hermeneutic, practice when exercised in its most advanced forms. The Dreyfus and Dreyfus Model is used here for two reasons: (a) to draw attention to what is inextricably lost to children and their teachers by continuing down the road of using gains on tests as the proxy for learning, and (b) to extricate learning from its isolated lock box and to place it once more within the social context that is required for humans to become proficient and engaged learners who are capable of a range of tasks, from following directions, to collaborative planning, to using available resources to innovate, and resolving emerging problems in new and effective ways. The Dreyfus and Dreyfus learning continuum reminds us that the ostensible goal today of preparing children to be successful in the work place, or the global economy (as the mantra goes), has been entirely unsupported and even negated by the kind of learning that more accountability-by-testing rigidly enforces. For as we can see that most standardized tests leave students stranded in Bloom's "recall" domain or the Dreyfuses' "novice" stage, the same tests promote an infantilized state of dependency and tunnel vision that all but the most lowly work tasks cannot possibly accept as desirable employee characteristics (Figure 4).

At the same time that demands for test score gains become more intensely institutionalized, entrenched, and politically desirable as the way

Novice-to-Expert scale (1)

Level	*Stage*	*Characteristics*	*How knowledge, etc. is treated*	*Recognition of relevance*	*How context is assessed*	*Decision-making*
1	**Novice**	Rigid adherence to taught rules and plans Little situational perception No discretionary judgement	Without reference to context	None	Analytically	Rational
2	**Advanced beginner**	Guidelines for action based on attributes or aspects (aspects are global characteristics of situations recognizable only after some prior experience) Situational perception still limited All attributes and aspects are treated separately and given equal importance	In context			
3	**Competent**	Coping with crowdedness Now sees actions at least partially in terms of longer-term goals Conscious, deliberate planning Standardized and routinized procedures		Present		
4	**Proficient**	Sees situations holistically rather than in terms of aspects Sees what is most important in a situation Perceives deviations from the normal pattern Decision-making less labored Uses maxims for guidance, whose meanings vary according to the situation			Holistically	
5	**Expert**	No longer relies on rules, guidelines, or maxims Intuitive grasp of situations based on deep tacit understanding Analytic approaches used only in novel situations or when problems occur Vision of what is possible				Intuitive

Figure 4 Adaptation of Dreyfus and Dreyfus Skill Acquisition model (Lester, 2005).

to keep the accountability engine chugging along—pulling, as it does, a massive education industry along with it—the education reform rhetoric has turned to an increasingly fanciful notion of preparing all children for college or some form of higher education. Fanciful, in that the exposure to ideas, practices, events, and learning contexts that would be required to enable children to be successful upon reaching college becomes increasingly remote, as teachers' careers and children's futures are legislated to become more dependent upon test results, thus reinforcing a testing rigor mortis that is further entrenched by punitive pedagogy and burgeoning curriculum content absent of the nutritive value required to build strong college-ready students.

When teacher effectiveness is defined by student academic gain rather than student learning, systems like TVAAS render the complex learning context with its many variables irrelevant. Constructed as it is from general statistical theories, TVAAS "is only loosely aligned with relevant theories in education" (Kupermintz, 2003, p. 297), and it steers the educational community away from its central purpose—the enabling of the transformative capacity of a child's mind, life, and future. Displacing that noble and ennobling aspiration is a "cynical calculus of the worth of different students to maximizing teachers' return on investment" (Kupermintz, 2003, p. 294).

In a workshop sponsored by the National Research Council and the National Academy of Education (2008), leading experts in educational testing and accountability, value-added modeling, and state and local data systems were invited to provide research-based guidance to policy makers related to the appropriate uses of value-added models (p. vii). Their work was published in *Getting Value Out of Value-Added: Report of a Workshop* (National Research Council and National Academy of Education, 2010). While summarizing the research on both the measurement issues such as what and how tests measure student achievement and analytic issues such as bias, precision, and stability of value-added estimates for educational assessment and accountability systems, the convened group of experts confirmed for policy makers that for exploratory research or as a screening tool for professional development needs, value-added modeling was beneficial as a low-stakes tool. However, when it came to using value-added modeling for determining school improvement status or the effectiveness of a teacher the participants withheld support for those applications "given the current state of knowledge about the accuracy of value-added estimates" (p. 25). The report highlighted some important points often forgotten in the ongoing debate of appropriate uses for value-added modeling in education. For example, the panel pointed out that "policy makers' goals are usually more ambitious than statistical methodology and data quality can support"

(p. 6). While available statistical tools such as value-added modeling are applied with success in business, industry, economic modeling, or medicine to assess the relationship between inputs and outputs, educational settings characterized by ongoing developmental and cultural flux provide a far from perfect fit for VAM, as the multiple variables that affect student learning are difficult to isolate and to keep stable long enough to measure with the level confidence that high stakes decisions require. On the relationship between test performance and socioeconomic status, the National Research Council (2010) report acknowledged the widely accepted research documenting a high correlation between achievement and socioeconomic status. The report also included the research findings of workshop participant, J. D. Willms (2008), Director of the Canadian Research Institute for Social Policy, that demonstrated a correlation between *rates* of academic growth and SES, "with those who start out with higher scores typically gaining at faster rates" (p. 6). Those students who start out with higher scores typically have greater individual, home, school, or community advantages than students who start out with lower scores. When using value-added models to isolate teacher effect by adjusting students' original scores to account for advantages and disadvantages, VAM may overestimate or underestimate the size of the effect teachers have on student learning, bringing into question the validity of claims made on the basis of biased estimates.

When asked if they could identify the most effective value-added model, the experts recruited by the National Research Council and National Academy of Education (2010) stated emphatically, "No value-added approach (or any test-based indicator, for that matter) addresses all the challenges to identifying effective or ineffective schools or teachers" (p. 58). These value-added experts challenged policy makers to analyze carefully the cost-effectiveness and the liabilities of potentially biased value-added information based on VAM, as Pennsylvania and Chicago administrators' comments, summarized in the report, found value-added information to be no more helpful than indicators in place prior to implementing value-added systems.

In 2008, after examining the research literature concerning many methodological issues related to EVAAS and finding discrepancies between the claims of Sanders and SAS and the findings of national assessment experts, Amrein-Beardsley (2008) asked a series of very important questions:

> Who protects [students and teachers in America's schools] from assessment models that could do as much harm as good? Who protects their well-being and ensures that assessment models are safe, wholesome, and effective? Who guarantees that assessment models honestly and accurately inform the

> public about student progress and teacher effectiveness? Who regulates the assessment industry? (p. 72)

In response to her own question, Amrein-Beardsley acknowledged that there are standards for reliable, valid and fair use of educational measurements, those developed by the American Educational Research Association, the American Psychological Association, and the National Council on Measurement in Education, of which she highlighted six that must be "addressed satisfactorily by EVAAS developers":

- High-stakes decision should not be made on the basis of a single test score.
- High-stakes tests must be validated for each intended use.
- The negative side-effects of a high-stakes assessment program must be fully disclosed to policy makers.
- The accuracy of achievement levels (based on gains in this case) must be established.
- Students with disabilities must be appropriately attended to.
- The intended and unintended effect of the testing program must be continuously evaluated and disclosed (pp. 72–73).

The question remaining is who enforces the standards? If states like Tennessee mandate the tools of the assessment industry to be used to evaluate students and teachers who have no power to alter the evaluation methods and instruments that control their learning and teaching, then who is it that regulates, with the authority of law, the assessment industry? Who ensures that these standards developed by the educational and therapeutic professions become industry standards that are maintained and enforced in the assessment industry? Other industries in this country, under the authority of regulation and statute, have been monitored for their use of natural resources or for the quality of the products they produce, and they have been held accountable by law under product liability statutes and case law. Who makes sure that all children have equal opportunity to a diverse and comprehensive education, the universal availability of which may be masked by questionable progress rates on an inadequate standardized test? Who makes sure that parents and teachers who must rely on the assessment industry to get it right are not misled or mistreated when 26% of teachers are misclassified as effective or ineffective by value-added measurements (Schochet & Chiang, 2010)? The assessment industry, as it is interposed in schools between teachers and children, represents an exception to the important type of monitoring and accountability for best practice and public protection that is applied without exception for the production of automobiles or bottled water.

After 20 years of using value-added assessment, educational achievement in Tennessee does not reflect a value in the information gained from an expensive investment in value-added assessment system. With $326,000,000 spent for assessment, the TVAAS, and other costs related to accountability since 1992,[12] the State's student achievement levels remain in the bottom quarter nationally (Score Report, 2010, p. 7). Tennessee received a D on K–12 achievement when compared to other states based on NAEP achievement levels and gains, poverty gaps, graduation rates, and Advanced Placement test scores (*Quality Counts 2011*, p. 46). Educational progress made in other states on NAEP [from 1992 to 2011] lowered Tennessee's rankings:

- From 36th/42 to 46th/52 in the nation in fourth-grade math[13]
- From 29th/42 to 42nd/52 in fourth-grade reading[14]
- From 35th/42 to 46th/52 in eighth-grade math
- From 25th/38 (1998) to 42nd/52 in eighth-grade reading.

The Public Education Finances Reports (U.S Census Bureau) ranks Tennessee's per pupil spending as 47th for both 1992 and 2009. When state legislators were led to believe that the teacher is the single most important factor in improving student academic performance, they found reason to justify lowering education spending as a priority. In the 2012 legislative session, Tennessee Governor Haslam led an unsuccessful attempt to repeal the average class size requirement of the Education Improvement Act of 1992 in order to fund nominal increases to teacher salaries. The urge to make educators "accountable" for improvements to education seemed as robust in 2012 as it was in 1992.

In summary, the evidence of 20 years of review and analysis by leading national experts in educational measurement, accountability, lead to the same conclusion when trying to answer Dr. Sanders' original question: Can student test data be used to determine teacher effectiveness? The answer: No, not with enough certainty to alter, create, or eliminate very important policies and protections concerning student learning environments and high-stakes personnel decisions. In turn, when we ask the larger social science question (Flyvbjerg, 2001): Is the use of value-added modeling and high stakes testing a desirable social policy for improving learning conditions and learning for all students? The answer must be an unequivocal "no," and it must remain so until assessments measure various levels of learning at the highest levels of reliability and validity, and with the conscious purpose of equality in educational opportunity for all students.

We have wasted much time, money, and effort to find out what we already knew: effective teachers and schools make a difference in student learning and students' lives. What the TVAAS and the EVAAS do not tell us, and what supporters of VAM seem oddly uncurious to know is what, how or why teachers make a difference? While test data and value-added analysis may highlight strengths and/or areas of needed intervention in school programs or subgroups of the student population, we can only know the "what," "how" and "why" of effective teaching through careful observation by knowledgeable observers in classrooms where effective teachers engage students in varied levels of learning across multiple contexts. And while this kind of knowing may be too much to ask of any set of algorithms developed so far for deployment in schools, it is not at all alien to great educators who have been doing this kind of knowledge since Socrates, at least.

4

What Is to Be Done?

Trying to fix an urban school without fixing the neighborhood in which it is embedded is like trying to clean the air on one side of a screen door.

—Jean Anyon (2004)

Reprise

Since the early twentieth century, the economic argument has remained a principal ingredient in rationalizing an education reform agenda based on standardized testing, and it mixes well when stirred with Americans' secular faith (Tyack & Cuban, 1995) in education to solve social problems, including socioeconomic ones. Whether believed by current reformers or simply applied in dogmatic fashion as an obligatory catechism offered by skeptical priests, the rhetoric of education as both the great social equalizer domestically and the great economic weapon internationally continues to drive the reform agenda. As we have seen in previous chapters, the education reform equilibrium in the United States has been regularly punctuated by public exclamations of alarmist rhetoric from those who control both media and message.

The Mismeasure of Education, pages 193–218

The first generation of scientific management enthusiasts in the early twentieth century argued, for example, that a new skills-based differentiated curriculum in K–12 schools would offer security against the chief economic competitor, Germany, where the educational system was based on an efficient sorting and preparation of students for future life roles. Education reformers steeped in efficiency goals and social engineering zeal attacked, then, the classical orientation of the school curriculum as outmoded, old-fashioned, and out of touch with the times. For reformers and visionaries like Bobbitt, Terman, and Cubberley, economic prosperity demanded that waste be eliminated by targeting schooling to students based on the adult roles they were assumed to someday inherit as the result of biologically determined abilities. Rather than getting caught up in "the exceedingly democratic notion that all are equal and that our society is devoid of classes," as Stanford University's Elwood P. Cubberley quaintly phrased it (Mondale & Patton, 2001), school-businessmen sought and attained an educational system aimed to achieve social control, cultural assimilation, and vocational sorting. By the time "intelligence" tests and achievement tests had been developed and deployed by the "scientific" education reformers after World War I to label and sort the future workforce, the differentiated vocational curriculum movement seemed poised to deliver a social and economic efficiency of scale that the American economic engine required to cement America's preeminent role. As noted earlier, however, an economic depression and the Second World War interrupted the plan, and the German spectacle of eugenics applied on a steroidal scale pushed back (or underground) the more extreme elements who expected schools to function as reliable social and economic sorting machines (Spring, 1976).

K–12 education after World War II witnessed the rise of the life-adjustment curriculum, whereby the life skill needs of the middle 60% of academic performers took precedent over the 20% at the top and the other 20% at the bottom. Schooling, then, in the late 1940s and early 1950s resembled a kind of moralistic and feel-good functionalism. As Joel Spring quips in the documentary (Mondale & Patton, 2001), *School: A History of American Public Education,* alongside the standard subjects, students were now learning "how to deal with their zits" and "whether or not to kiss on the first date."

By the mid-1950s, however, a new generation of education reformers like Admiral Hyman Rickover and history professor, Arthur Bestor (Bestor, 1953/1985) were decrying the loss of rigorous discipline-based school practices, and they exploited new fears of foreign technological and ideological domination to steer K–12 schools back toward traditional teaching and a rigorous curriculum focused on math, science, and history. The launch in 1957 of the Soviet satellite, Sputnik, came to represent in the mass media another example of the U.S. educational system asleep at the wheel, while a foreign nation drove away with the prize of first place in the space race. The grave security threats posed by the Soviet space advances were played up for an American public already cringing near their bomb shelters, and the political fallout forced the first huge infusion of federal dollars to beef up science and math curriculums in 1958. The congressional bill had a name that assured its passage: the National Defense Education Act.

By the time the United States landed the first man on the moon in 1969, just 12 years after Sputnik had signaled the apparent demise of American schools, the supposed superiority of Soviet education was already forgotten by the media, just as the superiority of the German schools early in the Century was forgotten at the end of the First World War. No one, in the media or elsewhere, gave credit to great American schools when Neil Armstrong and Buzz Aldrin walked on the moon in 1969, nor did anyone celebrate the accomplishments of U.S. schools when America exercised its industrial muscle to force Germany to the peace table in 1918. In both cases, reformers had used national insecurities and economic anxieties to announce a false educational crisis in order to win the curriculum controls and management systems that might have not been achieved so easily, otherwise.

Twice more in the years following the space race, education reformers with business interests and economic incentives played the foreign fear card to justify desired policy shifts in schools. During the Reagan years, *A Nation at Risk* (National Commission on Excellence in Education, 1983) produced a groundswell of anxiety that was spread through mass media, with claims that the diminished quality of U.S. schools constituted a form of "unilateral educational disarmament" (p. 5). Once again, reactionary reforms flared as a result, enough to turn schools toward "rigor" and test based accountability and away from the educational equity movement begun in the 1960s with ESEA. As a rationale for steering education policy onto an older road to reform, President Reagan claimed that, as a result of desegregation, the schools had been "charged with doing too much too fast," and that the goal of educational quality had been undermined by aspirations for social equality. Responding to the dire warnings of *ANAR*, economic motives supplanted egalitarian ones, and turning away from the educational equity agenda was justified on the basis of saving the American people from another foreign economic threat from Japan, which ostensibly had been triggered by bad U.S. schools. With the mass media willing once more to trumpet the impending catastrophe brought on by the failure of public schools, and with a public willing to believe any news about schools as long as it was bad (Bracey, as cited in Ohanian, 2012), *ANAR* had the desired effect of making more accountability-by-testing, increased standardization, more direct instruction, and more "choice" plans like school vouchers appear as the natural alternative, or patriotic response, for a nation determined to maintain its national sovereignty and economic survival in the face of educational meltdown.

The economic advances by Japan during the 1980s, then, were attributed to the collapse in quality of U.S. schools, which had been brought on, according to President Reagan, by an underlying "permissiveness" and a lowering of standards that accompanied school desegregation. Just ten years later, however, when the Japanese economic threat was eclipsed by an American economic boom such as the world had not seen before, neither the reformers nor the media credited the American success with the economic turnaround to improvements in U.S. schools, even though they were vehemently blamed for losing the economic race just a few years earlier.

At the beginning of the twenty-first century, reformers used the same kinds of anxious remonstrations and dire warnings that have become so successful in steering K–12 policy reforms to call for higher education reform based on similar conceptions of accountability testing and increased efficiencies. Quite suddenly, the concept of a K–16 national system found currency (Haycock, 1998) in the reformer literature, and it was soon followed by the call for a P–20 system, such as the one established in Florida in 2010 to create "a coordinated, seamless system for kindergarten through graduate school education" that "provides for local operational flexibility while promoting accountability for student achievement and improvement" (Florida Senate Website Archive, 2000–2013). Beginning in 2010 in Tennessee, university teacher education programs were rated by the State on how well their graduates, once hired, could raise value-added test scores, and in New York the State approved a new teacher education graduate school that required teacher education candidates to raise student test scores during their practicum, or else not receive their Masters Degree. With support from the primary teacher accreditation body, NCATE, (Green, 2011), the idea took hold quickly in New York, with the *New York Times* (Otterman, 2011) reporting "by 2013, New York will begin holding all graduate students in education accountable for student learning in their classrooms before they can get their degrees" (para. 24).

Education Reform and Business Opportunities

The more any quantitative social indicator is used for social decision-making, the more subject it will be to corruption pressures and the more apt it will be to distort and corrupt the social processes it is intended to monitor.

—Donald Campbell (as cited in Nichols & Berliner, 2007)

In 2005, the Spellings Commission (U.S. Department of Education, 2006) called for an accountability-based higher education version of vocational preparedness to help the United States maintain its lead in the knowledge economy. This rendition of reform promised to provide the antidote to "other countries... passing us by when education is more important to our collective prosperity than ever" (p. x). Echoing the rationale used by reformers since the 1980s, the Report contended that its proposed changes to higher education would allow, in the end, the United States to gain "a heightened capacity to compete in the global market place" (p. xiii). The Report supported closer linkages between K–12 and higher education, and it called for the same accountability measures in higher education that were being promoted for the next generation of testing in K–12:

> Student achievement, which is inextricably connected to institutional success, must be measured by institutions on a "value-added" basis that takes into account students' academic baseline when assessing their results. This information should be made available to students, and reported publicly in aggregate form to provide consumers and policy makers an accessible, understandable way to measure the relative effectiveness of different colleges and universities. (p. 4)

These recommendations met with a cool response from most colleges and universities, but by 2011 over a hundred institutions of higher education, including the University of Texas, were administering and reporting student results on the College Learning Assessment (CLA) (de Vise, 2012). The CLA is given to students as entering freshmen and at the end of their sophomore year to measure the "value added" knowledge attainment after two years of college. Efforts to expand the use of the CLA have been strongly supported by the Bill and Melinda Gates Foundation and the Lumina Foundation, the latter of which was formed in 2001 by the sale of the "nation's largest private guarantor and administrator of education loans" to SLM, Inc. (Sallie Mae), which was the "owner and manager of student loans for 5.3 million borrowers (Lumina Foundation, 2007, p. 3) Both foundations have worked in concert since Lumina's founding to push a variety of "advocacy philanthropy" initiatives aimed to increase college attendance among minorities and the poor (Lumina's focus), and to advance twenty-first century scientific management through technological applications to higher education planning, implementation, and delivery (Gates' focus). In a study (Hall & Thomas, 2012) presented in 2012 at AERA, researchers found that in both foundations,

> There has been a shift in the focus of foundations toward issues of completion, productivity, metrics, and efficiency—foundations are focusing on broad policy issues, including the ways in which higher education systems

> are arranged, their funding structures, how they are held accountable, and how they manage their data systems. (p. 12)

Hall and Thomas (2012) found Gates, Lumina, and other corporate foundations using strategies "to insert themselves in the public policy process" in ways that have paid great dividends in the corporate foundation exercise of power to steer K–12 public education agendas at the federal and state levels. Hall and Thomas interviewed policy experts who expressed a common concern and a deep irony that the foundation accountabilists never seem to acknowledge:

> the most disturbing element... is that, in America, we elect officials to determine the direction of the country, yet foundations are working to set the public policy agenda. Foundation officials are not elected, foundations do not pay taxes, and there are no accountability or transparency measures. It's not that they shouldn't have a voice, but trying to direct government is another thing.... (p. 31)

By seeding state government departments and university departments with lucrative grants, foundations such as Lumina and Gates effectively buy cooperation among public officials and knowledge workers who may, otherwise, question who stands to benefit most by increased college efficiencies in data analysis, transfer, storage, and retrieval, or they may wonder about motives for programs supported by a foundation created with funds from the student loan business to increase access to college for students who must borrow heavily to attend.

This kind of narrow instrumentalist approach extended to colleges and universities bodes ill for the future of the economy, the nation, and the health of the planet. For, even if foundation motives and "advocacy philanthropy" were entirely pure and without economic benefit for the companies that spawned the foundations or the cottage industries sprung up to promote foundation goals, there remains problems with this kind of social policy determination:

1. It weakens democracy by perpetuating anti-democratic control of public institutions.
2. It restricts the diversity of opinion and expertise that are required to solve the interlinking and systemic problems that threaten economic sustainability, the health of the ecosystems, and the continuation of civilization as we know it.
3. It narrows educational priorities to serve productivity needs that constrict the growth of knowledge at a most importune time in human history.

For those who view the schools' and the universities' core mission as foundational to creating and evolving knowledge and understanding to advance the autonomy and improved living for all people and cultures, the fixation by unelected plutocrats on a singular vision of what is fair for everyone except themselves expresses a level of arrogance for which no parallel exists in the national history. Public education policy steering by billionaires offers a real and present danger to the purpose and functioning of democratic institutions, as well as the likelihood for the kind of ethical dysfunction and reckless self-aggrandizement that earned for Wall Street investment bankers a reputation as casino capitalists (Sinn, 2010). Or, when foundation sponsored research takes precedent over independent scholarly research by the National Research Council, as in the case of Gates-funded research prevailing as NRC warnings about value added assessments were dismissed, there is the open invitation to grave policy errors arising from tunnel vision and knowledge advocacy posing as independent judgment (Baker, 2013). These possibilities loom at a unique juncture in planetary history from which the future of most species will be determined by the choices, educational and otherwise, that we humans make in the near term. The exigencies of our political, scientific, and cultural dilemmas will require many well-educated minds, spirits, and hands to make a sustainable road into the future, and the commitment and consensus-building required to choose a direction and the conveyance to get there should not be determined by opportunists with enough blind hubris to convince themselves, if no one else, that the destination and the vehicles have been pre-arranged by those who stand to expand and concentrate their power by those crucial choices.

Improving Rather Than Proving

By the 1980s the accountability movement that had originated in attempts to evaluate the effectiveness of ESEA Title I programs became solidified and deeply entrenched by a standards and testing movement driven largely by an ideological agenda aimed at establishing alternatives to public schools at public expense. Whereas previous efforts had been devoted to determining if Title I money was serving the needs of poor children, which was the liberal rationale for accountability, or if Title I money was being spent in the most efficient manner with some degree of state control, which was the traditional conservative rationale, accountability changed during the Reagan years. Even though evaluation experts like Dan Stufflebeam (1983) were pointing out in 1983 that "the most important purpose of evaluation is not to prove but to improve" (p. 283), the push by reformers following *A Nation at Risk* (National Commission on Excellence in Education, 1983) shifted from an accountability agenda based on "compliance and assistance" to a "compliance-dominant strategy" (Elmore & McLaughlin, 1982) that set out to "prove" the shortcomings of the existing system and to force compliance by imposing sanctions of increasing severity over the next three decades.

As accountabilist exertions increased, so did skepticism and resistance among educators, based largely on insights that had been ignored since the mid-1960s when they were first offered. During the planning and formulation of ESEA, educators at the state and local levels expressed reservations about federal evaluations to measure effectiveness of Title I implementation. With limited understanding of the compensatory strategies on which so much attention and money had been directed, educators acknowledged their lack of experience in implementing federal programs of a magnitude never before undertaken. To complicate the work of economists and social planners during the late 60s and early 70s, educators warned that using standardized tests for federal evaluation purposes would lead to teaching to the test, which was incompatible with best educational practices, and that such evaluations constituted a waste of scarce resources that would lead to the deprofessionalism of teaching (McLaughlin, 1974, pp. 8–11). Expressing a deep historical reservoir of resistance to federal intrusion in local education decision-making (Kaestle, 1983), educators and state departments of education worried that the new evaluations could be the "first step in the federal prescription of a national curriculum" (McLaughlin, 1974, p. 9).

Coming to Washington in 1980 with a long-standing animosity toward unions, Ronald Reagan used his rhetorical gifts to portray educators and their professional organizations as resistant to accountability reforms and protectors of the status quo. Such rhetoric led to more resistance and suspicion among educators, who viewed conservative initiatives as a threat to their profession and to public education. Positions hardened and trust eroded as accountability measures advanced rapidly. By the mid-1980s, 33 states had adopted minimum competency testing, by the mid-1990s, 18 states required seniors to pass standardized tests to earn a diploma (Heubert & Hauser, 1999, p. 15). Ten years after that, all schoolchildren in grades three through eight were tested annually under threat of school closure or loss of federal funds, while 25 states required high school proficiency tests. By 2010, six states required elementary age children to pass an annual state test (Horn, 2010) to be promoted to the next grade, and the same year Tennessee became the first state to legislate the use of value-added test scores to evaluate teachers.

Though steadfast in their commitment to compliance dominant strategies, education reform became increasingly shaped by ideological agendas and financial opportunism during the decades following *A Nation at*

Risk. In 1999, commentator Ron Unz (1999) expressed the rising level of consternation among accountabilists, whose frustrations belied a barely disguised enthusiasm for new possibilities and opportunities that could result from the continued wielding of the reform cudgel:

> If years of effort have failed to improve public education substantially, perhaps the task is simply impossible, and the system should be "blown up" or at least have enough holes knocked in it to allow frustrated parents to flee with their children to private or charter schools. (para. 2)

Eight years later, Susan Neuman, who served as Assistant Secretary of Education during the first years of NCLB implementation, told a reporter for *Time Magazine* (Wallis, 2008) that there were, indeed, federal officials in charge of implementing NCLB who had plans to supplant the public schools that they were supposedly working to improve:

> ...there were others in the department, according to Neuman, who saw NCLB as a Trojan horse for the choice agenda—a way to expose the failure of public education and 'blow it up a bit,' she says. "There were a number of people pushing hard for market forces and privatization." (para. 3)

Even as reform rationales have evolved over time, then, the negative effects of testing have remained constant. And as in the first decades of the previous century, the standardized tests used in the twenty-first century continued to effectively marginalize minorities, the poor, and immigrants. Low test results, too, were used to justify very different educational treatments and interventions from high performers, whose class privilege, economic status, and ethnic advantages did not necessitate narrowly focused scripted remediation in total compliance learning environments (Horn, 2003; 2011). By 2008, when America's first African-American president chose Arne Duncan as his Secretary of Education, the "No Excuses" corporate charter schools had become the most popular reform solution among policy makers and their corporate patrons. Ostensibly aimed to end educational inequity and inequality, the proliferating charter reform schools are more intensely segregated (Frankenberg, Siegel-Hawley, & Wang, 2010) than the marginalized public schools they replace, and they operate without publicly elected boards and outside the purview of public oversight or regulation. Sadly, the sorting and segregating in the early twenty-first century has much in common with the early twentieth century, when eugenicists first designed standardized tests for the same purpose. Even though total compliance charter reform schools staffed by non-professional neophyte teachers from Teach for America have been critiqued as efforts by corporate "colonizers" to contain and control minority populations (Warniment, 2012), these challenges have not penetrated the mainstream media. Meanwhile, the broad reach of corporate foundation grants or government grants written by corporate foundations continue to incentivize market solutions to education, conservative economic ideologies, and the social distancing of the poor (Stiglitz, 2012, pp. 160–162) in publicly funded, though corporate-run, schools.

Present Tense

Except for new sanctions directed at schools, educators, and children whose test results have long belied their economic disadvantage and socioeconomic isolation, the same strategies of more standardized testing accountability and tougher standards make recent education policy talk in 2013 largely indistinguishable from what it was three decades ago. Even as other areas of American institutional life may have found it difficult to maintain the reputation of "reformer" after generations of essentially the same formula applied with similar results, education reformers remain undeterred in their fixations by either history or increasing resistance, even as their motives and endgames continue to evolve in ways that muddy distinctions or erase boundaries between government and business, democracy and capitalism, philanthropy and investment, incentivizing and bribery.

After decades of highly anticipated reform success that remains unrealized, business elites, corporate foundations, philanthro-capitalists, and venture philanthropists (Libby & Horn, 2011) soldier on in their crusade to bring business inspired social efficiencies, privatization, and corporate governance to public education. Fortified by tax breaks for funding corporate charter reform schools and school voucher programs, recently re-labeled as "scholarship tax credit programs" (National Conference of State Legislators, 2012), and venture philanthropy and corporate advocacy philanthropy were able to grow into multi-billion dollar enterprises operated by Wall Street hedge funds (Gabriel & Medina, 2010) and tax-exempt foundations. Huge financial investments have yielded unprecedented levels of political and education policy influence, as noted by founder of the Economic Policy Institute, Jeff Faux (2012):

> It is well known, although rarely acknowledged in the press, that the reform movement has been financed and led by the corporate class. For over twenty years large business oriented foundations, such as Gates (Microsoft), Walton (Wal-Mart) and Broad (Sun Life) have poured billions into charter school start-ups, sympathetic academics and pundits, media campaigns (including Hollywood movies) and sophisticated nurturing of the careers of privatization promoters who now dominate the education policy debate from local school boards to the U.S. Department of Education. (para. 4)

As corporate influence has come to dominate the ways that the education policy agenda is implemented, then, more top-down testing mandates, higher stakes, and heavier sanctions have displaced most other school priorities, particularly in communities comprised of poor, minority, and immigrant populations. As Reagan Era enthusiasms for business management and market solutions came to dominate education policy talk and then implementation under subsequent presidents, the imposition of macro accountability policies based on high-stakes testing grew ever-more dependent upon heavier sanctions and threats to bring about compliance by educators whose skepticism matched their passive resistance to the reshaping of the teaching and learning process by forces ever more distant from the school room. Following passage of NCLB, schools in disadvantaged communities found themselves struggling even to stay open to educate the children of the poor, whose parents were encouraged to opt for the only alternative to their neglected and failure-designated public school: corporate reform charter schools. Upon the recommendations of corporate foundations and an increasingly influential education reform industry flush with cash from federal discretionary grants, the U.S. Department of Education grew its Charter School Program from $6 million annually in 1995 to $256 million in 2011 (Lazarin, 2011, p. 11). With the passage of NCLB and the subsequent introduction of RTTT grants, the federal government, too, provided other generous economic incentives to non-profit and for-profit corporations to help them open the preferred type of "No Excuses" reform charter schools to replace the most vulnerable urban public schools.[1] Allowed to operate without the services and protections (for both teachers and students) required of public schools, the most significant "public" aspect of the corporate reform charter schools remains the public tax dollars that fund them.

Through the spread of charter schools, contracted management, transportation, commercial curriculum, private tutoring, and testing services, the well-worn reform strategies based on more high stakes testing and nationalized curriculum expanded to claim a significant market share of the $600 billion spent each year on P-20 education. In late 2012, Rob Lytle, a partner in a Boston consulting firm, (Simon, 2012) outlined for a group of investors in Manhattan the imminent bonanza taking shape as national standards and national testing were scheduled to replace state and local standards and tests:

> Think about the upcoming rollout of new national academic standards for public schools.... If they're as rigorous as advertised, a huge number of schools will suddenly look really bad, their students testing way behind in reading and math. They'll want help, quick. And private, for-profit vendors

> selling lesson plans, educational software and student assessments will be right there to provide it.... You start to see entire ecosystems of investment opportunity lining up. It could get really, really big. (para. 2–3)

Educators and other concerned citizens of the nation and the world should not wait and wonder if Mr. Lytle or those he advises will notice the social and natural ecologies screaming for attention just behind the investment ecology that holds the attention of policy elites. For as surely as the last half of the twentieth century directed schools toward competing in a global economy that has concentrated power to economic institutions without national boundaries, the first half of the twenty-first century must be devoted to education aimed toward cooperating in global, national, and local ecologies to save our place on the planet. Otherwise, economies of the future, whether global, national, or local, will not matter for much.

What, Then, Is To Be Done?

John Dewey believed that we may proceed toward the future only so far as we are willing to examine our past. For Dewey, experience was comprised of a continuum of past, present, and future that intersected with our internal and external geographies in an ongoing interactive dance (Dewey, 1938). Experience, thus derived from the components of time (past, present, future) and space (internal and external), became organized by reflective and purposive thought directed toward action. If Dewey was correct, the current steady state of education reform, which is seemingly unable to break out of a fixation on high stakes testing, makes sense. For in perpetuating a brazen kind of anti-history that discards knowledge that scholars have gleaned from past reform efforts, education reformers have become doomed to repeat the failures that they appear determined to ignore. Take, for example, what was learned about implementation failures following the 1960s "reform initiatives" at the federal level that had to span various levels and layers of government and institutions (McLaughlin, 1987). Writing some 20 years after the initial Title I evaluations, McLaughlin (1987) noted that economists and sociologists, who were the "chief architects" of Great Society programs, were quick to assign blame when their "theories of scientific management" did not produce the results predicted by their "notions of hierarchical authority and bureaucratic control":

> Thus while economists interpreted disappointing program outcomes as market failure and sought solutions in incentives, sociologists and organization theorists saw signs of inadequate organizational control, and counseled new penalties and increased oversight. (p. 171)

Educators as "implementers" of policy appeared, then, as "resistant to change" or "just simply lazy" until second generation policy analysts concluded that "motivation and commitment (or will) reflect an implementer's assessment of the value of a policy or the appropriateness of a strategy" (pp. 172–174). What appeared to policy elites as a simple case of resistance that must be met with harsher control measures for policies to succeed reflected, instead, different judgments, reservations, and professional commitments by educators for which policy makers far removed from implementation sites had little or no understanding:

> Their [educators'] failure to implement as planners hoped may signal their assessment that new practices are not as good as the ones they replace or their uncertainty about outcomes for children. Motivated professionals, we have seen, generally make every effort to do their job well. Yet many early analyses assumed implicitly that the 'right' policy was that contained in policy directives. (p. 174)

Unfortunately, lessons learned by second generation policy analysts were lost on the next generation of reformers, whose laser focus on high-stakes testing from the 1990s forward missed or dismissed much of the scholarly and practical advice emanating from university departments, whose empirically based research studies were quickly being replaced by advocacy research of corporate-sponsored think tanks fronted as research centers and functioned as public relations and marketing annexes[2] for corporate education reform. A deepening tunnel vision resulted among politicians and their corporate patrons who sought to make reputations as education reformers, as in the Tennessee case we documented in earlier sections. Independent scholarship, then, from within universities was often ignored or treated as ad hoc support of the "resistance to reforms," which was attributed mainly to teachers and their professional organizations since the 1960s. After all, university researchers were teachers, too.

One last example may suffice to illustrate the final point that our journey here has led us to conclude: education reform is engaged in an ahistorical, recurrent, and vicious policy circle that willingly sacrifices the intellectual integrity, emotional well-being, and educational capacity of students and teachers, in order to protect and nourish a vast and growing interconnected network that represents a precocious educational version of the military industrial complex. To realize and to grow the corporate reform school mission, this newer form of corporate-governmental mutual parasitism depends upon continuing governmental largesse, continued investment from venture philanthropists, and a reliable and continuing supply of targets from among the most vulnerable and least valued within the public schools, whose low test scores are taken as a sign of continued resistance by both students and teachers. The charter schools offered as replacements for these low-scoring schools constitute, then, the only other choice to public schools suffering from generations of malignant neglect and the effects of poverty. Promoted by advocacy philanthropy, venture philanthropy, and government grants, the charters are run by corporate officers, formerly known as principals, to recruit young and compliant "corps members"[3] from the most privileged universities who receive six weeks of basic training before they are assigned to pacify disadvantaged school populations among America's urban poor. The result is a growing occupation of urban school systems, often in hostile territory where the indigenous people have come to resent the public school closures, the silencing of parent voices in public forums, and the harsh treatment of children (Parents for Responsible Education, n.d.). Education in the total compliance charter schools effectively subdues, indoctrinates, and pacifies children, and those who do not succeed there for academic or behavioral reasons end up in the remaining public schools, which are viewed increasingly as schools of last resort. The charterization of public education in urban America functions as the spearhead of the corporate education reform assault in 2013, and it could not be accomplished and carried forward without the high-stakes tests that supply the data, as well as the rationale, for new target schools and districts, as well as those teachers who stand in the way of the battle plans.

A decade before No Child Left Behind announced the war against the achievement gap, policy analysts who had closely studied and written about earlier reform efforts warned of negative outcomes from the push following the Charlottesville Conference in 1989 for more test based accountability and harsher sanctions to quell "continued resistance" to Reagan-Bush market-based education initiatives. In a special section in *The Phi Delta Kappan,* Milbrey McLaughlin (1991) wrote the Introduction to five articles by education scholars with extensive knowledge of policy reforms, and under her summary point number four, "*Test-based accountability plans often misplace trust and protection,*" McLaughlin offered these potential negative outcomes for "high-stakes testing schemes" (p. 250):

- Perverting incentives for teachers—encouraging them to avoid difficult students and difficult schools
- Discouraging classroom innovation, risk-taking, and invention
- Allocating "failure" disproportionately to nontraditional or at-risk students who need classroom activities constructed with an eye to their particular abilities, motivations, and interests
- Forcing out of the curriculum the very kinds of learning—higher-order thinking and problem solving that learning theorists and

> others say are most important to "increased national competitiveness" and success in the world marketplace (p. 250)

Just as reformers ignored warnings during the 1960s, we know now that these prescient warnings were ignored as well, even though they were offered ten years before NCLB became law in 2001 and almost 20 years before Race to the Top, which has served to buy alliances at the statehouse policy level for the continuing war that would accept "no excuses" for any outcome that did not result in subjugation or surrender of all educational territories.

What began for many as an idealistic battle against achievement gaps has become a myopic fixation on raising test scores at any cost, including the quality of education of those targeted for help and the professional careers of the helpers. Ironically, and this irony is little appreciated among the wider population as yet, the system has come to depend upon continued failure as measured by test scores in order to sustain and grow the corporate reform charter school outposts that now number over 5,500. Whether by plan or serendipity, the value-added modeling (VAM) allows regular public schools and charter schools (now legislatively uncapped in their growth potential in the first 12 states to win RTTT grants) to show progress as measured by student test score gains. So, even as the proficiency gaps in achievement levels continue to mirror the income disparities among groups, increases in value-added scores have come to foreground proficiency gaps, thus allowing charters to avoid the prior fate of public schools that were labeled as irredeemable failures for missing arbitrary testing targets established by states under pressure from NCLB. At the same time, the spread of non-profit or for-profit corporate charters is incentivized by continuing federal grants and state mandates to target the bottom 5% of public schools for transformation, restructuring, or turnaround, which may, at the discretion of state or municipality, convert public schools to charter status as a solution. And, even though focusing on the bottom 5% of schools assures a continuing set of annual targets, such a strategy for charter expansion shows little likelihood of success (Peltason & Raymond, 2013): "Taking the first available performance measure and using it to predict one-year increments going forward, 80% of [charter] schools in the bottom quintiles of performance remain low performers through their fifth year" (p. 4). With numbers like these for the bottom 20% of charter school start-ups, what could be the likelihood of success for the bottom 5%, particularly within five years?

To exemplify this example of implausible rhetoric and wishful thinking trumping empirical research, Tennessee's Education Commissioner, Kevin Huffman, declared publicly that in turning over Tennessee's bottom 5% of schools to the State's Achievement School District (ASD) for charter conversion or corporate contracting, the bottom 5% of schools will be brought "up to the top 25% in the state within five years."[4]

As long as American education policy continues to rank schools using scores, whether scores are from current state tests or the tougher tests being designed to align with a national curriculum adopted by 47 states in 2012, there will always be a bottom 5% of low performing schools, which offers plenty of room for the growth of corporate charters schools that will carry the torch for corporate education reform initiatives. The growth of charter schools encourages the further elimination of "resistance" to the intensification of social separation through segregated schools, which are staffed largely by young, minimally prepared recruits who impose total-compliance test-based curriculums that, if deemed successful, indoctrinate children (Horn, 2011) to behave in ways that defy the effects of socioeconomic inequality. Unfortunately, inequality cannot be cornered into the schools, treated with harsh instructional solvents designed to scrub away the effects of poverty, and then tested to make sure the residue has been alleviated. Nor can we pretend that the creation and nurturing of unequal schools will solve inequality, whether made unequal by minimally prepared teachers, the absence of basic services like school libraries, the preponderance of atrophied curriculums, or by the physical and psychic separation of the poor and disenfranchised. That such outcomes may be offered as a viable resolution to inequality in education, which is parroted as the "civil rights issue of our generation" (Change.gov, 2008), represents a minstrel version of social justice, paraded on the public stage for the benefits that may be derived from delusion or deception, or both. Though forgotten in rhetoric and in deed, the U.S. Supreme Court declared in a unanimous decision almost 60 years ago that "separate educational facilities are inherently unequal" (*Brown v. Board of Education*, 1954). We must stop pretending they are not,[5] or else risk a further erosion of the moral courage required to complete the forgotten goal and neglected task of building a quality system of public schools that serves the needs of all children.

Stepping Away from Education Re-form and the Mismeasure of Education

> As long as learning is connected with earning, as long as certain jobs can only be reached through exams, so long must we take this examination system seriously. If another ladder to employment was contrived, much so-called education would disappear, and no one would be a penny the stupider.
>
> —E. M. Forster, *Aspects of the Novel* (1927/1956)

Value-added assessment based on standardized test scores has become the preferred tool for mandated assessment programs that measure content mastery and skill development in Tennessee and elsewhere in the United States. The standardized test is the most widely used assessment tool in determining what and how students should know. As Gardner (1991) puts it, "the test is the ultimate scholastic invention, a 'decontextualized measure' to be employed in a setting that is itself decontextualized" (p. 132). Current "objective" assessment practices have served to enforce the teaching of certain skills and content (Shulman, 1987), while doing little or nothing to improve the art and science of teaching or the multifaceted processes of learning. As the reformer logic goes (with apologies to logicians), mandating, measuring, rewarding, and punishing are enough to bring about the improvements that are sought, without regard to resources, psychological factors, sociological realities, professional preparation, or even good will. These practices have been used to devise and implement teacher evaluation schemes that are unsupported by the best scientific evidence, and they have been used as a rationale to close schools, retain students, and to segregate students based on test scores and socioeconomic status. They have also been used as the chief reason to launch and expand charter schools and school voucher programs for which no consistent achievement advantages have been demonstrated by research. In addition, such assessment practices and results have been used to plan and implement costly and ineffective policies, programs, teaching practices, curriculum packages, and tutoring services that have re-directed educational resources toward the private sector. Their widespread use was used to justify the narrowing of federal research expectations toward quantifiable research, and they have been used to narrow the preparation of teacher candidates to follow the prescriptions demanded by standardized curriculum and tests. These same assessment practices have spawned a vast education industry (PBS, 2004) that preys on desperate schools willing to use much-needed federal funds to buy untried solutions with big promises and price tags; they have created a testing industrial complex whose billions in revenue are based on the expansion of testing programs without any apparent benefit beyond the companies that produce and sell the tests. Most importantly, these assessment practices have undergirded and helped to sustain the categorical inequalities of a society whose legacies of bigotry, patronizing practices, and the industrial application of quack science for oppressive ends should cause some pause and some precaution against repeating pasts that are quickly forgotten in the quest for the next wave of lucrative fixes. If insanity is, as Einstein noted, doing the same thing over and over again while expecting different results, then perhaps we are not insane. But by what label of madness should we attach to our unique insistence on doing the same things over and over again while presenting it as something different each time? Perhaps we should stick with the term "education re-form," and when it is encountered in one or more of its many adaptations, it should be examined closely, for one may find clearly visible the vestigial legs of Social Darwinism, still kicking.

Ending the Dependency on High-Stakes Standardized Tests

As we showed in earlier sections of this book, we have known for a hundred years where the testing gaps are located, thanks to standardized instruments devised by Lewis Terman, Edward Thorndike, and other education reformers intent upon bringing "defectives under the surveillance and protection of society" (Terman, 1916, p. 7). The low achievers are still where they have always been, there among the poor, the disenfranchised, and those handicapped by circumstance or biology, and they are there despite the naïve or cynical rhetoric used to justify the more tests in order, ostensibly, to not leave them behind. The achievement gaps remain gaping and the education debt (Ladson-Billings, 2006), now centuries old, remains unpaid. The biggest difference between 2013 and 1913 is that, instead of requiring the walling off of defectives for the protection of society, as Terman cheerfully admitted, we now call constant surveillance and total compliance "freedom" and "choice" and pretend that children and their parents prefer penal-style school settings and test prep to the more humane schools and real content that we find where middle class parents demand it. In the name of not leaving children behind, reform schoolers have applied more and more draconian compliance measures that allow a two-tiered school caste system, whereby the testing "defectives" are segregated, contained, and provided behavioral interventions that no middle class parent would allow.

In contrast to the high-stakes tests that have spawned this century's "orgy of tabulation" (Rugg, 1975), the NAEP assessments administered by the National Assessment Governing Board are low stakes tests that are selectively administered to scientifically selected samples of students all over the country, and these tests provide policy makers with valuable achievement data by gender, ethnicity, location, income, etc. NAEP is referred to as the Nation's Report Card, and data are gathered from each state (and a number of cities) for comparison purposes. NAEP tells us many things we need to know without testing every child every year and without labeling his school, his future prospects, or his teachers as failures. Linguist and researcher, Stephen Krashen, has made this analogy (Haag, 2012) in arguing for a scaling back of high-stakes testing: "When you go to a doctor, they don't take all your blood. Just a sample" (para. 11).

What Should Be Done to Restore Reliability and Validity to the Measurement of Education?

Simply put, there are no multiple-choice or constructed-response standardized achievement tests that measure all levels of learning as outlined by Dreyfus and Dreyfus (1986) or described by Bloom's Taxonomy (Anderson & Krathwohl, 2001) or elaborated in any other accepted schema that depicts the gradations of learning, from simple to complex. Under the best of circumstances, most standardized assessments can do no more than measure knowledge acquisition at the more basic levels with varying degrees of reliability and validity. When Secretary of Education, Margaret Spellings, reminded reporters during her tenure in Washington that "what gets tested gets taught" (Toppo, 2007), she neglected to note that the other side of the coin is equally true: what does not get tested does not get taught, especially in schools where children's low achievement on standardized tests mirrors their economic disadvantage. Because the assessments used in schools measure learning at basic levels, those teaching to the test are incentivized to keep teaching and learning at the most basic levels, thus denying children who are being remediated from more advanced and authentic learning opportunities.

The movement of student learning levels from novice to expert levels does not occur in neatly measured increments assumed in the equal intervals or vertical scales constructed for standardized tests. Moving from novice to expert learning requires learners to move back and forth from knowing a subject to doing a subject, from knowing information and skills employed in various disciplines to using information and skills to *do* science, history, mathematics, art and to effectively communicate about that work within these disciplines. Due to the importance of "contextual insight" and "good judgment" (Wiggins, 1993, pp. 208–209) that are needed to work at expert levels within any discipline, we cannot assess the "complexity and ambiguity" of disciplinary performance tasks while "maximizing standardization and reliability" of those tasks. The when, where, why, how, and how-much dimensions of using information to accomplish real tasks are diminished or eliminated altogether in the limited choices to standardized questions with only four or five potential responses. A student's correct response to finding *x* in a given or known algebra problem on a standardized test gives the teacher and student very little feedback regarding the student's ability to create an algebraic expression describing a real life situation for determining an unknown variable.

From the standardized question and answer, what does the teacher learn about the student's ability to decide when to use algebra in problem solving as opposed to geometry or calculus; or why the student selects a particular algebraic expression to describe a problem scenario; or how the student actually constructs the algebraic expression when faced with an unknown variable scenario? The most productive way to assess student understanding beyond strict adherence to rules is for teachers to observe and evaluate, using refereed criteria by educators and disciplinary professionals, student performance of real life tasks in either simulated or actual disciplinary contexts. For example, where do students' performances or output measures fall on the continuum of novice to expert when they work separately and together to develop a testable question concerning the health of a local wetland, design an experiment to explore the question, organize and interpret data collected, and present conclusions and recommendations to a city council, county commission, or local environmental organization?

For teachers to do this type of assessment well, they must have a conceptual understanding of the disciplines they teach and be well versed in disciplinary methods of inquiry and reporting. They must also understand how students learn and how to engage students in both knowing and doing, as well as how to give students the feedback they need to move to deeper levels of learning. Without adequate feedback from performance assessments, or with only feedback from general standardized assessment, it is difficult for teachers to focus on the multiple learning needs of students. The teacher must understand how and why the student constructs questions and answers to know where to effectively intervene, support, and extend the student's learning progression from novice to expert. This requires ongoing interactions among students and teachers that are not test-centered, teacher centered, or scripted.

The potential reliability of value-added manipulations to standardized achievement test scores is compromised when the tests are used as a proxy for the full gamut of student learning that occurs in classrooms, where teachers take students beyond the novice and beginning levels that standardized tests are designed to measure. To restore reliability to the measurement of learning, achievement tests and value-added modeling must be used for diagnostic purposes to gauge achievement within the limited confines of basic knowledge attainment. For example, one of the authors worked with teachers in an East Tennessee county to use both achievement tests and value-added gain scores to determine trends in student data sets, to formulate questions and hypotheses about those trends, and to examine teaching practices related to those trends. Upon examining reading scores over three years at one middle school, the pattern showed both decreasing scores for eighth grade boys in achievement and decreasing value-added scores for eighth grade reading. Not unexpectedly, economically disadvantaged boys fared worse than their more advantaged peers. In analyzing the achievement scores further, items related to comprehending text emerged as the most troublesome for students, but why for predominantly eighth grade boys? While examining the instructional methods, the amount of time spent, how students engaged with eighth grade texts, and the type of texts used in eighth grade classrooms, the most animated and interested discussion among the teachers was whether eighth grade boys from poor homes really did engage with texts like *Sarah, Plain and Tall* (a nineteenth century story about a widowed farmer living in the western United States, his decision to find a second wife, and their life together raising two children from his first marriage). If students did not engage with the text, teachers understood that valuable teaching time and learning time related to improving reading comprehension was lost.

If teachers were to use value-added assessment to determine if students were achieving as expected, to see if value-added assessment was congruent with the teachers' observations of students, and then, to examine testing categories that were consistently below expectation for these students, the teachers, then, could reflect on student performance and their own teaching practices. The standardized tests and the value-added assessments used thusly in a low-stakes, diagnostic way can help bring about needed change in classroom practices through teacher reflection, analysis, and discussion of assessment results—in this case, the selection of reading material based on student interest and comprehension improvement needs. In addition to curricular and instructional decision-making, assessment must be recognized as a valuable and necessary requirement of teachers' professional responsibilities with on-going professional development in diagnostic evaluation, and with time provided within the school day to complete this work with other teachers.

In Tennessee and other states as well, assessment policy has become walled off from the kinds of reflective formative teacher reflections that can lead to more complex and authentic manifestations of teaching and learning. This separation occurs because the emphasis of assessment is on higher scores rather than increased learning at more advanced levels that are not measured by the tests. When assessment of student performance is developed, scored, and interpreted outside the classroom, as it is in Tennessee, the crucial element of reflection in the teaching-learning interactions is diminished, and basic knowledge acquisition becomes isolated from more complex manifestations of learning. What recalibrates the teaching-learning process is focus on performance, reflection, and feedback about the performance, and adjusted practice by the student and the teacher based on new insights related to how and why to change the performance or the task to reach higher levels of expertise and understanding. Current assessment policies constrain practice by emphasizing mastery of decontextualized content knowledge and skill development within narrow confines, largely to the exclusion of other levels of learning and teaching that are required if students are to leave school knowing how to continue learning and with the desire and confidence to do so.

Because standardized test results are predicated largely on the socioeconomic status of test takers, disadvantaged children become even more stranded on one side of the infamous and omnipresent achievement gap for which so much rhetoric has been advanced, even as resources that could help narrow the gaps dwindle. The increasing rate of U.S. child poverty, which was over 23% in 2012 (UNICEF, 2012), has been accompanied by a ratcheting up in the importance of standardized test results. Poor children, whose improved test results are advertised as the palliative to poverty, continue to do poorly on the tests and are, thus, provided ameliorative "choices" that most often intensify segregation by class, race, and ability, while re-entrenching the kinds of direct instruction and narrowed curriculum that are further isolated from the kinds of advanced learning opportunities that remain available on the opposite side of the "gap" where family incomes and test scores flourish. By the time that the children at the low end of the curriculum caste system reach high school, they are further disadvantaged (Rothstein, 2004) by not having been taught how to think and approach subject matter and learning tasks that require more than indiscriminate consumption and regurgitation. High school courses to further remediate the children whose remediation has not worked in the earlier grades leave students less ready to do well on either the SAT and ACT that are used to determine college placement. Many drop out, end up in dead end jobs, marry and begin the process all over again for another generation. Those who do make it into colleges that will accept the low scores are more likely to fall prey to the marketing strategies of for-profit institutions that have extremely low student completion rates and extremely high college debt rates.

If value-added modeling offered some way to alter this tight and vicious miseducative circle that cements together the categorical inequality (Massey, 2008) that wall off the economic unfortunates who suffer its indignities, then we might be more receptive to its arrival and spread. On the contrary, what value-added modeling has contributed in the testing fairness formula by acknowledging different starting points in the testing race, it takes away by helping to conceal the chasms that constitute the inequalities that mark the very different starting points of the disadvantaged and the privileged. When gain scores become the currency used to purchase testing success, then the distances that children are left behind by economic disadvantage become less figural as score improvement moves into the foreground. When a poor child, then, enjoys a year's worth of test score growth just as the middle class child across town enjoys a year's worth of growth, the achievement gap will not have been finally closed, but the new measurements, nonetheless, will serve to confine our attention to a version of success that, indeed, masks the growing inequalities and inhumane school environments where the education debt (Ladson-Billings, 2006) remains unpaid.

As Accountability Has Advanced, Trust Has Receded

To restore validity and fairness to academic measurement, policy makers and implementers must focus on learning, rather than test scores for accountability purposes. This will require the development and use of locally produced curriculum and assessments that reflect the many contexts where learning takes place. Since these new assessments and curriculum cannot be standardized for purposes of high-stakes accountability, their development and use will require rebuilding a structure of trust among policy makers, educators, and educational leaders that has been severely battered down over the past quarter century by successive rounds of "test and punish" (Ravitch, 2011) reform strategies. Never in great abundance even before the modern reform era, trust in our education professionals depends, too, on a highly educated and professionally prepared teacher corps with compensation that allows for competition among other professions. This is a particularly difficult challenge to overcome, in light of (a) preference among corporate school reformers for teachers with minimal professional teacher training who serve limited stints in teaching before moving into other careers or into educational leadership roles for which they are even less prepared; (b) the damaged reputations of teachers that results from the barrage of blame for the low test performances among disadvantaged children; (c) the scuttling of successful educational practices, philosophies, and theory built up over decades of research that have been used to good results, ironically, by other countries (Sahlberg, 2011); (d) the spread of performance pay plans with proven track records of failure (Springer & Winters, 2009; Springer, et al., 2010) that have held down professional teacher pay; (e) the spreading use of value-added student scores to evaluate educators and make job security decisions; and (f) the broader ideological linkage of anti-unionism with efforts to limit or end collective bargaining and job security for teachers.

What is currently meant by achievement in the education reform vernacular is success at quick responses to decontextualized questions from among choices that sample a student's memory of subject information, facts, and the application of those facts to rule-bound situations. State assessments in Tennessee and elsewhere are high-stakes summative measurements of achievement that require memorization for knowledge acquisition and skill development of concepts at a level Dreyfus and Dreyfus (1980) would label as "novice" learning. On the other hand, performance indicators that reflect the conceptual and applied circularity based on knowing as doing and doing as knowing (Maturana & Varela, 1987) are recognized by teachers, parents, and students alike as the kinds of achievements that may positively impact a student's capacity and confidence to extend and deepen learning in and beyond school. Connected with the conceptual, then, are practices such as writing samples, projects, experiments, demonstrations, public performances, and/or portfolios that awaken and build prideful ownership of knowledge among learners. These capacities, too, can be assessed, as teachers make these judgments and assign grades[6] every day. Unfortunately, federal and education assessment policies do not require or even encourage these kinds of practice sessions in the art and science of living.

In our current test prep school environments, students, whether passing or failing, are often retained at novice or beginner levels of learning. There they experience each grade level as another year's worth of facts and skills to be quickly mastered and as quickly forgotten, rather than as opportunities for engagement with real-world experiences, simulations, and other tasks to improve performance and gain understanding of how new facts and skills are related to what they already know and understand. A child learns to read proficiently when he has a purpose for reading; the text is relevant; she understands how words convey meaning to objects, actions, and ideas in her home, classroom and neighborhood; and how symbols represent the sounds and words of her life. The child progresses in the performance of reading much faster with these understandings and conditions established first, rather than spending an entire school year with one initial consonant or vowel introduced per week and matched to pictures of objects beginning with the same consonant or vowel. Keeping learners confined by the rule-bound rigors of basic disciplinary knowledge acquisition, regardless of context or situation, does not allow them to progress to deeper learning that requires situational insight and decision-making for actionable problem solving. It is through real life simulations and direct experience that learners hone the ability to manipulate knowledge and skills and, thus, participate in the world as alterable rather than fixed.

Limiting assessments to standardized measures of performance for high-stakes accountability has produced "teacher-proof curricula" (textbooks, computer programs and teaching manuals with prescribed and scripted scope and sequence for daily lessons) since the 1960s, with each subsequent generation of educational policy makers doubling down on compliance tactics that push schooling even further from the possibility of autonomous, professional educators and educational leaders who are professionally prepared and trusted to do what is needed to best educate all children. To push for control and predictability of classroom practice for increasingly high-stakes test scores based on one-size-fits-all curricula in our classrooms is antithetical to the goal of producing caring, autonomous professionals who are reconciled to the need to create proficient and engaged learners who understand and engage the world they live in. The students in the test prep environments simply do not gain the experience and practice to grow the expertise needed to deal with the complexities of the world or to succeed with the problem-solving tasks that get much more complicated beyond school. Grant Wiggins (1993) maintained that "the simplest way to sum up the potential harm of our current tests is to say that we are not preparing students for real, 'messy' uses of knowledge in context—the 'doing' of a subject" (p. 207).

And yet, there is a deeper existential harm that is the result when teachers are turned into bank tellers (Freire, 1971/2000) and knowledge into deposits which teachers are responsible for depositing and auditing. A fixation on scores from standardized tests makes knowledge derived from other contexts irrelevant, and children without an understanding of how interacting social and cultural contexts shape the evolution of knowledge grow up ignorant of how meaning is created, how power is exercised and shared, and how their own lives and communities may be made better by their actions. Whether conscious or not, the effects of imposing the kinds of "banking concept of education" systems that continue to be touted as reform are lethal to learning to become autonomous and connected beings. They were critiqued by Freire (1971/2000) over forty years ago:

> It is not surprising that the banking concept of education regards... [children] as adaptable, manageable beings. The more students work at storing the deposits entrusted to them, the less they develop the critical consciousness which would result from their intervention in the world as transformers of that world. The more completely they accept the passive role imposed on them, the more they tend simply to adapt to the world as it is and to the fragmented view of reality deposited in them. (p. 73)

Whether students are being prepared for college or work, a prescribed scope and sequence for daily lessons limits student participation to listening and responding, without regard for the human need to interact and to question. In Freirean terms, students become receivers of communiqués, rather than active participants in communication. To cover the prescribed curriculum that will be assessed with a standardized instrument, direct instruction and practice worksheets are regularly chosen as the most efficient instructional methods, which increase teacher dependence upon the only feedback available—more testing results. By using score based teacher evaluations to ratchet up pressure to wring out higher scores from students, teachers are coerced to become active participants in the annulment of students' creative powers (Freire, 1971/2000, p. 73), rather than acting as caring educators reconciled to "putting… [the student] in complete possession of all his powers" and "to give him command of himself" (Dewey, 1897). Assessment systems designed to measure the aptitude and skills required of individuals, in cooperation with others, to direct and transform their own lives, and to offer the remediation when needed toward that end, would indicate the long-awaited arrival of education reforms that are authentic to the needs of social beings to nurture the values of democratic institutions, democratic living, and the equal opportunities to bring forth meaningful lives. For the dogged pursuit of any other educational outcomes, whether real or chimerical, to hinder or circumvent this most basic human need, there are truly no excuses.

Epilogue

The Mismeasure of Education

When . . . the future becomes reckless toward the past from which it derives, the compensating plans become, at best, scrap paper; they then project futures that will never come, and are thus, in a new way, museumlike.

—Odo Marquard (1989)

In John Goodlad's 1975 essay, *A Perspective on Accountability*, he quotes (1975) at some length from an essay (Murphy & Cohen, 1974) published the year before, which includes the following important insight, expressed concisely here: "American education has had an ongoing romance with technocratic approaches to accountability. Seeking better information seems less threatening and more up-to-date than redistributing political power" (Murphy & Cohen (1974), cited in Goodlad, 1975, p. 108). For decades now, Goodlad and others have shared this skeptical view of the efforts to apply more "scientific data gathering" as a way to push forward education programs aimed to compensate for long-standing inequalities, as the structural tampering that could affect the social power grid remains mostly off limits. As a result of the more timorous approach to social change, increased accountability and more test data became the primary girders for the education reform infrastructure, which over time claimed large portions of the available education resources. Significantly, Goodlad expressed doubts then that are still heard from educators and educational leaders two generations hence. And though harsher sanctions have come to be attached to the testing ac-

The Mismeasure of Education, pages 219–224

countability strategies over the decades, even the universal compliance and proficiency demands of the No Child Left Behind Act (NCLBA) have still not ushered in the compensatory outcomes promised to all those children of the 1960s or, now, to their grandchildren who remain left behind. And though each new reform decade promises greater rewards if only the implementers would implement and stop accepting excuses or looking for them, accountabilists and reformists have learned, if nothing else, that failure has its rewards. For until such time that the era of universal testing proficiency arrives minus the testing gaps, elite corporate reformists may continue to credit others for its non-arrival—whether those others are students, parents, teachers, or local school boards. By continually aiming their searchlight on the horizon for any slackers that can be spotted, reformists are able to keep attention focused on who is failing to perform, rather than whose policies have already failed, perhaps, and they save themselves from acknowledging that there may be other ways "to the top" (though, perhaps, less lucrative ones) with less impressive track records of consistent failure.

Each successive generation of repackaged reform, then, has required new policing measures, tougher sanctions, and fresh targets of blame in order for the accountability searchlight to remain directed downward as the testing edifice proceeds upward. This is clearly illustrated by the ongoing concerns expressed in an ad campaign by Exxon Mobil, whose CEO, Rex Tillerson, serves on the Board of Directors and Chair of the Education and Workforce Committee for the Business Roundtable (BRT). Until U.S. international test scores climb to heights that American child poverty rates have thus far made impossible to scale, Exxon Mobil may continue its national advertising of U.S. students' mediocre PISA rankings in math (25th) and science (17th), all the while ignoring America's more impressive ranking (2nd) in child poverty rates among the "richest countries" of the world (UNICEF, 2012). Where child poverty is low in the United States, Exxon Mobil should know that there is ample evidence to show that American students are doing very well in international test achievement comparisons and that economic disadvantage accounts significantly for lower U.S. PISA scores when compared to other Western nations (Carnoy & Rothstein, 2013).

In U.S. schools, for instance, with poverty rates below 10%, American students rank first in the world on PISA in both math and science, and where poverty is between 10 and 24.9%, American students score third behind Korea and Finland (Riddile, 2010). To deny or fail to acknowledge this prominent and undeniable feature of reality, while maintaining a studied disregard for needed structural changes for poverty rates and segregation to be brought down and learning rates raised up, adds, then, a deep moral stain to the frayed reformist banner that cannot be washed away by rhetorical bromides or even advertising campaigns.

Goodlad, writing 18 years after his 1974 essay, turned his own high beam on some of the darker assumptions underlying another generation of testing and accountability efforts just underway in 1992, the same year that VAM became law in Tennessee. Those assumptions remain very much with us today, and decisions based on those assumptions still hobble efforts aimed at equal access to a quality education for all children. The fifth assumption that Goodlad (1992) identified has led to some particularly regrettable outcomes:

> 5. The necessity of rigorously sustaining world-class standards (for fear of otherwise making a mockery of the whole system) will ensure a steady supply of test-failers (presumably accommodated by temporary job certificates), who will perform the plethora of mundane services that the more successful among us will increasingly require. (p. 233)

Two decades after Goodlad shined his light to expose this assumption, those "temporary job certificates" for test-failers are often referred to as "certificates of completion," and they are abundantly provided to students who have completed all high school course requirements except for passing the high school exit exams that reformers would like to make harder still. For with the implementation of the nation's next testing delivery system, the Common Core State Standards (CCCS), more and harder tests will be required than the ones that many poor children have consistently been failing now for many years. We may wonder, then, how many more students will find themselves giving up to "perform the plethora of mundane services that the more successful among us will increasingly require." We may be fairly certain that large numbers of them will end up in the school-to-prison pipeline (Alexander, 2010).

There are reasons to believe that this outcome may be avoided if available evidence accompanied by public demand continues to be mobilized. For the quick and scientifically dubious rise of value-added modeling since 2009 points to a foundation that is incapable of supporting the structure that corporate education reformists are racing to build. Such heedless practices are likely to increase the likelihood of an eventual collapse, and the added weight of more value-added high-stakes testing with validity and reliability pillars missing further weakens the structure. At the same time, warnings of possible collapse grow louder and have awakened concerns among parents who must send their children into this questionable environment, as well as from the teachers who must work there, and even from the children, themselves, who have sensed the danger imminent in educational structures built by flimsy measures with hasty methods. As social engineers and architects scratch their heads and as politicians fret about the potential outcome, the corporate funders issue orders to keep building without delay. A rickety version of the Tower of Babel proceeds, then, even as a growing crowd encircles the construction, speaking many languages but with a single message of opposition. Below are a few examples from recent history:

> In 2011, two principals from Long Island began collecting signatures (Winerip, 2011b) from fellow principals for a letter expressing opposition to the use of value-added test scores to evaluate teachers in their state. By late 2012, the letter had collected 1,635 signatories, which represents over a third of New York State principals. (New York Principals, 2013)
>
> Led by Heath Morrison from Charlotte-Mecklenburg Schools in Charlotte, North Carolina and Joshua Starr from Montgomery County, Maryland, a national consortium of superintendents in 2012 formed a "network of district leaders inside and outside North Carolina, to try to counteract the national testing craze." (Helms, 2012)
>
> At the beginning of the 2012–2013 school year, the local school board of Metro Nashville voted 5–4 to defy the State Board of Education's approval of a charter school in a Nashville suburb. (Fingeroot, 2012)
>
> In an historic action, the Texas House of Representatives in January 2013 responded to the growing chorus of parent protests against high stakes testing in Texas by passing a draft budget for 2014–15 that zeroed out funding for State of Texas Assessments of Academic Readiness (STAAR). In February 2013, Texas state Senator, Letitia Van de Putte introduced a bill "to reduce the onerous 15 end-of-course (EOC) exams required for graduation by the State of Texas Assessments of Academic Readiness (STAAR) testing system down to the most important three: Algebra I, English III and Writing III" (Van de Putte, 2013). Just days before, the Texas Senate passed a bill to "remove the state rule that ties end-of-course exams in high schools to 15% of the student's final course grade." (Parker, 2013)
>
> In late 2012 teachers at Seattle's Garfield High School announced they would not administer the next Measures of Academic Progress (MAP) test. The test was administered by principals in February 2013, but with strong parental support (Shaw, 2013) three-fourths of Garfield's ninth graders stayed home.
>
> Led by the student representative on the Portland School Board, Alexia Garcia, students of the Portland Student Union announced on February 1, 2013 that they would urge Portland students to boycott the Oregon Assessment of Knowledge and Skills (OAKS) test: "Alexia Garcia, a Lincoln High School senior, said the tests take away valuable class time and are ultimately unfair measures for both students and teachers." (Dungca, 2013)

In Nashville, Tennessee a group of parents and community members mobilized in February 2013 to oppose a corporate education reform bill hastily introduced in the State Legislature to create a state authorizer of charter schools and to pass a school voucher plan (Garrison, 2013). The statewide group known as Standing Together 4 Strong Community Schools was given prominent coverage Nashville's leading daily newspaper, the *Nashville Tennessean*.

These events and actions indicate, both geographically and institutionally, a growing turbulence among a variety of affected groups that may, indeed, alter the power dynamics of high-stakes testing policy at the local, state and federal levels. The longstanding skepticism of professional educators to testing accountability measures has now been taken up by parents, students, and school boards, and experience tells us that successful politicians are always on the lookout for public issues with support on the rise, rather than on the decline. The timing could not be worse for corporate education reform.

With the predominance of corporate power to effect business-friendly education reforms reaching a zenith just after the Great Recession of 2008, the widespread resentment toward Wall Street solutions by unaccountable billionaires has fueled a growing awareness that more of the same education reforms now directed by corporations with little oversight is likely to bring about disappointing results that will not end well. Too, pragmatic concerns among cash-strapped communities have led many taxpayers to bristle at the possibility that corporate interests could end up running the public schools at taxpayer expense. Adding to the growing unease is the realization, based on an extensive body of empirical research, that most charter schools score no higher than the public schools they are replacing (CREDO, 2009; Peltason & Raymond, 2013; Di Carlo, 2011); the ones that do have higher scores offer a harshly regimented, zero tolerance model that contributes to increased segregation and children who follow orders well but who think poorly. Additionally, total compliance boutiques like KIPP influence other urban schools to emulate their harsh policies, which increase the numbers of dropouts and pushouts (Advancement Project, 2010). Finally, with the school-to-prison pipeline having entered the mainstream of educational conversation nationally (Bahena, et al., 2012), policy makers are looking for any way to reduce dropouts, if for no other reason than the economic one. Finally, the threat of charter expansion to suburban school districts has awakened resistance (Mooney, 2013) among influential middle class parents who are becoming keenly aware of the economic drain to school budgets that comes with charter expansion.

The annual PDK/Gallup opinion polls during the first decade of this century showed that the more parents learned over the years about the No

Child Left Behind Act, the less they found it beneficial to their communities and the less they supported it (Bushaw & McNee, 2009). It appears that this same dynamic is at work with the latest initiatives demanded or incentivized by Race to the Top. Perhaps it should be expected, then, that corporate education reform implementation would resemble a round-the-clock project that is hurriedly hammered into place by participants racing against a clock they cannot see, with little incentive or opportunity for reflection and none for self-evaluation by the project directors, themselves. With a hundred years of effort already expended, surely they have concluded that time is running out.

Notes

Part 1

1. While Superintendent Cash no doubt was correct about making the front pages that day, he was incorrect in his claim that teachers are the most important single factor in the education of the child. The mistake is forgivable if we assume Cash simply misspoke as a result of his jubilation, but the same non-factual claim was being made that day in the Press Release from the BMGF Director of Education, College Ready, Vicki Phillips: "Decades of research and our own grant making provide clear evidence that supports the growing consensus among policymakers and parents alike that teachers matter most when it comes to student achievement" (http://www.gatesfoundation.org/press-releases/pages/intensive-partnership-for-effective-teaching-091119.aspx).
2. Although teacher observations count 50% of a teacher's overall evaluation score, the Tennessee Department of Education retains the power to revoke any observation results that do not align with student test scores, thus forcing observational data to conform to conform to test data. According to State Board of Education Teacher and Principal Evaluation Policy 5.201, the "Department of Education will monitor observation scores throughout the year and enforce consistent application of standards across districts. Upon the conclusion of the school year and relevant data collection, the department will publish evaluation results by district. Districts that fall outside the acceptable range of results, subject to student achievement scores, will not be approved to use alternate models for the following school year, and will be subject to additional training and monitoring by the department" (http://www.tn.gov/sbe/2011Novemberpdfs/IV%20G%20Teacher%20&%20Principal%20Evaluation%20Policy.pdf).
3. From the Program Description of the PBS Series, Africans in America, produced by WGBH Boston: Executive Producer, Orlando Bagwell (http://www.pbs.org/wgbh/aia/tvandbeyond/tvbeyonddescr.html)

The Mismeasure of Education, pages 225–232

4. Rice published *Scientific Management in Education* in 1913, just two years after the publication of Taylor's *Principles of Scientific Management,* which brought the industrial revolution to full fruition through assembly line mass production of goods. It is not a coincidence that schooling of that era and subsequent eras has come to be known as the "factory system" of education. See Callahan's *Education and the Cult of Efficiency* (1962) and Kliebard's *The Struggle for the American Curriculum* (2004) for detailed explications of the social efficiency movement in education.
5. The prevailing rationale for rejection of payments to sterilization victims was expressed by a North Carolina State Senator, Chris Carney: "If we do something like this, you open up the door to other things the state did in its history.... Some, I'm sure you'd agree, are worse than this" (Severson, 2012, June 20).
6. This was a term used by UC Berkeley zoology professor, Dr. Samuel Holmes, in a syllabus for one of his extension courses, "The Factors in the Evolution of Man." From the syllabus: "Made aware of the biological trend of his development, man will have it in his power to counteract, in a measure, the forces which are productive of racial decay, and to set in operation agencies by which the heritage of the race may be improved" (Retrieved from the Cold Springs Harbor website at http://www.dnalc.org/view/10238—The-factors-of-evolution-in-man-course-offered-by-Samuel-Holmes-at-University-of-California-Berkeley-1-.html)

   Holmes remained a staunch eugenics advocate after others in the scientific community came to see the errors of their ways. In fact, in 1939 Holmes published an essay in the prestigious journal, *Science,* in which he defended eugenics against what he viewed as "ill-founded opposition" that eventually would be "melted away like fog before the rays of the rising sun" (p. 357). Near the end of his essay, he tried to allay the fears of eugenics detractors with this admission, which underscored his shared commitment to a social agenda embraced by the Nazis, who would be rolling through Poland five months after Holmes's essay appeared:

   > ... as eugenicists, we are committed to no particular social, religious, political or economic creed, that we are no more concerned with the class war than the botanist or the astronomer, that we are quite willing that Mary should marry Jack or any one else provided their progeny will probably not be imbeciles, lunatics or otherwise a burden to society. (p. 357)

7. William Ryan coined the phrase, "blaming the victim," in his 1976 book of the same title, *Blaming the Victim.*
8. Karl Alexander (1997) traces the skeptical research related to school spending to economist Eric Hanushek, longtime Fellow at the conservative think tank, the Hoover Institution:

   > Hanushek's first literature review, titled "Throwing Money at Schools," covers 130 school-level and person-level analyses of basic "bread and butter" issues, including effects on student performance of pupil expenditures, class size, and teacher experience. His conclusion (1981:30): "Higher school expenditures per pupil bear no visible relationship to higher student performance." That was in 1981. Then in 1989, with

more studies in hand (N = 187): "There is no strong or systematic relationship between schooling expenditures and student performance." (Hanushek 1989:47)

Words like "strong" and "systematic" somewhat qualify the 1981 conclusion, but the impression stands, and people in high places take this work seriously. In a series of speeches in 1988, Former Secretary of Education William Bennett invoked Hanushek's work to conclude: "Money doesn't cure school problems. We've done 147 studies at the Department of Education and we cannot show a strong, positive correlation between spending more and getting better results." (cited in Baker 1991)

Such a sweeping conclusion is very likely wrong, however. For example, a recent meta-analysis (Hedges, Laine & Greenwald 1994:11) of Hanushek's 1989 data finds "substantially positive effects" for per pupil expenditures and for teacher experience and "typically positive" effects for teacher salary, administrative inputs, and facilities.

9. After his appointment in 2009, Secretary of Education, Arne Duncan, repeatedly claimed that "education is the civil rights issue of this generation" (http://chronicle.com/article/article-content/64567/). In laying out his similarly focused, though more aggressively privatized, education policy agenda in June 2012, the Republican contender, Mitt Romney also called education "the civil rights issue of our era" (http://www.nytimes.com/2012/05/24/us/politics/romney-calls-failing-schools-civil-rights-issue-of-our-era.html). Both political parties continue to embrace charter schools as a key policy initiative, even though charters have been found to have segregative effects, even in schools systems that are intensely segregated (Frankenberg, Siegel-Hawley, & Wang, 2010; Miron, Urschel, Mathis, & Tornquist, 2010).
10. See *Applications of social capital in educational literature: A critical synthesis* (Dika & Kusum, 2002) *Review of Educational Research*, Vol. 72, No. 1 (Spring, 2002), pp. 31–60.
11. Prior to his appointment as Secretary of Education, Alexander "had received $125,000 from Whittle as a paid consultant" (Bracey, 2002, p. 138). Bracey also reported in 2002 that Alexander made a hefty profit on a stock deal involving a Whittle company, Channel One, whereby Alexander "purchased Channel One stock for $10,000, which Whittle bought back for $330,000" (p. 138).

Part 2

1. The second Supreme Court loss came in a 1974 ruling against a school desegregation plan for Detroit and Wayne County, which mirrored a busing-based plan the Supreme Court had approved in 1971 for Charlotte and Mecklenburg County in North Carolina (*Swann v. Charlotte-Mecklenburg Board of Education*). In the Detroit case, known as *Milliken v Bradley*, the new majority on the Court, which was established in 1972 with Nixon's picks of Justice Powell and Renquist, struck down the initial ruling by Federal District Judge Stephen Roth and the subsequent state and federal appeals court rulings that upheld the Judge Roth's initial verdict. The 5–4 ruling in 1974 had the effect

of encouraging the continued de facto segregation of schools in the West and the North based on segregated housing patterns, and it opened the door to further court challenges to the school desegregation plans aimed to remedy de jure segregation in the South.

2. Based on an educator's years of experience and evaluation performance, he or she could apply for the Career Ladder Program for merit pay and the option of working under an extended contract—more hours for additional pay. It was the Career Ladder Program and the Extended Contract Program that created the most controversy in implementing Tennessee's Comprehensive Education Reform Act (CERA).
3. Senator Dunavant's 1987 Resolution for the State Certification Commission to study the "use of student progress or achievement, as measured by standardized testing or other appropriate measures as an indicator of successful teaching and effective schools" was only asking for what was already in State law, but in the early 1980s as CERA was constructed, few knew or cared about the concept of value-added assessment applied to education. Value added assessment was understood to be a measurement practice used in the production-function models of business and industry to evaluate very different processes and products, not teaching and learning.
4. It is important to remind the reader here that NCLB did not accept growth model scores based on national norm-referenced achievement tests like the California Achievement Test due to the lack of alignment between state standards and those tests. So how the Knox County educational specialists determined alignment in 1983 would have been important to note in the Sanders & McLean paper.
5. Albright and Womack were both businessmen and members of the Chambers of Commerce in their respective communities of Chattanooga and Murfreesboro.
6. Passed in 1994, the Goals 2000: Educate America Act (P.L. 103–227) included 8 major goals:

    a. All children in America will start school ready to learn.
    b. The high school graduation rate will increase to at least 90%.
    c. All students will leave grades 4, 8, and 12 having demonstrated competency over challenging subject matter including English, mathematics, science, foreign languages, civics an government, economics, the arts, history, and geography, and every school in America will ensure that all students learn to use their minds well, so they may be prepared for responsible citizenship, further learning, and productive employment in our nation's modern economy.
    d. United States students will be first in the world in mathematics and science achievement.
    e. Every adult American will be literate and will possess the knowledge and skills necessary to compete in a global economy and exercise the rights and responsibilities of citizenship.

f. Every school in the United States will be free of drugs, violence, and the unauthorized presence of firearms and alcohol and will offer a disciplined environment conducive to learning.
g. The nation's teaching force will have access to programs for the continued improvement of their professional skills and the opportunity to acquire the knowledge and skills needed to instruct and prepare all American students for the next century.
h. Every school will promote partnerships that will increase parental involvement and participation in promoting the social, emotional, and academic growth of children."

7. (Aizer, Gold, & Shcoen, 1999, p. 22)
8. TennCare Quarterly Report, 2003, p. 2 [http://www.tn.gov/tenncare/forms/leg0703.pdf]
9. The Tennessee NCLB target (AYP) for math in 2005 was 79% proficient/advanced and 83% for reading.
10. The changes to the mathematics framework introduced in 2005 for grades 4 and 8 were minimal, which allowed for the continued reporting of results from previous assessments beginning with 1990. The reading framework was updated in 2009. Results from special analyses determined the 2009 and subsequent reading assessment results could be compared with those from earlier assessment years (NCES, 2011, http://nces.ed.gov/nationsreportcard/mathematics/frameworkcomparison.asp; http://nces.ed.gov/nationsreportcard/reading/whatmeasure.asp).
11. See above.
12. It is interesting to note that the majority of the Chicago public supported the Chicago teachers in their 2012 strike, which can be attributed in part, we believe, to grievances that focused on student learning needs, infrastructure deficiencies, and the social justice implications of policies like test-based evaluations that teachers believed would drive wedges between them and their students.

Part 3

1. In addition to these competencies, the Kentucky Supreme Court listed five additional competencies as an outcome of an efficient system of education:
   - Sufficient oral and written communication skills to enable students to function in a complex and rapidly changing civilization;
   - Sufficient understanding of governmental processes to enable the student to understand the issues that affect his or her community, state, and nation;
   - Sufficient self-knowledge and knowledge of his or her mental and physical wellness;
   - Sufficient grounding in the arts to enable each student to appreciate his or her cultural and historical heritage;

- Sufficient training or preparation for advanced training in either academic or vocational fields so as to enable each child to choose and pursue life work intelligently.

2. The Small School Systems appealed their case to the Tennessee Supreme court twice more in order to require the state to include teachers' salaries as part of the BEP formula for equitable distribution of state education funding.
3. As noted in Part 2, the precipitous drop in 2010 scores can be partially accounted for by the fact that the ACT became mandatory for all high school juniors in 2010.
4. The defendants in TSSS v. McWherter asked the Court to consider the BEP when deciding the constitutionality of the state's education funding system. The Court's response: "While the Court can take judicial notice of the Educational Improvement act of 1992... [a]t the time of the trial of the case, the BEP had been proposed, but had not been enacted or funded. Funding, of course is crucial; an educational plan heavily dependent on additional funding provides little support for the defendants' contention that the public school system meets constitutional requirements" (quoted in Meyer et al., 1995, pp. 405–406).
5. "[The current] year's estimates of previous years' gains may have changed as a result of incorporating the most recent student data. Re-estimating all years in the current year with the newest data available provides the most precise and reliable information for any year and subject/grade combination. Find district and school information at the following: TVAAS Public https://tvaas.sas.com/evaas/public_welcome.jsp, TVAAS Restricted: https://tvass.sas.com/evaas.jsp" (Eckert & Dabrowski, 2010, p. 90).
6. Currently, Scotts Hill Elementary and Scotts Hill High School have been assigned to Henderson County and are no longer recognized schools in Decatur County.
7. Characteristics of this model are described in the 2004 RAND Report, *Models for Value-Added Modeling of Teacher Effects,* published in the Journal of Educational and Behavioral Statistics. RAND researchers, McCaffrey, Lockwood, and Hamilton collaborated with Koretz, Harvard Graduate School of Education, and Louis, from the Johns Hopkins Bloomberg School of Public Health. This report provides additional evidence that *who* is assigned to the teacher's classroom makes a difference in the outcome of teacher effectiveness. The authors concluded that the teacher effect data are reasonable estimates of student academic achievement "when all the schools in the sample serve similar student populations. However, student characteristics are likely to confound estimated teacher effects when schools serve distinctly different populations" making it very difficult to determine if it is the student background characteristics or the teacher that is having an impact on student learning (p. 67).
8. Tracking is a process used to group students of similar ability for an instructional purpose. An example would be grouping high performing math students in sixth grade who are on track to take Algebra I in eighth grade versus 9th grade. In a middle school schedule, this grouping often results in these same students being grouped together for other academic subjects as well.
9. The group included Jesse Rothstein (University of California-Berkeley), Linda Darling-Hammond (Stanford University, Stanford Center for Opportu-

nity Policy in Education), and Edward H. Haertel (Chair, National Research Council Board on Testing and Assessment).

10. The study was conducted under best case scenario conditions by restricting data to a sample of teachers who each taught at least 15 students per class in public elementary school self-contained classrooms or who taught middle school students who were taking only one math class per year. The students had no data missing (pp. 583–584).
11. The Sanders model incorporates multiple years of student test data to project what the expected academic gain score is for each student. The expected score is compared to the actual score in determining teacher value-added scores.
12. This information was gathered from the Office of Education Research and Accountability (2004) and the Tennessee State Budgets from 2004–2011.)
13. The changes to the mathematics framework introduced in 2005 for grades 4 and 8 were minimal, which allowed for the continued reporting of results from previous assessments beginning with 1990.
14. The reading framework was updated in 2009. Results from special analyses determined the 2009 and subsequent reading assessment results could be compared with those from earlier assessment years (NAEP, 2011, http://nces.ed.gov/nationsreportcard).

Part 4

1. In 2010, for instance, the KIPP charter school chain received a 50 million dollar grant to help expand the corporation's number of charters by 50%, and in 2011, the Washington, DC KIPP franchise garnered a Race the Top grant worth $10 million.
2. Examples abound, but two of the most active think tanks devoted to the conservative wing of the corporate education agenda are the Manhattan Institute and Fordham Institute. On the neoliberal side of corporate education reform agenda are Education Sector and the Education Trust). Spokespersons for these think tanks have been extremely successful in inserting their positions in newspaper stories on education issues, and reporters often quote these advocates as independent research voices.
3. The term, "corp member," comes from Teach for America (TFA), a nonprofit corporation that has received, since 1991, large infusions of money from private and public sources to send college graduates, largely White and female, into the most challenging teaching environments in America to serve two year stints. Former TFA teachers most often refer to themselves as "former Corps members."
4. Both Commissioner Kevin Huffman and Achievement School District Superintendent, Chris Barbic, have deep connections with corporate education reform. Huffman is former TFA "corp member" and executive in TFA, and Barbic is the former CEO of Uncommon Schools, one of the most popular and well-funded corporate reform charter school chains in the United States
5. As noted in earlier chapters, the power of shared social capital has been known since it was documented in the Coleman Report in 1966. Two recent treatments of the benefits of integration based on socioeconomic status are

Gerald Grant's (2009) *Hope and despair in the American city: Why there are no bad schools in Raleigh,* and a volume edited by Richard Kahlenberg (2012): *The future of school integration: Diversity as an education reform strategy.*

6. Even by the College Board's (Lewin, 2008) own estimate, student grades assigned by teachers in high school are better predictors of how students will do in college than high stakes tests like the SAT [http://www.nytimes.com/2008/06/18/education/18sat.html?ref=education&_r=0].

References

ACT, Inc. (1994). *1994 ACT Composite averages by state.* Retrieved from http://www.act.org/newsroom/data/1994/states.html

ACT, Inc. (2009). *ACT: The first fifty years, 1959–2009.* Retrieved from http://media.act.org/documents/ACT_History.pdf

ACT, Inc. (2011). *WorkKeys® skills assessment system.* Retrieved from http://www.act.org/newsroom/factsheets/workkeys.html

ACT, Inc. (2012). *2012 ACT National and state scores* [Data file]. Retrieved from http://www.act.org/newsroom/data/2012/states.html

Advancement Project. (2010). *Test, punish, and push out: How zero tolerance and high stakes testing funnel youth into the school-to-prison pipeline.* Washington, DC: Advancement Project. Retrieved from http://www.advancementproject.org/resources/entry/test-punish-and-push-out-how-zero-tolerance-and-high-stakes-testing-funnel

Aizer, A., Gold, M., & Shcoen, C. (1999). *Managed care and low-income populations: Four years' experience with TennCare.* Washington DC: The Kaiser Family Foundation. Retrieved from http://www.commonwealthfund.org/~/media/Files/Publications/Fund%20Report/1999/May/Managed%20Care%20and%20Low%20Income%20Populations%20%20Four%20Years%20Experience%20with%20Tenncare/aizer_tenncare_4yexperience_403%20pdf.pdf

Alapo, L. (2010, July 28). Proposed 'cut scores' for Tennessee students to get look. *Knoxville News Sentinel.* Retrieved from http://www.knoxnews.com/news/2010/jul/28/proposed-cut-scores-tennessee-students-get-look/

Alexander, K. (1997). Public schools and the public good. *Social Forces, 76*(1), 1–30.

Alexander, K., & Salmon, R. G. (1995). *Public school finance.* Boston, MA: Allyn & Bacon.

The Mismeasure of Education, pages 233–260

Alexander, M. (2010). *The new Jim Crow: Mass incarceration in the age of colorblindness.* New York, NY: The New Press.

Allen, G. (1986). The Eugenics Record Office at Cold Springs Harbor, 1910–1940: An essay in institutional history. *Osiris, 2*, 225–264.

Almy, S., & Theokas, C. (2010). *Not prepared for class: High-poverty schools continue to have fewer in-field teachers.* Retrieved from http://www.edtrust.org/sites/edtrust.org/files/publications/files/Not%20Prepared%20for%20Class.pdf

Amrein-Beardsley, A. (2008). Methodological concerns about the Education Value-Added Assessment System. *Educational Researcher, 37*(2), 65–75. doi: 10.3102/0013189X08316420

Amrein-Beardsley, A., & Collins, C. (2012). The SAS Education Value-Added Assessment System (SAS® EVAAS®) in the Houston Independent School District (HISD): Intended and unintended consequences. *Education Policy Analysis Archives, 20* (12). Retrieved from http://epaa.asu.edu/ojs/article/view/1096

An unfair school system and an unfair tax system. (1988, July 13). *Nashville Tennessean*, p. A8.

Anderson, J. (1988). *The education of Blacks in the South, 1860–1935.* Chapel Hill, NC: University of North Carolina Press.

Anderson, L. W., & Krathwohl, D. R., (Eds.). (2001) *A taxonomy for learning, teaching and assessing: A revision of Bloom's Taxonomy of educational objectives* (Complete edition). New York : Longman.

The Annie E. Casey Foundation. (2013). *2012 kids count data book: National and state-by-state data on key indicators of child well-being* (Tennessee state profile). Retrieved from http://datacenter.kidscount.org/DataBook/2012/Default.aspx

Anyon, J. (1997). *Ghetto schooling: A political economy of urban education reform.* New York, NY: Teachers College Press.

Aronson, J., Quinn, D., & Spencer, S. (1998). Stereotype threat and the academic underperformance of minorities and women. In J. K. Swim & C. Stangor (Eds.), *Prejudice: The target's perspective* (pp. 83–103). San Diego, CA: Academic.

Assembly to consider funding $400 million education program. (1989, September 25). *Nashville Banner*, p. B1.

Aud, S., Fox, M., & KewalRamani, A. (2010). *Status and trends in the education of racial and ethnic groups* (NCES 2010-015). U.S. Department of Education, National Center for Education Statistics. Washington, DC: U.S. Government Printing Office. Retrieved from http://www.air.org/files/AIR-NCESracial_stats__trends1.pdf

Ayres, L. (1909). *Laggards in our schools: A study of retardation and elimination in city school systems.* New York, NY: Charities Publication Committee.

Bach, D. (2004, April 26). Researcher blasts No Child Left Behind and vouchers. *Seattle Post-Intelligencer.* Retrieved from http://seattlepi.nwsource.com/local/170797_ecenter27.html

Bahena, S., Cooc, N., Currie-Rubin, R., & Kuttner, P. (Eds.). (2012). *Disrupting the school-to-prison pipeline.* Cambridge, MA: Harvard Educational Review.

Balfanz, R., Bridgeland, J. M., Bruce, M., & Fox, J. H. (2012). *Building a grad nation: Progress and challenge in ending the high school dropout epidemic.* A report by Civic Enterprises, Everyone Graduates Center at Johns Hopkins University, America's Promise Alliance, & Alliance for Excellent Education. Retrieved from http://www.americaspromise.org/~/media/Files/Our%20Work/Grad%20Nation/Building%20a%20Grad%20Nation/BuildingAGradNation2012.ashx

Ballou, D. (2002). Sizing up test scores. *Education Next.* Retrieved from www.educationnext.org

Ballou, D. (2005). *Value-added assessment: Lessons from Tennessee.* Retrieved from http://dpi.state.nc.us/docs/superintendents/quarterly/2010-11/20100928/ballou-lessons.pdf

Ballou, D., Sanders, W., & Wright, P. (2004). Controlling for student background in value added assessment of teachers. *Journal of Educational and Behavioral Statistics, 29*(1), 37–66. Retrieved from: http://www.jstor.org/stable/3701306

Baker, A., Xu, D., & Detch, E. (1995). The measure of education: A review of the Tennessee value added assessment system. Nashville, TN: Comptroller of the Treasury, Office of Education Accountability Report.

Baker, B. (2013, January 9). Gates still doesn't get it! Trapped in a world of circular reasoning. [Web log post]. Retrieved from http://schoolfinance101.wordpress.com/2013/01/09/gates-still-doesnt-get-it-trapped-in-a-world-of-circular-reasoning-flawed-frameworks/.

Baker, B., Sciarra, D., & Farrie, D. (2012). *Is school funding fair? A national report card* (2nd edition). Retrieved from http://www.schoolfundingfairness.org/National_Report_Card_2012.pdf

Baker, E. (1994). Educational reform through national standards and assessment. *American Journal of Education, 102*(4), 450–477.

Baker, J. (2011, September). King of the hill: Don Sundquist at a distance. *Memphis Magazine.* Retrieved from http://www.memphismagazine.com/Memphis-Magazine/September-2011/King-of-the-HillDon-Sundquist-at-a-Distance

Baker, K. (1991). Yes, throw money at schools. *Phi Delta Kappan, 72*(8), 4–6.

Barone, C. (2007). *Keeping achievement relevant: The reauthorization of 'No Child Left Behind.'* New York, NY: Democrats for Education Reform.

Barone, C. (2009, March). *Are we there yet?: What policymakers can learn from Tennessee's growth model* [Technical Report]. Washington, DC: Education Sector.

Barton, P. F., & Coley, R. J. (2010, July). *The black-white achievement gap: When progress stopped* [Policy Information Report]. Princeton, NJ: Educational Testing Service. Retrieved from http://www.ets.org/Media/Research/pdf/PICBWGAP.pdf

Bateson, G. (1972). *Steps to an ecology of mind: Collected essays in anthropology, psychiatry, evolution, and epistemology.* Chicago: University of Chicago Press.

Bateson, G. (1979). *Mind and nature: A necessary unity (Advances in Systems Theory, Complexity, and the Human Sciences).* New York, NY: Hampton Press.

Bellon report. (1988, April). *TEA News.*

Berliner, D., & Biddle, B. (1995). *The manufactured crisis: Myths, fraud, and the attack on America's public schools.* Reading, MA: Addison-Wesley.

Bestor, A. (1953/1985). *Educational wastelands: The retreat from learning in our public schools.* Urbana, IL: University of Illinois Press.

Betebenner, D. (2004). An analysis of school district data using value-added methodology (CSE Report 622). Retrieved from www.cse.ucla.edu/products/reports/r622.pdf

Beverley, R. (1722). *Of the servants and slaves of Virginia* (2nd ed). National Humanities Center. Retrieved from http://nationalhumanitiescenter.org/pds/amerbegin/power/text8/BeverlyServSlaves.pdf

Black, E. (2003). *War against the weak: Eugenics and America's campaign to create a master race.* New York, NY: Four Walls Eight Windows.

Bloom, B. (Ed.). (1956). *Taxonomy of educational objectives* (Book 1 Cognitive Domain). White Plains, NY: Longman.

Bobbitt, J. (1918). *The curriculum.* New York, NY: Houghton Mifflin.

Bock, R., & Wolfe, R. (1996, Jan. 23). *Audit and review of the Tennessee value-added assessment system (TVAAS): Preliminary report.* Nashville, TN: Comptroller of the Treasury, Office of Education Accountability Report.

Bracey, J. (2004). *Setting the record straight: Responses to misconceptions about public schools in the U. S.* (2nd ed.). Portsmouth, NH: Heinemann.

Bracey, J. (2009). *Education hell: Rhetoric vs. reality.* Alexandria, VA: Education Research Service.

Bradley, A. (1990, March 7). Tennessee reform program advances. *Education Week.* Retrieved from http://www.edweek.org/ew/articles/1990/03/07/09290053.h09.html

Braun, H. (2005). *Using student progress to evaluate teachers* (Policy Information Perspective). Retrieved from http://www.ets.org/Media/Research/pdf/PICVAM.pdf

Briggs, D., Weeks, J., & Wiley, E. (2008, April). *The sensitivity of value-added modeling to the creation of a vertical scale score.* Paper presented at the National Conference on Value-Added Modeling, Madison, WI. Retrieved from http://academiclanguag.wceruw.org/news/events/VAM%20Conference%20Final%20Papers/SensitivityOfVAM_BriggsWeeksWiley.pdf

The Bureau of TennCare. (2003, July 15). *TennCare Quarterly Report.* Nashville, TN: The Bureau of TennCare. Retrieved from http://www.tn.gov/tenncare/forms/leg0703.pdf

Bushaw, W., & McKee, J. (2009, September). The 41st PDK/Gallup Poll of the public attitudes toward the public schools. *The Phi Delta Kappan, 91*(1).

Callahan, R. E. (1962). *Education and the cult of efficiency: A study of the social forces that have shaped the administration of the public schools.* Chicago: The University of Chicago Press.

Carnoy, M., & Loeb, S. (2002). Does external accountability affect student outcomes? A cross-state analysis. *Educational Evaluation and Policy Analysis. 24*(4), 305–331. Retrieved from http://cepa.stanford.edu/sites/default/files/Does%20External%20Aaccountability%20affect%20student%20outcomes.pdf

Carnoy, M., & Rothstein, R. (2013). What do international tests really show us about U.S. student performance. Washington, DC: Economic Policy Institute. Retrieved from http://www.epi.org

Center for Business and Economic Research. (2003). Net enrollment, average daily membership, average daily attendance in public schools, Tennessee, selected scholastic years ending 1950–2001. In *Tennessee Statistical Abstract: 2003.* (p. 16.1). Knoxville, TN: University of Tennessee . Retrieved from http://cber.utk.edu/tsa/tsa03/ch16.pdf

Center for Business and Economic Research. (2005). *Education Crossroads.* Retrieved from http://educationcrossroads.utk.edu/Chapters/Foundation.pdf

Center for Business and Economic Research. (2007). *Education crossroads: Opportunities for you, me, and Tennessee.* Knoxville, TN: University of Tennessee. Retrieved from http://cber.utk.edu/tsa/tsa03/ch16.pdf

Center for Media and Democracy. (2012, April 17). *ALEC disbands task force responsible for stand you ground, voter ID, prison privatization, AZ's SB 1070.* Retrieved from http://www.prwatch.org/news/2012/04/11454/alec-disbands-task-force-responsible-stand-your-ground-voter-id-prison-privatizat

Chang, C. F. (2007, November). Evolution of TennCare yields valuable lessons [Electronic version]. *Managed Care 16* (11), 45–49.

Chang, C. F., & Steinberg, S. C. (2009, January). *TennCare timeline: Major events and milestones from 1992 to 2009.* Retrieved from http://healthecon.memphis.edu/

Change.gov. (2008). *President-Elect Obama nominates Arne Duncan as Secretary of Education.* Change.org. Retrieved from http://change.gov/newsroom/entry/president_elect_obama_nominates_arne_duncan_as_secretary_of_education/

Chantrill, C. (2013). Tennessee State 2010 spending by function [Data file]. Retrieved from http://www.usgovernmentspending.com/state_spending_2010TNrn

Chesteen, R. D. (1998). The Tennessee prison system: A study of evolving public policy in state corrections. In J. R. Vile & M. Byrnes (Eds.), *Tennessee government and politics: Democracy in the Volunteer State* (pp. 167–181). Nashville, TN: Vanderbilt University Press.

Cheung, A. (2004, September). *Prison privatization and the use of incarceration.* The Sentencing Project, Washington, DC. Retrieved from http://www.sentencingproject.org/search/search.cfm?search_string=Cheung

Chira, S. (1992). Whittle's school unit gains prestige and pressure. *New York Times.* Retrieved from http://www.nytimes.com/1992/05/27/education/whittle-s-school-unit-gains-prestige-and-pressure.html

Coleman. J. S. (1972). Coleman on the Coleman Report. *Educational Researcher, 1*(3), 13–14.

Coleman, J. S., Campbell, E., Hobson, C., McPartland, J., Mood, F., Weinfeld, F., et al. (1966). *Equality of educational opportunity.* Washington, DC: U.S. Government Printing Office.

College Board. (2009). *2009 college bound seniors: Total group profile report.* New York, NY: College Board. Retrieved from http://professionals.collegeboard.com/profdownload/cbs-2009-national-TOTAL-GROUP.pdf

Columbia Documents. (n.d). *Letter from Columbia College Dean Herbert Hawkes to Professor E. B. Wilson, June 9, 1922.* Retrieved from http://beatl.barnard.columbia.edu/learn/2008/DocumentsReadings/ColumbiaDocuments/ColumbiaDocuments/HHawkes1922.htm

Comprehensive Education Reform Act, *Tennessee Public Acts,* Chapter No. 7, pp. 20–65 (1984).

Conant, J. (1940). Education for a classless society: The Jeffersonian tradition. *The Atlantic Online.* Retrieved from http://www.theatlantic.com/past/docs/issues/95sep/ets/edcla.htm

Conant, J. (1943). Wanted: American radicals. *The Atlantic Online.* Retrieved from http://www.theatlantic.com/past/docs/issues/95sep/ets/radical.htm

Conant Suggests GI Bill Revision. (1945). *Harvard Crimson.* Retrieved from http://www.thecrimson.com/article/1945/1/23/conant-suggests-gi-bill-revision-pentering/

Conover, C., & Davis, H. (2000, February). The role of TennCare in health policy for low-income people in Tennessee, Occasional Paper No. 33. Retrieved from http://www.urban.org/PDF/occa33.pdf

Corcoran, S., Jennings, J., & Beveridge, A. (2011). *Teacher effectiveness on high- and low stakes tests.* Retrieved from https://files.nyu.edu/sc129/public/papers/corcoran_jennings_beveridge_2011_wkg_teacher_effects.pdf

Corrections Corporation of America. *About CCA.* Retrieved from http://www.cca.com/about

Cour, K. (2002). *Multiple choices: Testing students in Tennessee.* Nashville, TN: Tennessee Comptroller of the Treasury, Office of Education Accountability Report.

CREDO. (2009). *Multiple choice: Charter school performance in 16 states.* Stanford, CA: Center for Research on Education Outcomes. Retrieved from http://credo.stanford.edu/reports/MULTIPLE_CHOICE_CREDO.pdf http://credo.stanford.edu

Cubberley, E. (1922). *A brief history of education: A history of the practice and progress and organization of education.* New York, NY: Houghton Mifflin.

Darnell, R. (1995–96). *Tennessee blue book: Bicentennial edition (1796–1996).* Nashville, TN: State Government Publication.

Dawley, A. (1993). *Struggle for justice: Social responsibility and the liberal state.* Cambridge, MA: Harvard University Press.

Debray, E. (2006). *Politics, ideology, & education: Federal policy during the Bush and Clinton administrations.* New York, NY: Teachers College Press.

de Vise, D. (2012, March 16). College accountability: A closer look. *Washington Post.* Retrieved from http://www.washingtonpost.com/blogs/college-inc/post/college-accountability-a-closer-look/2012/03/16/gIQAECG7GS_blog.html

Dewey, J. (1897, January 16). My pedagogic creed. *School Journal, 54*(3), 77–80. Retrieved from http://dewey.pragmatism.org/creed.htm

Dewey, J. (1907). *The school and society.* Chicago: University of Chicago Press.

Dewey, J. (1938). *Experience and education.* New York, NY: Touchstone.

Di Carlo, M. (2011). Explaining the inconsistent results of charter schools. *Shanker blog: The voice of the Albert Shanker Institute.* Retrieved from http://shankerblog.org/?p=4229

Dillon, S. (2009, October 27). After complaints. Gates Foundation opens education aid offer to all states. *New York Times.* Retrieved from http://www.nytimes.com/2009/10/28/education/28educ.html

Dillon, S. (2011, August 8). Overriding a key education law. *New York Times.* Retrieved from http://www.nytimes.com/2011/08/08/education/08educ.html?pagewanted=all

Dorn, S. (2007). Accountability Frankenstein: Understanding and taming the monster. Charlotte, NC: Information Age Publishing.

Dreyfus, S., & Dreyfus, H. (1980). A five-stage model of the mental activities involved in directed skill acquisition. Washington, DC: Storming Media.

Dreyfus, H, & Dreyfus, S. (1986). *Mind over machine: the power of human intuitive expertise in the era of the computer.* New York, NY: Free Press.

Dungca, N. (2013, February 1). Portland Public Schools students push standardized test boycott. *The Oregonian.* Retrieved from http://www.oregonlive.com/portland/index.ssf/2013/02/portland_public_schools_studen_1.html

Dunn, M., Kadane, J., & Garrow, J. (2003). Comparing harm done by mobility and class absence: Missing students and missing data. *Journal of Educational and Behavioral Statistics, 28,* 269–288.

Eckert, J. M., & Dabrowski, J. (2010). Should value-added measures be used for performance pay [online exclusive]? *Phi Delta Kappan, 91*(8), 88–92. Retrieved from www.pdkintl.org

Economic Policy Council. (2010, August). *Problems with the use of student test scores to evaluate teachers* (Issue Brief #278). Washington, DC: Baker, E. L., Barton, P. E., Darling-Hammond, L., Haertel, E., Ladd, H. F., Linn, R. L., Ravitch, D., Rothstein, R., Shavelson, R. J., & Shepard, L. A.

Edmiston, K. D., & Murray, M. N. (1998). Finances of Tennessee state government. In J. R. Vile & M. Byrnes (Eds.), *Tennessee government and politics: Democracy in the Volunteer State* (pp. 197–198). Nashville, TN: Vanderbilt University Press.

The Educational Improvement Act, *Tennessee Public Acts,* Chapter No. 535, pp. 19–49 (1992).

Elementary and Secondary Education Act of 1965, Pub. L. 89–10, 79 Stat. 27, 20 U.S.C. ch. 70.

Elmore, R., & McLaughlin, M. (1982). Strategic choice in federal education policy: The compliance-assistance trade-off. In A. Lieberman and M. McLaughlin (Eds.), *Policy Making in Education*, (pp. 159–194). Chicago: The University of Chicago Press.

Everhart, R. B. (Ed.). (1982). *The public school monopoly: A critical analysis of education and the state of American society.* San Francisco: Pacific Institute for Public Policy Research.

Faux, J. (2012). Education profiteering; Wall Street's next big thing? *Huffington Post.* Retrieved from http://www.huffingtonpost.com/jeff-faux/education-wall-street_b_1919727.html

Fingeroot, L. (2012, September 11). Metro defies state, denies Great Hearts. *Nashville Tennessean.* Retrieved from http://www.tennessean.com/article/20120911/NEWS04/309110094/Metro-defies-state-denies-Great-Hearts

Fisher, T. (1996, January). A review and analysis of the Tennessee value-added assessment system. Nashville, TN: Tennessee Comptroller of the Treasury, Office of Education Accountability Report.

Florida Senate Website Archive. (2000–2013). *The 2010 Florida statutes (including Special Session A).* Retrieved from http://archive.flsenate.gov/Statutes/index.cfm?App_mode=Display_Statute&Search_String=&URL=1000-1099/1000/Sections/1000.02.html

Flyvbjerg, B. (2001). *Making social science matter: Why social inquiry fails and how to make it succeed again.* Cambridge: Cambridge University Press.

Forster, E. M. (1927/1956). *Aspects of the nowel.* New York, NY: Harvest. novel-http://books.google.com/books?id=FLS1tVUXawC&q=stupider#v=onepage&q=stupider&f=false

Frankenberg, E., Siegel-Hawley, G., & Wang, J. (2010). *Choice without equity: Charter school segregation and the need for civil rights standard.* Retrieved from http://civilrightsproject.ucla.edu/research/k-12-education/integration-and-diversity/choice-without-equity-2009-report/

Freire, P. (1971/2000). *Pedagogy of the oppressed* (30th Anniversary ed.). New York, NY: Bloomsbury Academic.

French, R. L. (1984/1985). Dispelling the myths about Tennessee's Career Ladder Program [Electronic version]. *Educational Leadership, 42*(4), 9–15.

Full new funding for state schools may take time. (1988, Nov. 18). *Nashville Banner,* p. B1.

Gabe, T. (2012). *Poverty in the United States: 2011.* Washington, DC: Congressional Research Service.

Gabriel, T., & Medina, J. (2010, May 10). Charter schools' new cheerleaders: Financiers. *New York Times.* Retrieved from http://www.nytimes.com/2010/05/10/nyregion/10charter.html?pagewanted=all&_r=0

Gamoran, A., & Long, D. (2006). *'Equality of Educational Opportunity': A 40-year perspective.* Madison, WI: Wisconsin Center for Educational Research.

Gardner, H. (1991). *The unschooled mind: How children think and how schools should teach.* New York, NY: Basic Books.

Garrison, J. (2013, February 12). State charter authorizer bill singles out Nashville, Memphis. *Nashville Tennessean.* Retrieved from (http://www.tennessean.com/article/20130212/NEWS02/302120076/State-charter-authorizer-bill-singles-out-Nashville-Memphis

Getting teacher evaluation right: A challenge for policy makers: An AERA-NAEd research briefing before the U. S. Senate Committee on Health, Education, Labor & Pensions [Slides 53–68], 112th Cong. (2011, September 14) (testimony of Audrey Amrein-Beardsley). Retrieved from http://legacy.aera.net/uploadedFiles/Gov_Relations/AERA%20-%20NAE%20briefing%20_%20Combined%20Slides%20(9-20).pdf Amrein-Beardsley

Glass, G. (1972). The many faces of 'educational accountability.' *The Phi Delta Kappan, 53*(10), 636–639.

Glass, G. (1994, December 10). Re: Fairness of value-added ratings for teachers in unequal circumstances [Online forum comment]. Retrieved from http://gvglass.info/TVAAS/

Glazerman, S., & Max, J. (2011, April). *Do low income students have equal access to the highest performing teachers?* (NCEE Evaluation Brief). Washington, DC: Institute of Education Sciences, National Center for Education Evaluation and Regional Assistance. Retrieved from http://ies.ed.gov/ncee/pubs/20114016/pdf/20114016.pdf

Goals 2000: Educate America Act, 20 U.S.C. § 5801 (Supp. 1994).

Goldhaber, D. (2002). The mystery of good teaching [Electronic version]. *Education next, 2*(1), para 8.

Goldhaber, D., & Chaplin, D. (2011). *Assessing the "Rothstein Falsification Test." Does it really show teacher value-added models are biased?* (CEDR Working Paper 2011-5). Retrieved from http://www.cedr.us/publications_teacherq.html

Goldhaber, D., Liddle, S., Theobald, R., & Walch, J. (2010). *Teacher effectiveness and the achievement of Washington students in mathematics* (Working paper no. 2010-6.0). Seattle, WA: University of Washington, Center for Education Data & Research. Retrieved from http://www.cedr.us/publications.html

Gonzalez, T. (2012, July 17). TN education reform hits bump in teacher evaluation. *The Tennessean.* Retrieved from http://www.wbir.com/news/article/226990/0/TN-education-reform-hits-bump-in-teacher-evaluation

Goodlad, J. (1975). A perspective on accountability. *The Phi Delta Kappan, 57*(2), 108–112.

Goodlad, J. (1992). On taking school reform seriously. *The Phi Delta Kappan, 74*(3), 232–238.

Gould, S. J. (1996). *The mismeasure of man* (revised ed.). New York, NY: W. W. Norton.

Governor's Communication Office. (2007, September). Bredesen addresses United States Chamber of Commerce Institute for a Competitive Workforce summit (speech). Washington, D. C. Retrieved from http://media.timesfreepress.com/pdf/2007/sept/bredesen_commerce_0926.pdf

Grant, G. (2009). *Hope and despair in the American city: Why there are no bad schools in Raleigh.* Cambridge, MA: Harvard University Press.

Green, E. (2011, Februrary 14). A new graduate school of education, Relay, to open next fall. *Gotham Schools.* Retrieved from http://gothamschools.org/2011/02/14/a-new-graduate-school-of-education-relay-to-open-next-fall/

Green, H., Smith, C., & S. Hydorn. (1995, June). *Funding Tennessee schools: From reform to restructuring.* Tennessee Advisory Commission on Intergovernmental Relations Report. Nashville, TN: TACIR.

Grounard, D. J. (2006). *At the intersection of political culture and the policy process: An evolution of the Tennessee Value-Added Assessment System through the Tennessee Legislature.* Unpublished doctoral dissertation. Virginia Polytechnic Institute and State University–Blacksburg.

Guarino, C., Reckase, M., & Wooldrigde, J. (2011, April 23). *Can value-added measures of teacher performance be trusted?* (Working paper #18). East Lansing, IL: Michigan State University, The Education Policy Center. Retrieved from http://education.msu.edu/epc/library/documents/Guarino-Reckase-Wooldridge-2011-Value-Added-Measures-v2.pdf

Haag, M. (2012, February 16). Would giving poor students more books solve the achievement gap? *Dallas Morning News.* Retrieved from http://education blog.dallasnews.com/tag/stephen-krashen/

Hall, C., & Thomas, S. (2012). *'Advocacy philanthropy' and the public policy agenda: The role of modern foundations in American higher education.* Paper presented at the Annual Meeting of the American Educational Research Association, Vancouver, Canada, April 2012.

Hall, G. S. (1904). *Adolescence: Its psychology and its relations to physiology, anthropology, sociology, and education, Volume 2.* New York, NY: Appleton.

Halsall, P. (1997). *Modern history sourcebook: Herbert Spencer: Social Darwinism, 1857.* Retrieved from http://www.pbs.org/wgbh/amex/carnegie/people events/pande03.html

Haney, W., & Raczek, A. (1994). *Surmounting outcomes accountability in education.* Chestnut Hill, MA: Center for the study of testing, evaluation, and educational policy. Retrieved from http://digilib.bc.edu/reserves/ed466/hane/ed46603.pdf

Harris, D. (2010). Clear away the smoke and mirrors of value-added. *Phi Delta Kappan, 91*(8), 66–69. Retrieved from www.pdkintl.org

Harris, D., & Sass, T. (2009, September). *What makes for a good teacher and who can tell?* (Working paper No. 30). Washington DC: The Urban Institute, National Center for Analysis of Longitudinal Data in Education Research (CALDER).

Haycock, K. (1998). Good teaching matters ... a lot. *Thinking K–16, 3*(2), 3–14.

Heher, A. (2004). TennCare revam faced shortfall: Governor declares health plan negotiations at an impasse, delays further action for a week. *Chattanooga Times Free Press.* Retrieved February from http://www.tnjustice.org/wp-content/uploads/2011/01/Chatt-TFP-article-re-budget-shortfall.pdf

Helms, A. (2012, December 21. Morrison: New state tests waste tax dollars. *Charlotte Observer.* Retrieved from http://www.charlotteobserver.com/2012/12/21/3739031/morrison-177-state-tests-waste.html#storylink=cpy

Henderson, C., Jr., & Henderson, C. (1979). Analysis of covariance in mixed models with unequal subclass numbers. *Communications in Statistics-Theory and Methods, 8*(8), 751–787

Heubert, J., & Hauser, R. (Eds.). 1999. *High stakes: Testing for tracking, promotion, and graduation.* Washington, DC: National Academies Press. Retrieved from http://www.nap.edu/catalog.php?record_id=6336

Hofstadter, R. (1955). *Social Darwinism in American thought, 1860–1915* (rev. ed). Boston: Beacon Press.

Horn, J. (2005, August 8). Jeb Bush and "integrity that is unquestioned" [Web log post]. Retrieved from http://www.schoolsmatter.info/2005/08/jeb-bush-and-integrity-that-is.html

Horn, J. (2007). The LEAP for accountability? Ideology and practice of testing in a Louisiana urban elementary school. In M. Brown, Ed.), *Still not equal: Expanding educational opportunity in society* (pp. 111–143). New York, NY: Peter Lang.

Horn, J. (2010). *Ten years after the LEAP: How long does it take to hit rock bottom?* Paper presented at the 19th Annual National Evaluation Institute. Williamsburg, Virginia, October 7–9, 2010.

Horn, J. (2011). Corporatism KIPP, and cultural eugenics. In P. Kovacs, (Ed.), *The Gates Foundation and the future of U. S. 'public schools'* (pp. 80–103). New York, NY: Routledge.

Horn, J., & Libby, K. (2011). The giving business: The New Schools Venture Fund. In P. Kovacs, (Ed.), *The Gates Foundation and the future of U. S. 'public schools'* (pp. 168–185). New York, NY: Routledge.

Humphreys, T. (2010, January 17). Humphrey: Education reform walked legislative hallways. *Knoxville News Sentinel.* Retrieved from http://www.knoxnews.com/news/2010/jan/17/education-reform-walked-legislative-hallways/

Hunter, G. (1914). *A civic biology: Presented in problems.* New York, NY: American Book Company.

Hunter, G., & Whitman, W. (1922). *Civic science in the community.* New York, NY: American Book Company.

Hunter, G, & Whitman, W. (1935). *Science and our world of progress.* New York, NY: American Book Company.

Hunter, M. (1982). *Master teaching: Increasing instructional effectiveness in elementary and secondary schools, colleges, and universities.* Thousand Oaks, CA: Corwin Press, Inc.

Institute on Taxation & Economic Policy. (2009, November). *Tennessee: State & local taxes in 2007.* Retrieved from http://www.itepnet.org/wp2009/tn_whopays_factsheet.pdf

Jacob, B., Lefgren, L., & Sims, D. (2008, June). *The persistence of teacher-induced learning gains* (Working Paper 14065). Retrieved from http://www.nber.org/papers/w14065

Jefferson, T. (1787/1853). *Notes on the State of Virginia.* Richmond, VA: J. W. Randolph. Retrieved from http://books.google.com/books/about/Notes_on_the_State_of_Virginia.html?id=DTWttRSMtbYC

Jennings, J. (1992). Lessons learned in Washington, D.C. *The Phi Delta Kappan, 74*(4), 303–307.

Johnson, A. (2001). *Privilege, power, and difference.* New York, NY: McGraw Hill.

Jones, J. (2012, August 6). Road to the top 25 percent begins today—ASD update. *ASD News.* Retrieved from http://www.achievementschooldistrict.org/road-to-the-top-25-percent-begins-today/

Kaestle, C. (1983). *Pillars of the republic: Common schools and American society, 1780–1860.* New York, NY: Macmillan.

Kahlenberg, R. (2001, Summer). Learning from James Coleman. *The Public Interest, 144,* 54–72.

Kane, T., & Staiger, D. (2001, August 13). Rigid rules will damage schools. *New York Times.* Retrieved from http://www.nytimes.com/2001/08/13/opinion/rigid-rules-will-damage-schools.html

Kantor, H. (1991). Education, social reform, and the state: ESEA and federal education policy in the 1960s. *American Journal of Education, 100*(1), 47–83.

Kantor, H., & Lowe, R. (1995). Class, race, and the emergence of federal education policy: From the New Deal to the Great Society. *Educational Researcher, 24*(3), 4–21.

Karier, C. (1983, Spring). G. Stanley Hall: A priestly prophet of a new dispensation. *Journal of Libertarian Studies, 3*(1), 35–60.

Kenrick, C. (2011). Stanford dean shares research on 'stereotype threat.' *Palo Alto News Online.* Retrieved from http://www.paloaltoonline.com/news/show_story.php?id=23064

Keese, N. (1990). *Educational decision making in the Tennessee state legislature.* Unpublished doctoral dissertation. The University of Tennessee—Knoxville.

Keese, N., & Huffman, J. (1998). Education in the Volunteer State. In J. R. Vile & M. Byrnes (Eds.), *Tennessee government and politics: Democracy in the Volunteer State* (pp. 151–166). Nashville, TN: Vanderbilt University Press.

Keveles, D. (1998). *In the name of eugenics: Genetics and the uses of human heredity.* Cambridge, MA: Harvard University Press.

Kliebard, H. (2004). *The struggle for the American curriculum, 1893–1958* (3rd ed.). New York, NY: RoutledgeFalmer.

Koedel, C., & Betts, J. (2009, July). *Does student sorting invalidate value-added models of teacher effectiveness? An extended analysis of the Rothstein critique.* Retrieved from http://economics.missouri.edu/working-papers/2009/WP0902_koedel.pdf

Ku, L., & Wachino, V. (2004, November 15). *The potential impact of eliminating TennCare and reverting to Medicaid: A preliminary analysis* (A Center on

Budget and Policy Priorities Report). Retrieved from http://www.cbpp.org/cms/index.cfm?fa=view&id=1384

Kupermintz, H. (2003). Teacher effects and teacher effectiveness: A validity investigation of the Tennessee Value Added Assessment System. *Educational Evaluation and Policy Analysis, 25*(3), 287–298.

Kupermintz, H., Shepard, L., & Linn, R. (2001, April). Teacher effects as a measure of teacher effectiveness: Construct validity considerations in TVAAS (Tennessee Value Added Assessment System). In D. Koretz (Chair), *New work on the evaluation of high-stakes testing programs.* Symposium conducted at the meeting of National Council on Measurement in Education (NCME) Annual Meeting, Seattle, WA.

Kyle, J. (1998, August). The privatization debate continues: Tennessee's experience highlights scope of controversy over private prisons. *Corrections Today, 60*(5), para 5, 18, 24, 25.

Ladson-Billings, G. (2006). From the achievement gap to the education debt: Understanding achievement in U. S. schools. *Educational Researcher, 35*(7), 3–12.

Ladouceur, R. (2011). Database: Eugenics in college biology textbooks. [Web log post]. Retrieved from http://www.textbookhistory.com/?p=2077

Lagemann, E. (2000). *An elusive science: The troubling history of education research.* Chicago: University of Chicago Press.

Laughlin, H. (1922). *Eugenical sterilization in the United States.* Chicago: Psychopathic Laboratory of the Municipal Court of Chicago. Retrieved from http://books.google.com/books/about/Eugenical_Sterilization_in_the_United_St.html?id=KuESAAAAYAAJ

Lawmakers may stay for school reform. (1990, Nov. 18). *Nashville Tennessean,* p. B1.

Lazarin, M. (2011). *Federal investment in charter schools: A proposal for reauthorizing the Elementary and Secondary Education Act.* Washington, DC: Center for American Progress. Retrieved from http://www.americanprogress.org/wp-content/uploads/issues/2011/10/pdf/charter_investment.pdf

Legislative minutes, Tennessee House Education Committee, January 23, 1990. Nashville, TN: Tennessee State Library and Archives. (testimony of Dr. William Sanders and Representative John Bragg).

Legislative minutes, Tennessee House Education Committee, February 12, 1991. Nashville, TN: Tennessee State Library and Archives. (testimony of Commissioner Charles E. Smith).

Legislative minutes, Tennessee House Education Committee, April 8, 1991. Nashville, TN: Tennessee State Library and Archives. (testimony of Tennesseans for Limited Taxation Association).

Legislative minutes, Tennessee House Education Committee, March 3, 2004. Nashville, TN: Tennessee State Library and Archives. (testimony of former State Senator Andy Womack, Paul Changas, Vernon Coffey, Dr. William Sanders, Representative Les Winningham).

Legislative minutes, Tennessee House Education Oversight Committee, July 12, 1989. Nashville, TN: Tennessee State Library and Archives. (testimony of Dr. Brent Poulton).

Legislative minutes, Tennessee Joint Education Oversight Committee, December 17, 1987. Nashville, TN: Tennessee State Library and Archives. (testimony of Commissioner Charles Smith, Dr. Brent Poulton, Senator Leonard Dunavant, Senator Robert Rochelle, Representative Leslie Winningham).

Legislative minutes, Tennessee Senate Education Committee, March 6, 1991. Nashville, TN. Tennessee State Library and Archives. (testimony of John Parish, Dan Frierson, Senator Ray Albright).

Legislative minutes, Tennessee Senate Education Committee, April 17, 1991. Nashville, TN: Tennessee State Library and Archives. (testimony of Senator Ray Albright).

Lemann, N. (1995). The structure of success in America. *The Atlantic Online.* Retrieved from http://www.theatlantic.com/past/docs/issues/95sep/ets/grtsort1.htm

Lemann, N. (1999). *The big test: The secret history of the American meritocracy.* New York, NY: Farrar, Straus, & Giroux.

Lewin, T. (2012, March 6). Black students face more discipline, data suggests. *New York Times.* Retrieved from http://www.nytimes.com/2012/03/06hh/education/black-students-face-more-harsh-discipline-data-shows.html?_r=0

Libby, K. (2010, August 11). What Shelton's waiver tells us about the Gates Foundation and the DOE. [Web log post]. Retrieved from http://www.schoolsmatter.info/2010/07/what-shelton-waiver-tells-us-about.html

Linn, R. (2001). *The design and evaluation of educational assessment and accountability systems.* Los Angeles: National Center for Research on Evaluation, Standards, and Student Testing. Retrieved from http://www.cse.ucla.edu/products/reports/TR539.pdf

Lipscomb, S., Teh, B., Gill, B., Chiang, H., & Owens, A. (2010, September). *Teacher and principal value-added research findings and implementation practices* [Final Report]. Cambridge, MA: Mathematica Policy Research, Inc.

Livingston, S. G. (1998). State policy, global economy: The political economy of foreign investment in Tennessee. In J. R. Vile & M. Byrnes (Eds.), *Tennessee government and politics: Democracy in the Volunteer State* (pp. 202–215). Nashville, TN: Vanderbilt University Press.

Lockwood, J., McCaffrey, D., Hamilton, L., Stecher, B., Le, V., & Martinez, F. (2006). *The sensitivity of value-added teacher effect estimates to different mathematics achievement measures.* Retrieved from http://www.rand.org/content/dam/rand/pubs/reports/2009/RAND_RP1269.pdf

Lombardo, P. (Ed.) (2011). *A century of eugenics in America: From the Indiana experiment to the human genome project.* Bloomington, IN: Indiana University Press.

Lumina Foundation for Education. (2007). *From the ground up: An early history of the Lumina Foundation for Education.* Indianapolis, IN: Lumina Foundation.

Marquard, O. (1989). Farewell to matters of principle. New York, NY: Oxford University Press.

Martin, D., Overholt, G., & Urban, W. (1976). *Accountability in American education: A critique.* Princeton, NJ: Princeton Book Company.

Massey, D. (2008). *Categorically unequal: The American stratification system.* New York, NY: Russell Sage Foundation.

Master Plan For Tennessee Schools: Preparing for the 21st Century. (1990). State Board of Education Document. Nashville, TN: Tennessee Board of Education.

Mathison, S. (2009). Public good and private interest in educational evaluation. In W. Ayers, T. Quinn, & D. Stovall (Eds.), *Handbook of social justice in education,* (pp. 5–14). New York, NY: Routledge.

Maturana, H., & Varela, F. (1987). *The tree of knowledge: The biological roots of human understanding.* Boston: Shambhala Publications.

McCaffrey, D., & Lockwood, J. (2008, November). *Value-added models: Analytic Issues.* Paper presented at the National Research Council and the National Academy of Education, Board of Testing and Accountability Workshop on Value-Added Modeling, Washington DC.

McCaffrey, D., Lockwood, J., Koretz, D., & Hamilton, L. (2003). Evaluating value-added models for teacher accountability. Retrieved from http://www.rand.org/pubs/monographs/MG158.html

McCaffrey, D., Lockwood, J., Koretz, D., Louis, T., & Hamilton, L. (2004). Models for value-added modeling of teacher effects. *Journal of Educational and Behavioral Statistics, 29*(1), 67–101.

McCaffrey, D., Sass, T., Lockwood, J., & Mihaly, K. (2009). The intertemporal variability of teacher effect estimates. *Education Finance and Policy, 4*(4), 572–606.

McCarthy, M. (1994). The courts and school finance reform. *Theory into Practice* (Finaning Education), *33*(2), 89–97.

McCartney, S. (2011, November). Child poverty in the United States 2009 and 2010: Selected race groups and Hispanic origin. *American Community Survey Briefs.* Retrieved from http://www.census.gov/prod/2011pubs/acsbr10-05.pdf

McLaughlin, M. (1974). *Evaluation and reform: The Elementary and Secondary Education Act of 1965, Title I.* Santa Monica, CA: Rand.

McLaughlin, M. (1987). Learning from experience: Lessons from policy implementation. *Education Evaluation and Policy Analysis, 9*(2), 171–178.

McLaughlin, M. (1991). Test-based accountability as a reform strategy. *The Phi Delta Kappan, 73*(3), 248–251.

McLean, R., & Sanders, W. (1983). *Objective component of teacher evaluation: A feasibility study.* Unpublished manuscript.

McLean, R., Sanders, W., & Stroup, W. (1991). A unified approach to mixed linear models. *The American Statistician, 45*(1), 54–64.

McNeil, M. (2009, September 23). Gates spreading 'Race to the Top' help to all states. *Education Week.org*. Retrieved from http://blogs.edweek.org/edweek/campaign-k-12/2009/09/all_states_now_eligible_for_ga.html

McWherter, N. (1989, Sept. 25). Press conference release. Collection of Governor McWherter's Papers. Nashville, TN: Tennessee State Library and Archives.

Menand, L. (2001–2002). Morton, Agassiz, and the origins of scientific racism in the United States. *The Journal of Blacks in Higher Education, 34*, 110–113.

Menand, L. (2002). *American studies*. New York, NY: Farrar, Straus, & Giroux.

Metro Nashville Public Schools. (2004, February 11). Tennessee accountability concerns. Document used in the testimony of Paul Changas. Legislative minutes, Tennessee House Education Committee, March 3, 2004. Nashville, TN: Tennessee State Library and Archives.

Meyers, T., Valesky, T., & Hirth, M. (1995). K–12 funding in Tennessee: Equity now—adequacy coming. *Journal of Education Finance, 20*(4), 394–409.

Millman, J. (1981). Student achievement as a measure of teacher competence. In J. Millman (Ed.), *Handbook of teacher evaluation* (pp. 146–166). Beverly Hills, CA: Sage Publication.

Millman, J. (1997). How do I judge thee? Let me count the ways. In J. Millman (Ed.), *Grading teachers, grading schools: Is student achievement a valid evaluation measure?* (pp. 243–247). Thousand Oaks, CA: Corwin Press, Inc.

Millman, J., & Schalock, H. (1997). Beginnings and introductions. J. Millman (Ed.), *Grading teachers, grading schools: Is student achievement a valid evaluation measure?* (pp. 3–8). Thousand Oaks, CA: Corwin Press, Inc.

Miron, G., Urschel, J., Mathis, W., & Tornquist, E. (2010). *Schools without diversity: Educational management organizations, charter schools, and the demographic stratification of the American School System*. Boulder and Tempe: Education and the Public Interest Center & Education Policy Research Unit. Retrieved from http://epicpolicy.org/publication/schools-without-diversity

Mondale, S., & Patton, S. (2001). *School: The story of American public education*. Boston: Beacon Press.

Mooney, J. (2013). In local battles against charters, Florence Township joins the fray. *NJS Spotlight*. Retrieved from http://www.njspotlight.com/stories/13/02/10/in-local-battles-against-charters-florence-township-joins-the-fray/

Moore, L. (2012, November 7). Shelby County sales tax increase fails. *The Commercial Appeal*. Retrieved from http://www.commercialappeal.com/news/2012/nov/07/no-headline—sales_tax/

Mosteller, F. (1995, Summer/Fall). The Tennessee study of class size in the early school grades. *Critical Issues for Children and Youths, 5*(2), 113–127. Retrieved from http://www.princeton.edu/futureofchildren/publications/docs/05_02_08.pdf

Mosteller, F., & Moynihan, D. (1972). *On equality of opportunity.* New York, NY: Random House.

Murphy, J., & Cohen, D. (1974, Summer). Accountability in education—the Michigan experience. *The Public Interest,* 53–54.

Nashville Health Care Council. (2013). *Health care industry contributes $30 billion annually to Nashville economy.* Retrieved from http://arxllc.com/component/content/article/37-arx-news-and-information/80-healthcare-industry

National Academy of Sciences. (2009). *Letter report to the U. S. Department of Education on the Race to the Top fund.* Washington, DC: National Academies of Sciences. Retrieved from http://www.nap.edu/catalog.php?record_id=12780

National Center for Education Statistics. (2003). *State & county estimates of low literacy.* Retrieved from http://nces.ed.gov/naal/estimates/StateEstimates.aspx

National Center for Education Statistics. (2011). *Mathematics framework changes.* Retrieved from http://nces.ed.gov/nationsreportcard/mathematics/frameworkcomparison.asp

National Center for Education Statistics. (2011). *NAEP state comparisons.* Retrieved from http://nces.ed.gov/nationsreportcard/states/

National Center for Education Statistics. (2011). *State snapshot report.* Retrieved from http://nces.ed.gov/nationsreportcard/states/

National Center for Education Statistics. (2011). *What does the reading assessment measure?* Retrieved from http://nces.ed.gov/nationsreportcard/reading/whatmeasure.asp

National Commission on Excellence in Education. (1983). *A nation at risk: The imperative for educational reform.* U.S. Government Printing Office. Retrieved from http://datacenter.spps.org/uploads/SOTW_A_Nation_at_Risk_1983.pdf

National Conference of State Legislators. (2012). *Tuition tax credits.* Washington, DC: NCSL. Retrieved from http://www.ncsl.org/issues-research/educ/school-choice-scholarship-tax-credits.aspx

National Council on Teacher Quality. (2011, October). *State of the states: Trends and early lessons on teacher evaluation and effectiveness policies.* Retrieved from http://www.nctq.org/p/publications/docs/nctq_stateOfTheStates.pdf

National Education Access Network. (2008). *Litigation: Kentucky.* Retrieved from http://www.schoolfunding.info/states/ky/lit_ky.php3

National Research Council and National Academy of Education. (2010). *Getting value out of value-added: Report of a workshop.* Committee on Value-Added Methodology for Instructional Improvement, Program Evaluation, and Educational Accountability, Henry Braun, Naomi Chudowsky, and Judith Koenig, Editors. Center for Education, Division of Behavioral and Social Sciences and Education. Washington, DC: The National Academies Press.

NCLB Reauthorization: Strategies for Attracting, Supporting, and Retaining High Quality Educators, of the U. S. Senate Committee on Health, Education,

Labor, and Pensions (Roundtable discussion), 110th Cong., (March 6, 2007) (testimony of William L. Sanders). Retrieved from http://www.help.senate.gov/hearings/hearing/?id=0d85163f-0e42-33fe-8eb1-bf5692ef251f

NEA. (2011). *Rankings and estimates: Rankings of the states 2011 and estimates of school statistics 2012.* Washington, DC: National Education Association. Retrieved from http://www.nea.org/assets/docs/NEA_Rankings_And_Estimates_FINAL_20120209.pdf

New York Principals. (2013). *Updated APPR paper with signatories.* Retrieved from http://www.newyorkprincipals.org/waiver-request/updatedapprpaperwithsignatories-6

Newton, X., Darling-Hammond, L., Haertel, E., & Thomas, E. (2010). Value-added modeling of teacher effectiveness: An exploration of stability across models and contexts. *Education Policy Analysis Archives, 18* (23). Retrieved from http://epaa.asu.edu/ojs/article/view/1096

Nichols, S., & Berliner, D. (2007). High-stakes testing and the corruption of America's schools. *Harvard Education Newsletter, 23*(2). Retrieved from http://www.hepg.org/hel/article/237

Nickerson, B., & Deenihan, G. (2002). From equity to adequacy: The legal battle for increased state funding of poor school districts in New York. *Fordham Urban Law Journal, 30* (4), 1341–1392.

Nixon, R. (1969, November 3). *Address to the Nation on the war in Vietnam.* Yorba Linda, CA: Nixon Presidential Museum and Library. Retrieved from http://www.nixonlibrary.gov/forkids/speechesforkids/silentmajority/silentmajority_transcript.pdf

Nixon, R. (1970, March 3.) *Special message to Congress on education reform.* The American Presidency Project. Retrieved from http://www.presidency.ucsb.edu/ws/?pid=2895

No Child Left Behind: Can Growth Models Ensure Improved Education for All Students, of the U.S. House Committee on Education and Workforce, 109th Cong., (July 27, 2006) (testimony of William L. Sanders). Retrieved from http://archives.republicans.edlabor.house.gov/archive/hearings/109th/fc/nclb072706/sanders.htm

No guarantee for poor areas. (1988, Nov. 27). *Nashville Tennessean,* p. A1.

Nye, B., Konstantopoulos, S., & Hedges, L. (2004). How large are teacher effects?" *Educational Evaluation and Policy Analysis, 26*(3), 237–257.

Ohanian, S. (2012, September 18). [Review of the book *The same thing over and over: How school reformers get stuck in yesterday's ideas*]. *Education Review.* Retrieved from http://www.edrev.info/reviews/rev1196.pdf

Olsen, L. (2004, November 17). 'Value Added' models gain in popularity: Growth yardstick appeals to states. *Education Week, 24(*12). Retrieved from http://www.edweek.org/ew/articles/2004/11/17/12value.h24.html

O'Neil, D. (1998–2012). *Adapting to climate extremes.* Retrieved from http://anthro.palomar.edu/adapt/adapt_2.htm

Orfield, G., & Lee, C. (2006). *Racial transformation and the changing nature of segregation.* Cambridge, MA: The Civil Rights Project at Harvard University.

Otterman, S. (2011, October 21). Ed school's pedagogical puzzle. *New York Times.* Retrieved from http://www.nytimes.com/2011/07/24/education/edlife/edl-24teacher-t.html?pagewanted=all&_r=0

Papay, J. (2011). Different tests, different answers: The stability of teacher value-added estimates across outcome measures. *American Educational Research Journal, 48*(1),163–193.

Parents for Responsible Education. (n.d.). *PURE: Building powerful public school parents and communities.* Retrieved from http://pureparents.org/?page_id=2

Parker, K. (2013, February 6). Senate passes first bill, would end 15 percent testing. *San Antonio Express-News.* Retrieved from http://blog.mysanantonio.com/texas-politics/2013/02/senate-passes-first-bill-would-end-15-percent-testing/

Partnership for the Assessments of Readiness for College and Careers (PARCC). (n.d.). *Our clients: Achieve, Inc.* Retrieved from http://www.education-first.com/our-clients/achieve-inc

Payton, R. (1991, February 12). *TEA president's presentation for the state legislature.* Collection of Governor McWherter's Papers. Nashville, TN: Tennessee State Library and Archives.

PBS. (2004, March 26). *NOW transcript 03.26.04.* New York, NY: Public Affairs Television. Retrieved from http://www.pbs.org/now/transcript/transcript313_full.html

PBS Frontline. (1995–2013). *Secrets of the SAT: Americans instrumental in establishing standardized tests.* Retrieved from http://www.pbs.org/wgbh/pages/frontline/shows/sats/where/three.html

PBS/WGBH. (1999). *Herbert Spencer.* Retrieved from expehttp://www.pbs.org/wgbh/amex/carnegie/peopleevents/pande03.html

Pellegrino, J. W. (2010). *The design for an assessment system for the face to the top: A learning sciences perspective on issues of growth and measurement.* Paper presented at the Exploratory Seminar: Measurement Challenges Within Race to the Top Agenda meeting of the Center for K–12 Assessment & Performance Management (December, 2009). Retrieved from http://www.k12center.org/publications.html

Peltason, E., & Raymond, M. (2013). *Charter school growth and replication, Volume 1.* Stanford, CA: CREDO. Retrieved from http://credo.stanford.edu/pdfs/CGAR%20Growth%20Volume%20I.pdf

Peevely, G., & Ray, J. (2001). Does equalization litigation effect a narrowing of the gap of value added achievement outcomes among school districts? *Journal of Education Finance,* 26(4), 463–476.

Phil Bredesen, Former Governor of Tennessee: Why he matters. *The Washington Post.* Retrieved from http://www.washingtonpost.com/politics/phil-bredesen/gIQA610s9O_topic.html

Popham, W. (1997). The moth and the flame: Student learning as a criterion of instructional competence. In J. Millman (Ed.), *Grading teachers, grading schools: Is student achievement a valid evaluation measure?* (pp. 264–274). Thousand Oaks, CA: Corwin Press, Inc.

Potts, K. (2012). *Homeless students in Tennessee public schools.* Nashville, TN: Tennessee Comptroller of the Treasury, Offices of Research and Education Accountability legislative brief. Retrieved from http://www.comptroller.tn.gov/Repository/RE/Homeless%202012.pdf

Public Education Governance Reform Act (PEGRA). (1984). Tenn. Code Ann. § 49-1-302.

Quaid, L., & Blankinship, D. (2009, October 25). Gates' largesse sways government spending. *NBC News.* Retrieved from http://www.nbcnews.com/id/33469415/ns/us_news-education/#.UTFFxLR8xSU

Quality counts, 2011: Uncertain forecast. (2011, January 13). *Education Week.* Retrieved from http://www.edweek.org/ew/toc/2011/01/13/index.html

Rampell, M. (2009, August 27). SAT scores and family income. *New York Times.* Retrieved from http://economix.blogs.nytimes.com/2009/08/27/sat-scores-and-family-income/

Ravitch, D. (1972). [Review of the book *On equality of educational opportunity* edited by F. Mosteller & D. Moynihan]. *Change, 4*(4), 62–64. Retrieved from http://www.jstor.org/stable/40161459

Ravitch, D. (2010). *The death and life of the great American school system: How testing and choice are undermining education.* New York, NY: Basic Books.

Reagan, R. (1983). *Remarks on receiving the final report of the National Commission on Excellence in Education.* Retrieved from http://www.reagan.utexas.edu/archives/speeches/1983/42683d.htm

Rebell, M. (2002). Educational adequacy, democracy, and the courts. In T. Ready, C. Edley, Jr., & C. E. Snow (Eds.), *Achieving high educational standards for all: Conference summary* (pp. 218–267). Washington, D. C.: National Research Council, Division of Behavioral and Social Sciences and Education.

Reckase, M. (2004). The real world is more complicated than we would like. *Journal of Educational and Behavioral Statistics, 29*(1), 117–120.

Rice, J. (1913). *Scientific management in education.* New York, NY: Hinds, Noble, & Eldredge.

Riddile, M. (2010, December 15). *PISA: It's poverty not stupid.* [Web log post]. National Association of Secondary School Principals. Retrieved from http://nasspblogs.org/principaldifference/2010/12/pisa_its_poverty_not_stupid_1.html

Rippa, S. (1996). *Education in a free society: An American history* (8th ed.). New York, NY: Longman.

Rivlin, A. (1973). Measuring performance in education. In M. Moss (Ed.), *The measurement of economic and social performance* (pp. 411–438). Cambridge, MA: National Bureau of Economic Research. Retrieved from http://www.nber.org/chapters/c3619

Roberts, J. (2009, November 18). Memphis City Schools accepts $90 million Gates Foundation grant. *Memphis Commercial Appeal.* Retrieved from http://www.commercialappeal.com/news/2009/nov/18/memphis-city-schools-formally-accepts-90-million-g/

Roberts, J. (2010, July 31). Tennessee student scores plunge in new proficiency test: Failure rate tops 50% on tougher standards. *The Commercial Appeal.* Retrieved from http://www.commercialappeal.com/news/2010/jul/31/student-scores-plunge-in-new-test/

Roberts, J. (2012, October 22). Achievement School District gets jolt: Low test scores. *The Commercial Appeal.* Retrieved from http://www.commercialappeal.com/news/2012/oct/22/achievement-school-district-gets-jolt-low-test/

Rodriguez v. San Antonio Independent School District, 411 U.S. 1 (1973).

Rose v. Council, 790 S.W.2d 186, 60 Ed. Law Rep. 1289 (1989). Retrieved from http://www.schoolfunding.info/states/ky/ROSEvCBE.PDF

Rosen, C. (2004). *Preaching eugenics: Religious leaders and the American eugenics movement.* New York, NY: Oxford University Press.

Rothstein, J. (2008). *Student sorting and bias in value added estimation: Selection on observables and unobservables.* Retrieved from http://www.wcer.wisc.edu/news/events/vam%20conference%20final%20papers/studentsorting&bias_jrothstein.pdf

Rothstein, J. (2009, January). *Student sorting and bias in value added estimation: Selection on observables and unobservables* [Working Paper No. 14666]. Retrieved from www.nber.org/papers/w14666

Rothstein, J. (2010). Teacher quality in educational production: Tracking, decay, and student achievement. *The Quarterly Journal of Economics,* 125(1), 175–214.

Rothstein, R. (2004). *Class and schools: Using social, economic, and educational reform to close the black-white achievement gap.* New York, NY: Teachers College Press.

Rugg, H. (1975). Curriculum-making and the scientific study of education since 1910. *Curriculum Theory Network, 4*(4), 295–308. Retrieved from http://www.jstor.org/stable/1179267

Ryan, W. (1976). *Blaming the victim.* New York, NY: Vintage.

Ryan, C., & Siebens, J. (2012, February). *Educational Attainment in the United States: 2009* (Current Population Report P20-566). Retrieved from http://www.census.gov/prod/2012pubs/p20-566.pdf

Sahlberg, P. (2011). *Finnish lessons: What can the world learn from educational change in Finland?* New York, NY: Teachers College Press.

Sanders, W. (2003, April). *Beyond No Child Left Behind.* Paper presented at the Annual Meeting of the American Educational Research Association, Chicago, IL.

Sanders, W., & Horn, S. (1994). The Tennessee value-added assessment system (TVAAS): Mixed model methodology in educational assessment. *Journal of Personnel Evaluation in Education, 8*(1), 299–311.

Sanders, W., & Horn, S. (1998). Research findings from the Tennessee Value-Added Assessment System (TVAAS) database: Implications for educational evaluation and research. *Journal of Personnel Evaluation in Education, 12*(3), 247–256.

Sanders, W., & Rivers, J. (1996, November). *Cumulative and residual effects of teachers on future student academic improvement* [Research Progress Report]. Knoxville, TN: University of Tennessee Value-Added Research and Assessment Center.

Sanders, W., Wright, S., Rivers, J., & Leandro, J. (2009, November). *A response to criticisms of SAS® EVAAS®* [White Paper]. Retrieved from http://www.sas.com/resources/asset/Response_to_Criticisms_of_SAS_EVAAS_11-13-09.pdf

Saletan, W. (2012, January-February). The mismeasure of Stephen Jay Gould. *Discover Magazine.* Retrieved from http://discovermagazine.com/2012/jan-feb/59#.UTN9U7R8ylI

SAS. (2011). *SAS® EVAAS® for K–12* [Product Brief]. Retrieved from http://www.sas.com/resources/product-brief/SAS_EVAAS_for_K-12.pdf

Sass, T. (2008, November). *The stability of value-added measures of teacher quality and implications for teacher compensation policy* [Brief 4]. Washington, D.C.: The Urban Institute, National Center for Analysis of Longitudinal Data in Education Research (CALDER).

Schelzig, E. (2011, March 21). Haslam locates money for CCA-run prisons amid cuts. *The Associated Press.* Retrieved from http://www.knoxnews.com/news/2011/mar/21/haslam-locates-money-cca-run-prison-amid-cuts/

Schmader, T., & Johns, M. (2003). Converging evidence that stereotype threat reduces working memory capacity. *Journal of Personality and Social Psychology, 85*(3), 440–452.

Schochet, P., & Chiang, H. (2010). *Error rates in measuring teacher and school performance based on student test score gains* (NCEE 2010-4004). Washington, DC: National Center for Education Evaluation and Regional Assistance, Institute of Education Sciences, U.S. Department of Education.

Selden, S. (1999). *Inheriting shame: The story of eugenics and racism in America.* New York, NY: Teachers College Press.

Serrano v. Priest, 18 Cal. 3d 728, 135 Cal. Rptr. 345, 557 P.2d 929 (1976)

Severson, K. (2011, December 9). Thousands sterilized, a state weighs restitution. *New York Times.* Retrieved from http://www.nytimes.com/2011/12/10/us/redress-weighed-for-forced-sterilizations-in-north-carolina.html?ref=us

Severson, K. (2012, January 11). Payment set for those sterilized in program. *New York Times.* Retrieved from http://www.nytimes.com/2011/12/10/us/redress-weighed-for-forced-sterilizations-in-north-carolina.html?ref=us

Severson, K. (2012, June 20). Payment for victims of eugenics shelved. *New York Times.* Retrieved from http://www.nytimes.com/2012/06/21/us/north-carolina-eugenics-compensation-program-shelved.html?_r=0

Shaw, L. (2013, February 5). Parents joining teachers' test boycott as Garfield High principals give exam. *Seattle Times.* Retrieved from http://seattletimes.com/html/localnews/2020294766_garfieldtestxml.html

Shulman, L. (1987). Knowledge and teaching: Foundations of the new reform. *Harvard Education Review, 57*(1), 1–21. Retrieved from http://people.ucsc.edu/~ktellez/shulman.pdf

Sigler, J. (1997). *Education: Ends and means* (Lynchburg College Symposium Readings (Volume 9). Lanham, MD: University Press of America.

Simon, S. (2012a, August 2). *Private firms eyeing profits from U. S. public schools.* New York, NY: Thompson Reuters. Retrieved from http://in.reuters.com/assets/print?aid=INL2E8J15FR20120802

Simon, S. (2012b, August 2). Privatizing public schools: Big firms eyeing profits from U.S. K–12 market. *The Huffington Post.* Retrieved from http://www.huffingtonpost.com/2012/08/02/private-firms-eyeing-prof_n_1732856.html

Sinn, H. (2010). *Casino capitalism: How the financial crisis came about and what needs to be done now.* New York, NY: Oxford University Press.

Smith, C. (1987, October 15). *Text of prepared remarks to the Legislative Oversight Committee.* Collection of the Governor McWherter's Papers. Nashville, TN: Tennessee State Library and Archives.

Smith, C. (1988, January 27). *Tennessee State Department of Education news release.* Collection of Governor McWherter's Papers. Nashville, TN: Tennessee State Library and Archives.

Smith, C. (1990). *Goals and objectives of the 21st century challenge plan.* Nashville TN: State Department of Tennessee. (Submitted to and approved by the Legislative Oversight Committee on Education February, 1990. Submitted and approved by the State Board of Education March, 1990.)

Smith, M. J. (2004, April). *The Education Improvement Act: A progress report.* Nashville, TN: Tennessee Comptroller of the Treasury, Office of Education Accountability Report.

Snodgrass, W. (1990, February). *Performance audit.* Nashville, TN: Comptroller of the Treasury, Office of Education Accountability Report.

Spring, J. (1976). *The sorting machine: National education policy since 1945.* New York, NY: Longman.

Springer, M., Ballou, D., Hamilton, L., Le, V., Lockwood, J., McCaffrey, D., Pepper, M., & Stecher, B. (2010). *Teacher pay for performance: Experimental evidence from Project on Incentives in Teaching.* Nashville, TN: National Center on Performance Incentives at Vanderbilt University. Retrieved from https://my.vanderbilt.edu/performanceincentives/files/2012/09/POINT_REPORT_9.21.102.pdf

Springer, M., & Winters, M. (2009. *New York City's School-wide bonus Pay program: Early evidence from a randomized trial.* Nashville, TN: National Center on Performance Incentives at Vanderbilt University. Retrieved from https://my.vanderbilt.edu/performanceincentives/files/2012/10/200902_SpringerWinters_BonusPayProgram15.pdf

State Collaborative on Reforming Education. (2010). *The state of education in Tennessee (Annual Report).* Retrieved from http://www.tnscore.org/wp-content/uploads/2010/06/Score-2010-Annual-Report-Full.pdf

Stedman, L., & Kaestle, C. (1985). The test score decline is over: Now what? *The Phi Delta Kappan, 67*(3), 204–210.

Steele, C. (1997). A threat in the air: How stereotypes shape intellectual identity and performance. *American Psychologist, 52*(6), 613–629.

Steele, C. (1999, August). Thin ice: Stereotype threat and black college students. *Atlantic.com.* Retrieved from http://www.theatlantic.com/magazine/archive/1999/08/thin-ice-stereotype-threat-and-black-college-students/304663/

Steele, C., & Aronson, J. (1995). Stereotype threat and the intellectual test performance of African Americans. *Journal of Personality and Social Psychology 69*(5), 797–811.

Steinberg, J., & Henriques, D. B. (2001, May 21). When a test fails the schools, careers and reputations suffer: None of the above. *The New York Times.* Retrieved from http://events.nytimes.com/learning/general/specials/testing/21EXAM.html

Stern, A. (2005). *Eugenic nation: Faults and frontiers of better breeding in modern America.* Berkeley, CA: University of California Press.

Stewart, B. (2006). *Value-added modeling: The challenge of measuring educational outcomes* (A Carnegie Challenge Paper). New York, NY: Carnegie Corporation.

Stiglitz, J. (2012). *The price of inequality: How today's endangered society endangers our future.* New York, NY: W. W. Norton.

Strauss, V. (2012, September 19). Is The New York Times wrong (again) on teacher evaluation? *The Washington Post.* Retrieved from http://www.washingtonpost.com/blogs/answer-sheet/post/is-the-new-york-times-wrong-again-on-teacher-evaluation/2012/09/19/fed2cee2-026e-11e2-91e7-2962c74e7738_blog.html

Stufflebeam, D. (1983). The CIPP Model for Program Evaluation. In G.F. Madaus, M. Scriven, and D. Stufflebeam (Eds.), *Evaluation Models: Viewpoints on Educational and Human Services Evaluation.* Boston: Kluwer Nijhof.

Synnott, M. (2010). *The opened door: Discrimination and admissions at Harvard, Yale, and Princeton, 1900–1970.* Piscataway, NJ: Transaction Publishers.

Tax Foundation. (2012). State and local sales tax rates as of January 1, 2012. Retrieved from http://taxfoundation.org/sites/taxfoundation.org/files/docs/state%26local_sales%26use_rates_jan2012-20120216.pdf

Taylor, B. (2010). *Horace Mann's troubling legacy: The education of democratic citizens.* Lawrence, KS: University Press of Kansas.

Taylor, F. (1911/1967). *The principles of scientific management.* New York, NY: W. W. Norton.

TEA plan similar to governor's goals. (1989, Nov. 3). *Nashville Banner,* p. A6.

TEA to tell teachers' view of school needs. (1989, Nov. 3). *Nashville Tennessean*, p. A1.

Tennessee Accountability Concerns. (2004, February 11). *Position paper from Metro Nashville School System submitted to the Tennessee House Education Committee, 103rd General Assemby*, (testimony of Paul Changas, Director of Assessment for Metro Nashville School System).

Tennessee Advisory Council on Intergovernmental Relations (TACIR) and University of Tennessee Center for Business and Economic Research (CBER). (2008). *The local government response to the basic education program: Equity, spending, and local tax effort.* Nashville, TN: TACIR.

Tennessee Commission on Children and Youth. (1992, November). *Diagnosis: Indicators of the health and safety of young Tennesseans* [A Tennessee KIDS COUNT Project Report]. Retrieved from http://www.aecf.org/upload/publicationfiles/diagnosis.pdf

Tennessee Education Association (TEA). (2012). *Salary data.* Nashville, TN: TEA. Retrieved from http://teateachers.org/salary-data

Tennessee First to the Top Act of 2010, *Tennessee Public Acts*, Chapter No. 2, pp. 1–10.

Tennessee Justice Center. (n.d.). *Health reform and the lessons of TennCare.* Retrieved from http://www.tnjustice.org/resources/tenncare/tenncare-vs-affordable-care-act/

Tennessee Small School Sys. v. McWherter, 851 SW 2d 139 (1993)

Tennessee Small School Systems, et al. v. Ned Ray McWherter, et al. No. M2001-01957-SC-R3-CV, October 8, 2002, S. Ct. Tenn. Retrieved from http://nces.ed.gov/edfin/pdf/lawsuits/TSSS_v_McWherte_III.pdf

Tennessee State Board of Education. (2007, January 26). *Advisory council on teacher education and certification recommendation* (Agenda report item: II.B.). Retrieved from http://www.tn.gov/sbe/2007Januarypdfs/II%20B%20Advisory%20Council%20Recommendation.pdf

Tennessee State Department of Education. (2005). *2005 Tennessee Report Card.* Retrieved from http://www.k-12.state.tn.us/rptcrd05/state2.asp

Tennessee State Department of Education. (2011). *2011 Tennessee Report Card.* Retrieved from http://edu.reportcard.state.tn.us/pls/apex/f?p=200:1:1407925225289977::NO

Tennessee State Department of Education. (2012). *2012 Tennessee Report Card.* Retrieved from http://edu.reportcard.state.tn.us/pls/apex/f?p=200:1:1407925225289977::NO

Tennessee State Department of Education. (2012). *Teacher evaluation in Tennessee: A report on year 1 evaluation.* Retrieved from http://www.tn.gov/education/doc/yr_1_tchr_eval_rpt.pdf

Tennessee State Department of Finance & Administration. (2012). *The Budget, Fiscal Years 2004–2011.* Retrieved from http://www.tn.gov/finance/bud/archive.shtml

Terman, L. (1916). *The measurement of intelligence.* Cambridge, MA: Riverside Press. Retrieved from http://www.gutenberg.org/files/20662/20662-h/20662-h.htm

The Neshoba Democrat. (Nov. 15, 2007). *Transcript of Ronald Reagan's 1980 Neshoba County Fair speech.* Retrieved from http://neshobademocrat.com/main.asp?SectionID=2&SubSectionID=297&ArticleID=15599&TM=60417.67

Thomas, D. (1990, November). *Tennessee education for the 21st century* (Report to Governor Ned McWherter). Nashville, TN: State Board of Education.

Thorndike, E. (1906). *The principles of teaching based on psychology.* Syracuse, NY: Macon-Henry Press. Retrieved from http://books.google.com/books/about/The_principles_of_teaching.html?id=eDBCAAAAIAAJ

Tighter budget control to avoid more tax hinted. (1988, November 15), *Nashville Tennessean,* pp. B1, B2.

Toppo, G. (2007, January 18). How Bush education law has changed our schools. *USA Today.* Retrieved from http://usatoday30.usatoday.com/news/education/2007-01-07-no-child_x.htm

21st century schools education aim of McWherter. (1990, Jan. 27). *Nashville Tennessean,* p. A1.

Twenty-five percent of TennCare enrollees cut; Child coverage preserved. (2005, March). *Healthcare Financial Management, 59*(3), 18.

Tyack, D., & Cuban, L. (1995). *Tinkering toward utopia: A century of public school reform.* Cambridge, MA: Harvard University Press.

UNICEF. (2012). *Measuring child poverty: New league tables of child poverty in the world's rich countries.* Florence, Italy: Innocenti Research Centre. Retrieved from http://www.unicef-irc.org/publications/660

Unz, R. (1999, May 3). Voucher veto. *The Nation.* Retrieved from http://www.onenation.org/9905/050399a.html

Urban, W., & Wagoner, J. (2008). *American education: A history* (4th ed). New York, NY: Routledge.

U.S. Census Bureau. (2011). *Public education finances: 2009* (G09-ASPEF). Washington, DC: U.S. Government Printing Office.

U.S. Chamber of Commerce. (2007). *Leaders and laggards: A state-by-state report card on educational effectiveness.* Retrieved from http://www.uschamber.com/reportcard/2007

U.S. Department of Education. *Race to the Top application for initial funding* (January 18, 2010) (CFDA Number: 84.395A). Retrieved from http://www2.ed.gov/programs/racetothetop/phase1-applications/tennessee.pdf

U.S. Department of Education. (2006, February 22). *Under No Child Left Behind, states submit growth model proposals, outside peer reviews selected* (Press release). Retrieved from http://www2.ed.gov/news/pressreleases/2006/02/02222006.html

U.S. Department of Education. (2010, April). *Interim report on the evaluation of the growth model pilot project.* Washington, DC: Office of Planning, Evaluation and Policy Development, Policy and Program Studies Service.

U.S. Department of Education. (2011, January). *Final report on the evaluation of the growth model pilot project.* Washington, DC: Office of Planning, Evaluation and Policy Development, Policy and Program Studies Service.

U.S. Department of Education. (2012, July 16). *Statement from U.S. Secretary of Education Arne Duncan on "Teacher Evaluation in Tennessee: A Report on Year 1 Implementation"* (Press release). Retrieved from http://www.ed.gov/news/press-releases/statement-us-secretary-education-arne-duncan-teacher-evaluation-tennessee-report

U.S. Department of Education. (2006). *A test of leadership: Charting the future of U. S. higher education.* Washington, DC: ED Pubs, Education Publications Center.

U.S. Office of Education. (1918). *Cardinal principles of secondary education: A report of the Commission on the Reorganization of Secondary Education.*

Washington, DC: U. S. Government Printing Office. Retrieved from http://archive.org/details/cardinalprincipl00natiuoft

Van de Putte, L. (2013, February 11). Time to end excessive testing in Texas' public schools. *Houston Chronicle.* Retrieved from http://www.chron.com/opinion/article/Time-to-end-excessive-testing-in-Texas-public-4269750.php

Vinoski, M. (1996). An analysis of the concept and uses of systemic educational reform. *American Educational Research Journal, 33*(1), 53–85).

Wade, P. (2002, April 8). TennCare: Criminal probe looks at access med plus, where money went. *The Commercial Appeal.* Retrieved from www.freerepublic.com/focus/news/662151/posts

Wainer, H. (2011). *Uneducated guesses: Using evidence to uncover misguided education policies.* Princeton, NJ: Princeton University Press.

Wallis, C. (2008, June 8). No Child Left Behind: Doomed to fail? *Time Magazine.* Retrieved from http://www.time.com/time/nation/article/0,8599,1812758,00.html

Warniment, G., & Longhurst, J. (2012). *Promise and pitfalls: Place-based education and marginalized students.* Paper presented at the Annual Meeting of the American Educational Research Association, Vancouver, Canada, April 2012.

Weeks, K. (1988). *A study of the Tennessee Foundation Program.* Nashville, TN: Tennessee State Board of Education.

Weider, B. (2012, August 22). ACT shows 60% of high school seniors not college-ready. *Governing: The States and Localities.* Retrieved from http://www.governing.com/news/state/mct-seniors-not-college-ready.html

Wiggins, G. (1993). *Assessing student performance: Exploring the purpose and limits of testing.* San Francisco: Jossey-Bass.

Wilburn, S. (1996). *A qualitative study of legislated assessment policy in Tennessee.* (Doctoral dissertation). Retrieved from Dissertation Abstracts database. (UMI No. 9735368)

Wilgoren, J. (2001, July 17). State school chiefs fret over U. S. plan to require testing. *New York Times.* Retrieved from http://www.nytimes.com/2001/07/17/national/17EDUC.html

Willms, J. (2008). *Seven key issues for assessing "value-added" in education.* Paper prepared for the workshop of the Committee on Value-Added Methodology for Instructional Improvement, Program Evaluation, and Educational Accountability, National Research Council, Washington, DC, November 13–14. Retrieved from http://www7.nationalacademies.org/bota/VAM_Workshop_Agenda.html

Wilms, W., & Chapleau, R. (1999, November 3). The illusion of paying teachers for student performance. *Education Week, 19*(10), 34, 48. Retrieved from http://www.edweek.org/ew/articles/1999/11/03/10wilms.h19.html

Wilson, K. (1990, Feb. 28). Schools need monitoring, funds: adviser. *Nashville Banner,* p. B6.

Winerip, M. (2011a, November 6). In Tennessee, following the rules for evaluations off a cliff. *New York Times.* Retrieved from http://www.nytimes.com/2011/11/07/education/tennessees-rules-on-teacher-evaluations-bring-frustration.html?pagewanted=all

Winerip, M. (2011b, November 27). Principals protest role of testing in evaluations. *New York Times.* Retrieved from http://www.nytimes.com/2011/11/28/education/principals-protest-increased-use-of-test-scores-to-evaluate-educators.html?pagewanted=all&_r=0

Wissner, S. (1990, Sept. 29). Alexander's better schools plan graduates to remedial. *Nashville Tennessean,* pp. A1, A8.

Word, E., Johnston, J., Bain, H., Fulton, B., Zaharias, J., Achilles, C., Lintz, M., Folger, J., & Breda, C. (n.d.). *The state of Tennessee's student/teacher ratio (STAR) project: Final summary report 1985–1990.* Nashville, TN: Tennessee Department of Education. Retrieved from http://d64.e2services.net/class/STARsummary.pdf

Wraga, W. (1998). The comprehensive high school and educational reform in the United States: Retrospect and prospect. *The High School Journal, 81*(3), 121–134.

Wray, H. (1986). Cells for sale. *Southern Changes, 8*(3), 3–6. Retrieved from http://beck.library.emory.edu/southernchanges/article.php?id=sc08-3_011

Wright, S., Horn, S., & Sanders, W. (1997). Teacher and classroom context effects on student achievement: Implications for teacher evaluation. *Journal of Personnel Evaluation in Education, 1*(1), 57–67.

Index

A

B

The Mismeasure of Education, pages 261–271

C

D

E

Q

R

S

T

U

V

W

X

Y

Z

CPSIA information can be obtained at www.ICGtesting.com
Printed in the USA
BVOW05s2049200214

345556BV00003B/13/P